the power of superfoods

by Sam Graci, Nutritional Researcher

Guest authors

Harvey Diamond, co-author of *Fit For Life*

Professor David Schweitzer, Ph.D., M.D.

Jeanne Marie Martin, Superfoods Recipes

Foreword by Dr. Julian Whitaker, M.D.

Prentice Hall Canada Inc.
Scarborough, Ontario

Canadian Cataloguing in Publication Data

Graci, Sam, 1946–
    The power of superfoods: 30 days that will change your life

Includes index.
ISBN 0-13-021223-7

1. Nutrition.   2. Food.   I. Title.

RA784.G722 1999   613.2   C99-931848-3

This book is printed on recycled paper using vegetable-based inks.

Prentice-Hall Canada Inc.
Scarborough, Ontario

Original hardcover edition © 1997

Prentice-Hall, Inc., Upper Saddle River, New Jersey
Prentice-Hall International (UK) Limited, London
Prentice-Hall of Australia, Pty. Limited, Sydney
Prentice-Hall Hispanoamericana, S.A., Mexico City
Prentice-Hall of India Private Limited, New Delhi
Prentice-Hall of Japan, Inc., Tokyo
Simon & Schuster Southeast Asia Private Limited, Singapore
Editora Prentice-Hall do Brasil, Ltda., Rio de Janeiro

ISBN 0-13-021223-7

Director, Trade and Marketing: Robert Harris
Acquisitions Editor: Dean Hannaford
Editor: Jennifer Glossop
Copy Editor: Liba Berry
Assistant Editor: Joan Whitman
Cover Design: Mary Opper / Sarah Battersby
Interior Design: Mary Opper / Sarah Battersby
Production Coordinator: Shannon Potts
Page Layout: Craig Swistun

2 3 4 5 WEB 03 02 01 00 99

Printed and bound in Canada

Visit the Prentice Hall Canada Web site! Send us your comments, browse our catalogues, and more: **www.phcanada.com**.

Contents

Author's Note

This is the first book I have had the privilege to write. I hope that you will read it carefully and consider changing your eating habits to a more healthful and powerful program. You will never regret it.

For more than a quarter of a century, more than half my life, I have focused on nutritional research. My dream is to relieve suffering and allow humanity optimal good health for a better world.

Consequently, I have never charged money for a lecture series, preferring to share my knowledge in a free and natural style.

To be consistent with my ideals, this book is written on 100 percent recycled paper; typed with biodegradable vegetable inks; contains a tree clause that for every 100 books sold, the Girl Guides or Boy Scouts of Canada and/or the United States will plant a tree.

Except for a small advance to cover the costs associated with writing this book, I will receive no money from the sale of *The Power of Superfoods*. One hundred percent of all profits will go to not-for-profit groups that directly feed young children or malnourished seniors in North America.

If you know of such a group, please send the pertinent information to:

In Canada	*In the United States*
Please Feed Our People	Please Feed Our People
317 Adelaide St. West, Suite 501	c/o Sam Graci
Toronto, ON M5V 1P9	Orange Peel Enterprises, Inc.
	2183 Ponce de Leon Circle
	Vero Beach, FL 32960

Disclaimer

The ideas and advice contained in this book are based upon the experience and training of the author, as well as scientific information currently available. They are not intended to replace the services of a trained health professional or to substitute for careful medical evaluation and treatment by a qualified, licensed health professional.

Before initiating any of the programs or suggestions described herein, consult and work closely with a knowledgeable licensed health professional. The author and publisher do not recommend changing, eliminating, or adding to your diet any medications, hormones, or nutrients without consulting a personal physician. They specifically disclaim any liability arising directly or indirectly from the use of this book.

Acknowledgments

I owe a great debt to many people who have encouraged my personal growth and helped to bring this volume to fruition.

I am forever grateful to Elvira Patricia Graci, my wife of 27 years, whose gracious ways, loving kindness, and conscientious thoughtfulness to all encourages me to grow daily into a true human being. Her love of God and its manifestation in her life as love for all her sisters and brothers leaves me wonderstruck.

My mother, Grace Graci, who has passed on, demonstrated in her living and her dying that calm loving awareness of the eternal, ever-present Divinity is the birthright of us all. Even today she is a vibrant pole star in my life.

My father, "Papa Joe" Graci, found himself critically ill at 85 years of age. He put to practice all my nutritional suggestions, reversed the course of his health, and until his death in October 1998 at the age of 93, tirelessly encouraged seniors to adopt a healthful lifestyle and superior nutritional program. Many are very glad they did. Good work, Papa Joe.

My late father-in-law, Ronnie Deauville, was a quadriplegic for 37 years of his magnificent life. He was at the height of his Hollywood singing career as a lead singer for Ray Anthony, the Glen Gray Band, and The Tex Beneke–Glen Miller Band, when a car accident crippled his four limbs. This brilliant man examined all the current research on health to find ways for his malfunctioning body to operate at an optimal level. He introduced me to Dr. Erwin Stone, Dr. Linus Pauling, Dr. Abram Hoffer, Dr. Evan Shute, and Dr. Norman Walker, all great humanitarians, each of whom mentored my nutritional awareness and to whom I am indebted. To Patty Deauville, Ronnie's wife and my mother-in-law, who first encouraged me to write this book, thank you for your faith and patience. I owe you a great deal of gratitude.

Thanks also to Diana English, for her typing, patience, and goodwill; without her tireless efforts my words would not be in this book. Thanks to Jennifer Glossop, my editor, and copy editor Liba Berry; their enthusiastic support made it a pleasure to write *The Power of Superfoods*. And a very special thank-you to Hart Hillman, president of the PTR division at Prentice Hall Canada, for encouraging me to share the information contained here, to improve your health. His advice made endless good sense. Thank you for your perseverance.

I am also tremendously grateful to the many people across Canada, the United States, and Europe who attended my lectures and expressed their desire for a book of this kind. One of those people is Robert Harris; another, Mrs. Hilda Densmore (my ardent supporter); and another, my treasured V.J. To all of you, my humble but sincere gratitude.

Dr. Julian Whitaker, M.D., Dr. David Schweitzer, Ph.D., M.D., Harvey Diamond, and Jeanne Marie Martin are four people whose efficacy, dedication, clarity, and humanitarianism I greatly admire. I am most fortunate to count them as good friends and as contributors to this book.

Jude Deauville, Stewart Brown, and Joe Graci, my older brother, have been consistent in their support and have worked tirelessly to bring superior good health to everyone. They are blessed with real spirit, and each is a loving, active supporter of my nutritional research. An equally appreciative thank-you to Scott Riley, David Miller, Elise Maxheleau, Richard Goldwater, Kevin Donoghue, Susan Peterson, Peggy Dace, Glynnis Mileikowsky, Sharon MacFarland, and Bill Faloon for their dedication to humanity's welfare and superior health. And thank you to you, the reader, for using the dietary strategies in this book to achieve optimum health.

Foreword

We're in the midst of a health revolution. What steps can we take for optimum health? Surely we are the first generation who ever seriously asked the question. All generations before us were faced with a more prominent challenge of gaining material security. In fact, the final frontier just might be the pursuit of life at its fullest: Optimum Health.

Optimum Health requires three fundamental things: 1) nutritious fueling of our bodies; 2) reasonable nutritional supplementation; and 3) exercise to train our muscles and heart as well as to keep us limber and comfortable.

You hold in your hands a fascinating book that you can use immediately. As its author points out, our genetic makeup for the ingestion, digestion, and absorption of foods, and their utilization, is the same today as it was thousands of years ago when we were hunter-gatherers. However, our environment, and consequently our food, has changed dramatically. To "eat naturally" today, we must become hunter-gatherers of foods that truly do nurture us, and not consume foods that fill us only to drag us down. Sam Graci has written a book that is chock-full of tips on how to do just that. Sam shows you how to immediately incorporate healthy eating habits into your daily lifestyle, and how to use Superfoods to accelerate healing and achieve optimum health.

Sam draws an appropriate analogy between the engine and our bodies. This book is about food that will "fuel our bodies with high-octane fuels that give each of us more miles per gallon as well as a cleaner running molecular engine." Its intent is for you to look better, feel better, enjoy a more permanently enhanced quality of life, and a fortified immune system that will prevent degenerative disease later in life. I personally follow and enthusiastically endorse the healthy recommendations Sam sets out so clearly in *The Power of Superfoods*.

Most of us are more concerned with the quality of our lives rather than the length of it. This is a handbook for quality living. Perhaps as important as the material contained here is the enthusiasm and commitment of its writer. Anyone who reads this book cannot doubt Sam Graci's sincerity and his insatiable desire to help. Sam takes your hand and leads you, step-by-step, toward Optimum Health.

If you are reading this foreword, you probably have the book. Congratulations! You have made giant strides toward the final frontier.

Dr. Julian Whitaker, M.D., author of *Shed 10 Years in 10 Weeks*, and of the highly acclaimed newsletter *Health and Healing*

Introduction

The Power of Change

HEALTH REFLECTION

At what age will you give up trying?

What good is inspiration if it is not backed by action?
Anthony Robbins, author and inspirational speaker

If we did all the things we are capable of doing,
we would be pleasantly surprised.
Dr. Peter Papadogianis, N.D., M.Sc.

"Happy birthday to you! Happy birthday to you, Papa Joe!," our family's happy voices echoed as we celebrated my father's ninety-second birthday. Vibrant, independent, and healthy, Papa Joe is an inspiration to us all.

Suddenly, one of my nephews called out, "May you live to be a happy and healthy 120, Papa Joe!"

My nephew intended this as a good-humored toast, but is it more than that? Can we live to be healthy at 90, 100, or 120? What health quality and life expectancy should we expect of our bodies?

Papa Joe started life with some health advantages. He was a laborer most of his life, beginning in 1917 with a horse and buggy. Later he owned a produce store. He worked hard and that kept him strong and robust.

When he was about 65, Papa Joe retired. His medicine cabinet was soon stocked with antacids, over-the-counter painkillers, constipation remedies, arthritic-joint rubs—an entire arsenal to defend him from the ills and pains that afflicted him. He trusted those concoctions wholeheartedly. Aging, he believed, was inevitable. He felt vulnerable. Despite my training as a nutritional researcher, I had no influence on him.

Then, at the age of 85, Papa Joe became critically ill. At the time, I was on a lecture tour in California, and my older brother, Joe Jr., rushed him to the hospital. The diagnosis wasn't favorable. My father had an internal rupture, and the bleeding, in spite of the best treatment, just would not stop. An air of failing hope surrounded him.

That night in a dream he heard my voice tell him to make changes in his life. These diet and exercise suggestions were ones he had heard before, but this time he listened. The next day Papa Joe signed himself out of the hospital and began to make drastic changes in his lifestyle and diet. These changes were so powerful and decisive that they fully revived his health, and today, at 92, he is healthier than when he was 65.

Another example of the dynamic power of change is my remarkable sister-in-law. Lani was an outstanding athlete. At 15 she was a diving champion in Florida. Lani loved high-risk activity and would dive off bridges and swim across treacherous waterways. At the age of 17, she dived into the ocean from a seawall in Jacksonville, Florida. Unfamiliar with the location she hit the bottom hard. She broke her neck and was left a quadriplegic with a life expectancy of five years.

In addition to limpness of the arms and legs, quadriplegics suffer from loss of muscle power and nerve sensation, urinary tract infections, lung infections, central nervous system infections, gastrointestinal ulcerations, osteoporosis, bedsores, bowel blockage, excruciating pain, spinal block, and other illnesses that can suddenly end life. In 1958, the date of the diving accident, there were no helpful treatments for spinal cord injuries. Lani's muscle spasms were so strong that aides had to hold her down when they dressed her. Eventually a neurological specialist severed her motor nerves to prevent the severe spasms. Confined to a wheelchair, she went on to graduate from the University of Florida. From there, she went to the University of Alabama where she did graduate work in clinical psychology. Later, as an employee of the Department of Health and Rehabilitative Services in the state of Florida, she promoted legislation to make public buildings, sidewalks, and restrooms in the United States wheelchair accessible. In 1976, President Gerald Ford honored Lani as Disabled Employee of the Year.

Lani continued to experience illnesses and, invariably, once or twice a year, she ended up in the hospital. In 1989 when Lani was 48 years old and had been a quadriplegic for 31 years, she asked me to assist her with a nutritionally balanced diet that would rebuild her immune system, end her chronic pain, reduce her bladder infections, restore her energy, and allow her bowel movements to return naturally. She wanted to transform her life and health. She kept making positive affirmations, which are most effective in bringing about positive, long-term changes. Her determination was outstanding, but even I quietly wondered if it was not too late.

In 1990, I began to work with Lani. Today she has a fuller range of movement with her arms; the progression of osteoporosis has stopped; she has eliminated many medications, and experiences much more energy.

What are those changes that so dramatically altered Lani's and Papa Joe's health? That is what this book is about—changes to your lifestyle that will revive or influence your health for the better, at any age, under any conditions.

Average Life Spans

- 100,000 years ago—Neo-Paleolithic life span was 18 years
- 1797—approximately 25 years
- 1898—approximately 48 years (almost doubled)
- 1998—approximately 80 years (almost doubled again)
- 2018—anti-aging researchers predict potential life spans of 90 to 120 years for those following specific anti-aging protocols

Are the Effects of Aging Inevitable?

We are all aware of the aging process. Each year brings a deterioration of some bodily system. Is this then our inescapable destiny? What should be the life expectancy of our bodies?

After a quarter of a century of nutritional research, I have concluded that progressive deterioration can be slowed, and that the human body can operate efficiently in a youthful state well into our nineties or maybe even to 120.

Today, anti-aging researchers agree that many of the symptoms we associate as biomarkers of aging—wrinkled skin, memory loss, hearing difficulties, lack of vigor and energy, cancer, arthritis, weight gain, osteoporosis, degenerative disease, lack of enthusiasm, hair loss, loss of lean muscle mass and strength—may be more associated with improper nutrition than chronological aging.

Generally, aging begins when a person is about 25 years old. At that time, many of the body's natural functions begin to decline, like a waterfall. Many destructive chemicals form that gradually destroy the integrity of cell walls. One group of these chemicals is called free radicals. The obvious external decline in the skin's flexibility and elasticity, both associated with aging, are the handiwork of uncontrolled free radicals.

Damage to arteries is done by oxygenated cholesterol. Cholesterol and fat leak through the endothelial tissue of the outer artery and into the muscle layer of the artery. The muscle cells begin to multiply, covering the cholesterol particles. The resulting buildup is called plaque. The plaque keeps accumulating until the artery is blocked or even completely closed.

Another example of the body's deterioration is the formation of cancer cells. Once they are initiated and begin to multiply unopposed, the host tissue or skin is eventually destroyed.

In addition, over time, requirements for some nutrients, such as calcium, vitamin D, and vitamin B_{12}, rise in part because our bodies become less efficient at absorbing or manufacturing them, or, as with calcium, because nutrient needs escalate.

However, while nutrient needs increase, calorie needs decline. Dr. Richard Weindrich of the University of Wisconsin has shown that animals fed 35 to 50 percent fewer calories in their middle years live longer and healthier without most of the chronic diseases associated with advanced age.

Aging is a continuum, not a sudden event. The nutritional missteps that lead to ailments from heart disease to osteoporosis in our sixties or seventies, begin in the middle years. In short, it's not years alone that

Trends Similar in Men and Women

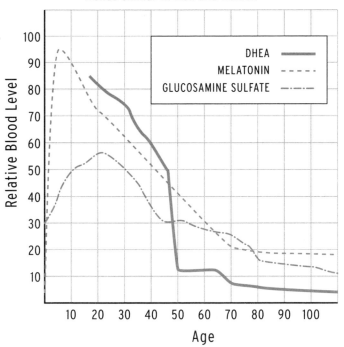

Levels of vital hormones and nutrients drop dramatically after age 25.
Source: With permission from *Health Realities*, Queen and Company Health Communications, Inc.

cause bodily deterioration but the diet and lifestyle we choose. The sooner we make healthier choices the better!

Revitalize Your Life

"Hey, you're going to die of something, right?" This is the excuse people generally cite for not taking care of their physical health. Since ultimately everyone perishes, they rationalize, they shouldn't do anything to sustain their health. The astounding power of control they have over their health and the aging process itself is something they fail to understand or believe.

How can you stop or slow the premature aging process? One significant way is by eating nutrient-rich foods that I call Superfoods. Each of the 100 trillion cells in your body wants to operate at optimal efficiency. Each cell has a built-in, automatic repair and rejuvenation mechanism. Superfoods can fundamentally change the chemistry in your body and give layer upon layer of protection to each of your 100 trillion cells against the chemical assaults that are fundamental to the premature aging process.

This book will help you realize the power you never imagined you had. It will show you a new way to understand aging, and help you counter the feeling that age makes us increasingly vulnerable to disease. Disease is not your inescapable destiny. If you believe it is, you need a shift in your view of aging and an equally attainable goal. You do not need to accept the consequences of premature aging. By following the recommendations contained here, you will allow your cells to operate at an optimal level for many more years without the regrettable "shut-down" most people experience beginning at 25.

The choice is yours! Papa Joe and Lani are only two examples of the many people who have experienced the power of change. They made a positive decision to use Superfoods properly to sustain, accelerate, and heighten their health. And they succeeded in realizing these goals.

What if you did not wait until 85? What if you decided today to make significant counteractions by choosing Superfoods to fundamentally change the chemistry in your body? If you begin to make significant changes now, you can adopt nutritional strategies to defend each and every one of the 100 trillion cells in your body against degenerative diseases and premature aging. The National Institute on Aging in Washington, D.C., reports that if the onset of Alzheimer's disease could be delayed by five years, the United States and Canada would save $40 billion in annual health-care costs.

Whether you enjoy eating meat, are on a vegetarian diet, a lactose-reduced diet, a vegan diet, whether you are a committed junk-food eater, follow a macrobiotic diet, an athletic-enhancing diet, or a diet of your own creation, I want to show you the way we are specifically designed to eat in harmony with our long-standing genetic makeup. So welcome along and *bon appétit!*

Eating Your Way to Better Health

HEALTH REFLECTION

Every single food you eat today directly dictates your health tomorrow.

*Mankind's food supply has changed remarkably in recent years,
but his digestive apparatus has not.*
Dr. Abram Hoffer, Guide to Eating Well for Pure Health

Food is the most intimate consumer product.
Ralph Nader, consumer advocate

What diet fits our human genetic makeup? To better understand our bodies' needs, let's track back to our roots.

Humans evolved as hunters of animals and gatherers of plants. From archeological finds and the remains of primitive hunter-gatherer societies, scientists estimate that our ancestors' diet consisted of about two-thirds unprocessed plant food—fruits, nuts, seeds, legumes, and fiber-rich vegetables—and the rest comprised lean meat or fish. An article in the 1985 *New England Journal of Medicine* surmises the typical diet of Neo-Paleolithic man supplied two to five times the amount of vitamins and minerals that today's foods do.

Once our ancestors began farming, their diet changed. Grains—especially wheat, corn, and rice—became a dietary staple. Domesticated animals, especially cattle, became the prime protein source, and cow's milk became a standard part of our diet. The farmers also ate a narrower range of vegetable foods than the hunters and gatherers had. Furthermore, most domesticated vegetables contained a higher ratio of starch to protein than their former wild forms, which suited our genetic digestive systems better.

Where Are We Today?

What does your diet have to do with the development of the human species? Simply put, our genes have not changed in 10,000 years; only our diet has. It now includes many more fats, sugars, less fiber, and more refined carbohydrates.

Have these changes helped humanity?

Let's tally the score. The U.S.D.A.'s survey of 11,658 Americans showed that on an average day:

- 41 percent did not eat any fruit;
- 72 percent did not eat vitamin C–rich fruits;
- 80 percent did not eat vitamin A–rich fruits and vegetables;
- 82 percent did not eat cruciferous vegetables like broccoli, brussels sprouts, cabbage, cauliflower, etc.; and
- 84 percent did not eat high-fiber, whole-grain foods.

And what are the consequences of our departure from our ancestors' diet?

- Since 1950, the overall incidence of cancer has increased by 44 percent, with breast cancer and male colon cancer up by 60 percent and prostate cancer up by nearly 100 percent.
- In 1987, there were 230,000 heart bypass surgeries in the United States, and in 1990 this figure was up to 392,000; cardiovascular disease is on the rise.
- In 1993, 47,000 people under the age of 44 had a heart attack in the United States.
- 33 percent of all North Americans are overweight, up from 25 percent just a decade ago.

Our North American Diet Is a Killer

The consequences of changing our diet from one comprising lean protein, lots of vegetables, water, some fruit, and moderate amounts of whole grains, to the standard North American diet, has caused a variety of diseases and conditions, among them candida (harmful yeast overgrowth), lack of vigor, indigestion, and increased levels of body fat. With the increased consumption of fatty protein has come a sharp increase in carbohydrate consumption and a reduced intake of vegetables. In our lack of wisdom, we have even created alternatives to water—carbonated soft drinks, coffee, and alcohol.

Paleolithic versus Modern Diet

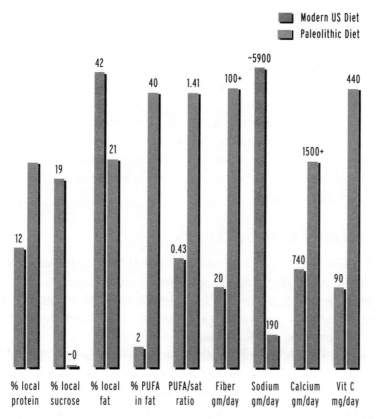

Source: The Paleolithic Prescription, by S. Boyd Eaton, Marjorie Shostak, and Melvin Konner. New York: Harper & Row. 1988.

Two out of three people in North America will die of cancer or heart disease. Many researchers estimate that approximately 50 percent of all cancers as well as 75 percent of all heart disease, are related to diet. Some foods increase our likelihood of cancer and heart disease, while other foods can cut that likelihood in half. Too much total fat, too much sugar, too many calories, too much red meat, not enough enzymes, not enough exercise, not enough water, not enough fiber are the prime dietary culprits. According to the Harvard Report on Cancer Prevention (November 1996), the lifestyle choices we make determine our risk for two-thirds of all cancers.

Problems that were rare a generation ago are now prevalent. Children experience behavioral disturbances, ear infections, speech and hearing difficulties, dental decay, obesity, and violence towards themselves or others.

These are now accepted as part of growing up in North America. This is how many begin life today!

As our bodies mature, we have other conditions to contend with: heart disease, chronic fatigue syndrome, cancer, osteoporosis, arthritis, thin hair, poor skin, excess weight, and inflammation of the stomach and intestines have all reached epidemic proportions in adults. This is how many end their lives today!

And yet, the only problems that traditional Western medicine, which is designed after a "disease model" rather than a "health model," generally attributes to foods are those of malnutrition or obesity; in other words, clinical variables that can be measured in numbers. The intrinsic qualities of good foods are ignored.

Eating Your Way to Better Health

You do have a choice. Instead of the standard North American diet, you can choose foods that contain powerful, natural nutrients that have a built-in capability to neutralize free radicals and spare your body from premature aging. You can return to a simple, nutrient-rich diet that genetically supports superior good health.

To achieve optimum good health from food, you must first understand the degree to which your body is affected by what you put into your mouth. It is startling to realize that the average North American consumes, on average, approximately 4.8 pounds of food daily. This means that in an average lifetime of 80 years, approximately 70 tons of food will pass through your stomach. Imagine 70 pickup trucks full of food rolling up to your front lawn and dumping their loads into one large pile. This is a huge mountain of food to consume and process.

Computer technicians use the descriptive phrase "garbage in equals garbage out," which means that the quality of information retrieved depends upon the initial input. Similarly, improperly fueling our bodies puts demands on our performance, stamina, and ultimately on our appearance. Increasingly, we realize that we are not just what we eat but what we absorb.

If I challenged a group of my fellow researchers to take a large bowl of organically grown, colorful fruits and vegetables into the laboratory, and convert those fruits and vegetables into disease-fighting killer T-cells, memory, emotions, bones, muscles, skin, they would never come out of the laboratory again. Your body, this wondrous organism that is always seeking perfection, has the ability to digest, absorb nutrients, courier them to exact spots in the body and, finally, to eliminate wastes before they become toxic. Your body can perform all these tasks with a precision beyond that of any computer program or our wildest imaginings.

The human body was designed to convert nutrients found in nature's foods into skin, hair, eyes, brains, bones, muscles, nerve impulses, organs, and glands. Our health depends on the digestion, absorption, and interaction of those naturally occurring nutrients. Unsuspecting folks who wolf down a double cheeseburger, large iced soda, and greasy, salt-laden fries do not understand how they are disrupting the exquisite precision of a functioning body. Even those on "good diets" may not appreciate the necessary exactness that allows a human body to run optimally. A deficiency of even the tiniest amount of nature's nutrients can simultaneously begin the premature aging of your inner metabolic process and your appearance.

To function, we require protein, vitamins, minerals, and micronutrients in various amounts. These nutrients are available in selected foods. The body is designed to find, isolate, and transport each nutrient, whether it is vitamin C or an amino acid, to a specific site where it is needed in the body.

Nutrients required in small amounts are referred to as micronutrients. One micronutrient is iodine. As an example of the capability and precision with which your body operates, let us examine the body's use of iodine. Most nutritionists recommend that we consume 150 micrograms (mcg) of iodine daily. A microgram is one-millionth of a gram, less than the weight of the ink from one word in this sentence. A microgram would fit on one-quarter of a pin head. Every day your body painstakingly locates and isolates the few molecules of iodine it finds in sea salt, seafood, Swiss chard, garlic, soybeans, lima beans, Nova Scotia dulse, and so on. Once isolated, the body's transport system couriers those molecules directly to the thyroid gland, situated at the base of the throat. The iodine brought into the thyroid, molecule by molecule, eventually allows the thyroid to produce and deliver powerful hormones called thyroxin and triiodothyronine into the bloodstream. These hormones regulate normal rates of growth in children, and in adults control metabolic rates associated with mood and energy supply. The nutrient must be available before the magic of the body can unfold. If the nutrient iodine is missing, regardless of our self-image or demands of the day, we lack energy and an upbeat mood.

Likewise, powerful, natural nutrients in fresh fruits, vegetables, sea vegetables, grains, yogurt, and protein reduce the plaque buildup in the arteries. Other powerful, natural nutrients in foods and water shield the body from environmental pollutants such as automobile exhaust, excessive sun, factory pollutants, and cigarette smoke; still other natural nutrients in foods and water tackle runaway cancer cells and either destroy them or prevent them from proliferating at one or more stages of development. Cancer cells feed ravenously at the expense of the rest of the body. Thirty-five to 40 percent of all cancer patients die of cachexia, or wasting of the body. Principally, they die of starvation.

Some foods contain ingredients that modify hormones associated with premenstrual syndrome (PMS), menopause, mood swings, and energy loss. You have only to take advantage of these foods to unleash the enormous power they contain. Foods from your refrigerator, cupboard, or fresh-fruit bowl are the most powerful modulator of your body chemistry. Food is the strongest drug directly influencing your body chemistry.

Food is very intimate. Many times a day we take the time to consume food to sustain and nourish our mental and physical body. What could be more intimate than incorporating and making something part of our bodies. Let us stop and think, in this intimate process, what foods we are choosing to become an actual part of us. Ask yourself: Do I want this food to become part of the 100 trillion cells in my body? Is this the food I want in the building blocks of each cell in my body?

One Step Backwards for a Huge Leap Forward

Our ancestors died earlier than we do, but they died of causes we have mostly controlled, such as deadly infectious diseases, an untamed environment, complications of childbirth, and accidents. We die of illnesses that were uncommon in their world. Our illnesses are encouraged by a modern-day environment that is rife with health hazards.

Current research increasingly indicates that reintroducing essential dietary strategies of our forebears' lifestyle dramatically increases our potential for optimum health and accelerated healing. By taking a step back in time we can restructure our faulty diet, with realistic possibilities for improvement. We can turn many foods into "wonder drugs" to combat cancer, heart disease, chronic fatigue, or degenerative diseases. The diet that will do this is a low-calorie diet that supplies adequate amounts of protein, fiber, essential fat, low-glycemic carbohydrates, macronutrients and micronutrients, all extremely critical for maintaining a high nutritional status. (The glycemic index is the rate at which a carbohydrate is absorbed into the bloodstream; the lower the glycemic index for a food, the slower the rate of absorption and the more constant the blood-sugar level or energy level. The higher the glycemic index for a food, the faster it will raise blood-sugar levels and therefore increase insulin secretion.)

Some Basic Guidelines

- To properly maintain your physical energy and mental acuity throughout the day, eat three meals each day and two to three snacks with no more than four hours between each one.
- Eat some protein at each of your three meals.
- Build your immunity to disease by consuming a wide variety of colorful fruits and vegetables.
- Only eat low-fat or fat-free protein sources. If you eat meat, eat free-range animals raised without antibiotics or growth hormones.
- Eat a low-fat diet.
- Eat a low-salt diet.
- Eat a low-sugar diet.
- Eat a high-fiber diet.
- Eat organic, unprocessed foods.
- Avoid consuming overly processed foods, processed meats, and food additives.
- Avoid or limit both alcohol and tobacco consumption.
- Drink clean water.
- Exercise daily.

6 POINT SUMMARY

- Eating is intimate. You have to eat, so you might as well eat wisely.
- Food is the most powerful drug you will ever take. Common foods in your refrigerator, cupboard, or fresh-fruit bowl can age-proof your cells.
- Our genetic structure was designed to function on a low-fat, lean protein diet, with lots of fresh vegetables and a little fruit.
- We may eat a lot of food but find very few of the necessary nutrients to sustain good health, unless the food is absolutely right.
- A diet of lean protein, water, high vegetable content, some fruit, and a few whole grains was our ancestors' diet. This diet is simple, unprocessed, and supports our genetic makeup.
- Our North American diet is a killer and does not support our genetic makeup.

6 POINT ACTION PLAN

- Do not wait for illness to dictate your need for change. Be decisive, take control of your health now!
- When you eat, enjoy the experience. Begin to feel the intimate experience of incorporating that food into each of the 100 trillion cells in your body.
- Set your priorities to eat more health-giving foods every time you eat. If not now, when?
- If your body is malfunctioning, realize that it is not being fueled properly.
- Chew all foods well. Your stomach processes a lot of food but unfortunately has no teeth. You are what you absorb, not just what you eat.
- Cut down—and eventually cut out—all red meat and dairy (except yogurt).

An Introduction to Superfoods

Humanity's mind, stretched to a new idea,
never goes back to its original dimensions.
Oliver Wendell Holmes

When you take care of something, it lasts a long time.
Zen saying

Ten thousand years ago our ancestors did not have houses, health care, or protection from the environment. Every day they faced physical danger, including the chance that they might end up on some predator's evening menu. And not all dangers were large: viruses, bacteria, parasites, yeasts, molds, dirt, and hazardous substances also posed threats of disease and disability. To protect themselves biochemically, their bodies learned to defend and repair themselves.

Many of our ancestors succumbed to early deaths, but others thrived on what nature provided—an incredible variety of colorful whole foods, each with a unique biological complex of vitamins, minerals, cell salts, organic water, fiber, antioxidants, and phytochemicals. Once in the body, these "toxic garbage collectors" moved about freely, protecting cells, organs, and the bloodstream.

Let's look at two groups of these protectors—antioxidants and phytochemicals.

Antioxidants

The human body uses oxygen to liberate energy from some proteins, carbohydrates, and fats. A by-product of this process, called oxidation, is the creation of molecules that are missing one electron. Although these so-called free radicals are an absolutely necessary part of normal, healthy body metabolism, they are unstable because they steal electrons from other molecules, damaging proteins, cell membranes, and causing a buildup of cellular debris; in short, causing disease and premature aging. Moreover, uncontrolled free radicals are thought to cause the devastation associated with heart disease, cancer, arthritis, stroke, cataracts, Alzheimer's disease, and other health problems.

To protect itself against free radicals, the body produces cellular police called antioxidants. Antioxidants easily give an electron to a free radical to allow the electron to become stable. This balance between necessary free radicals and protective antioxidants has guaranteed our survival for thousands of years. In today's technologically advanced environment, however, we face an enormous increase in free-radical-generating stresses, including environmental pollutants, radiation, pesticides, herbicides, food preservatives, physical overexertion, illness, excess sun, excess iron in the diet, poor nutrition, cigarette smoke, chronic infection, oxidized fat, medications, alcohol, drugs, automobile exhaust, barbecue smoke, paint fumes, odorless fumes from toxic-dump sites, fumes from synthetic carpets, and unnoticed sulfur dioxide from faroff industrial fumes carried in the wind. On top of this, dust, dirt, parasites, bacteria, viruses, yeast, stale air in our homes or workplaces, fungicides, herbicides on foods, mercury in our dental fillings, PCBs, aluminum in cookware, antibiotic residues and various veterinary compounds found in animal meats (poultry, turkey, red meat, dairy products) threaten our health daily.

More than 100,000 industrial chemicals (called xenobiotics) are used today and about 1,000 new chemicals are introduced worldwide each year. All are tested for the potential to cause cancer and birth defects, but not for the effects on the human endocrine and reproductive systems, where they could cause severe hormone mimicking implicated in a wide range of human and wildlife health problems.

Combine all this with the emotional stress we confront on a daily basis and it is no wonder many feel that we face "a free radical storm." The result of too many free radicals on a system depleted of enzymes is devastating. Cells become severely damaged and can no longer function or reproduce properly, which lead to nearly every facet of the decline associated with disease and premature aging.

The Encouraging News: Antioxidants and Phytochemicals

Despite this grim picture, there is good news. In addition to the antioxidants our bodies produce, nature provides us with hundreds of antioxidants in the foods we eat. Phytochemicals (from the Greek *phyto*, meaning "plant") are naturally occurring compounds that plants create for their own protection and survival; they take the form of enzymes, pigments, and hormones. They give plants their color, odor, and taste. Some, like beta-carotene, are well known, but 90 percent of phytochemicals are still unidentified. Beta-carotene is the carotenoid that gives carrots their orange color, but there may be as many as 600 different carotenoids in foods. The most commonly known antioxidants and phytochemicals (some prefer "phytonutrients") are vitamin C, vitamin E (alpha, beta, and gamma tocopheryls), beta-carotene, selenium, chromium, zinc, grape seed extract, ginkgo biloba, bilberry, green tea, and alpha lipoic acid.

Many years have passed since the discovery that vitamin C prevents scurvy, that thiamin (vitamin B_1) wards off beriberi and that calcium protects against rickets. Recently, nutritional scientists have focused on promising research that hints at the potent power of phytochemicals to prevent modern plagues such as cancer, heart disease, diabetes, arthritis, premature aging, and immune deficiency.

In the late 1970s, research in Japan demonstrated that green tea can prevent cancer-cell initiation, that garlic can lower cholesterol, and that chlorella, a freshwater green microalgae, can stop cancer cells from spreading. The substances responsible were the catechins in green tea, the sulfur in garlic, and the chlorophyll in chlorella.

Where to Find Phytochemicals and Antioxidants

Phytochemicals and antioxidants protect plants against free radicals, parasites, bacteria, viruses, insects, and strong sunlight. When we eat plants, their phytochemicals and antioxidants also protect our bodies from damage, infection, and disease. In other words, the thousands of phytochemicals that can help you live stronger and longer are right there in your produce market or in bins of legumes.

These substances work best in natural combinations—as they're found in food. You need to eat a variety of plant foods to get broad-spectrum protection. Phytochemicals in plants are not injured by cooking. Antioxidants are more sensitive to heat. Lightly steam or sauté vegetables so they remain crunchy-tender. Also try to consume some raw vegetables daily.

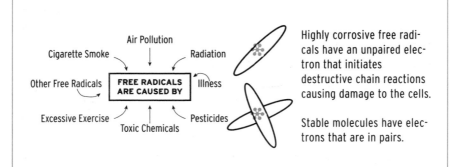

Air Pollution
Cigarette Smoke — Radiation
Other Free Radicals — **FREE RADICALS ARE CAUSED BY** — Illness
Excessive Exercise — Pesticides
Toxic Chemicals

Highly corrosive free radicals have an unpaired electron that initiates destructive chain reactions causing damage to the cells.

Stable molecules have electrons that are in pairs.

The physical and mental deterioration typically associated with aging isn't necessarily a condition of human maturity, but of excess free radicals.

Dietary antioxidants help:

- maximize life span
- prevent cell damage
- slow the aging process
- speed wound healing
- prevent arthritis

- protect against heart disease
- prevent cancer
- eliminate allergies
- prevent mental deterioration
- decrease endogenous free radical reactions

Without antioxidants we would perish within hours, because of free radical destruction. Antioxidants are molecules that contain several easily removable electrons. Without destroying itself, the antioxidant is able to donate an electron to a free radical, thereby neutralizing its violent potential and rendering it harmless.

antioxidant

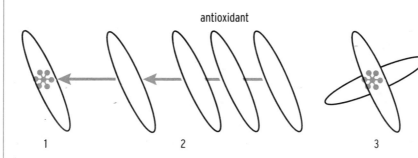

1   2   3

1. The highly corrosive free radical has one electron.
2. The antioxidant donates one electron to the free radical.
3. The free radical is now stable.

12 Food Groups with Beneficial Phytochemicals and Antioxidants

1. RED AND ORANGE FRUITS AND VEGETABLES Acerola berries, carrots, red and yellow peppers, cantaloupe, squash, watermelon, pumpkins, strawberries, raspberries, red currants, peaches, and mangoes are all high in carotenoids. Studies demonstrate that carotenoids decrease the risk of heart disease and cancer, enhance mental functioning, prevent cataracts and macular degeneration of the eyes, and support immune functions.

   Tip: Eat seasonal, locally grown, organic produce.

2. GREEN CRUCIFEROUS VEGETABLES Broccoli, arugula, bok choy, brussels sprouts, cabbage, cauliflower, turnips, collards, rapini, kohlrabi, and kale block tumor growth, retard colon cancer, boost immunity, and prevent polyps in the colon. They speed the removal of estrogen from the body, which helps to suppress breast cancer. They increase the body's production of glutathione peroxidase, which may be the most important enzyme system in the body to slow down the aging of cells. Cancer can begin with a carcinogenic molecule—when the food you eat or the air you breathe invades a cell. But if indoles found in cauliflower, or sulforaphane, found in broccoli, also reaches the cell, they activate a group of enzymes that whisk the carcinogen out of the cell before it can cause any harm.

   Tip: Dice raw cruciferous vegetables very fine and add them to salads or as garnishes to cooked stews, casseroles, soups, entrées, just prior to serving.

3. TOMATOES All varieties of tomatoes are high in lycopene, which prevents macular degeneration in the eyes and devastating chain reactions of oxygen-free radical molecules. As anticancer agents, tomatoes are linked in particular to lower rates of pancreatic and cervical cancer.

   Tip: Eat a variety of all colored tomatoes.

4. BEANS, NUTS, SEEDS, PEAS, LEGUMES All types are good, especially if they are soaked and sprouted before cooking to reduce both their phytic-acid content and enzyme inhibitors that interfere with protein digestion. Organic soy sprouts contain genistein, which is especially antagonistic to breast cancer cells. Seed foods like soybeans contain protease inhibitors (PI), a substance that can partially protect the seed from digestion. New evidence suggests that PIs may stop tumor growth. Researchers at the National Cancer Institute in Bethesda, Maryland, have found what appears to be potent anticancer

properties in soy called isoflavones and phytoestrogens. Each of these foods slows tumor growth in some way. They contain essential fats you need daily (especially flaxseed, pumpkin seed, hemp seed, black currants, and borage).

Tips: • Eat soy sprouts daily.
- Soy foods should be either fermented (such as tofu or miso) or soaked, sprouted, and cooked to help with digestion.
- Sprout sunflower and red clover seeds at home.

5. YOGURT About 70 to 80 percent of the world's population cannot digest lactose, the sugar in dairy. Since the lactose in milk is removed in fermentation, lactose-intolerant people can, however, eat yogurt. The active culture of bacteria (lactobacillus) contained in yogurt can fortify the immune system. Yogurt in the diet raises the level of natural beneficial killer T-cells and raises the internal production of the substance interferon that destroys cancer cells. Yogurt in the intestines actually blocks carcinogens, or cancer-causing agents: the more yogurt eaten, the less chance of breast cancer developing.

Tips: • Each day, consume 1 to 2 cups of organic, "live-cultured" yogurt (or acidophilus) or probiotic cultures (active "healthy" bacteria) grown on brown rice. Eat only unsweetened, plain, white yogurt, since the sugar was intended to be digested and moved out of the stomach in 15 minutes.
- Never mix yogurt with fruit or sweeteners such as honey or maple syrup. The protein in yogurt remains in the stomach, being digested, for $1\frac{1}{2}$ hours. When the sugar from fruit or a sweetener mixes with the protein, it languishes in the stomach for the $1\frac{1}{2}$ hours. This causes a fermentation process that produces both alcohol and more sugar that feed yeast, called candida albicans, that rapidly multiply, initiating a yeast infection.
- Fat-free dry cottage cheese is also recommended.

6. ORGANIC WHOLE GRAINS Whole wheat, barley, spelt, buckwheat, brown rice, unpolished basmati rice, rye, oats, quinoa, millet, amaranth, and kamut are all high-fiber grains. They prevent constipation, eliminate extra estrogen and carcinogens from the colon, and are antiparasitic. Grains protect against colon cancer, regulate cholesterol levels, and help prevent high blood pressure. They help regulate insulin, stabilize blood-sugar levels, and keep bowel transit times regular.

Tip: Experiment and eliminate wheat from your diet for a month, as a majority of the population have a wheat intolerance. In its place try other grain combinations, especially the natural sourdough combinations that help correct the acidic pH in the intestinal tract.

7. HERBS All herbs, including milk thistle, echinacea, Siberian ginseng, licorice root, ginkgo biloba, Japanese green tea, grape seed extract, European bilberry, hawthorn, turmeric, ginger, cinnamon, capsaicin (cayenne), and clove have powerful anticancer powers, act as potent antioxidants to prevent cell walls from aging, and are anti-inflammatory against arthritis and rheumatic diseases. They keep facial skin elastic and flexible. They are antibacterial, antiviral, antiparasitical, and boost "good" HDL cholesterol. They lower the risk of heart disease. Grape seed and skins contain resveratrol, perhaps the most potent anticancer phytochemical.

Tip: Use a full-spectrum grape extract daily.

8. ONIONS AND GARLIC Since the dawn of civilization, onions and garlic have been used to treat a host of illnesses successfully. They are broad-range antibiotics that combat bacteria, viruses, and intestinal parasites. Onions and garlic lower blood pressure, blood cholesterol, and prevent dangerous blood clotting. Both are at the top of the list as cancer-preventing foods. Garlic, a member of the lily family, may be the most important herb to strengthen the immune system. Raw garlic is more powerful than its cooked counterpart. The volatile odor in garlic contains allicin, a substance which is formed when the enzyme alliase reacts to allin, and which is the source of its pungent odor. The enzyme is inactivated when heated. Diallyl sulfide (DAS), organosulfides, and selenium are compounds of garlic that have been shown to inactivate potent carcinogens.

Tip: I eat raw garlic each day and have no garlic odor. Before you go to sleep, finely chop two cloves of garlic and place on a tablespoon. Swallow this with water and do not chew.

9. CITRUS FRUITS Grapefruit, oranges, tangerines, lemons, and limes collectively deactivate carcinogens, help prevent lung disease, reduce cholesterol, protect against cataracts, and boost immunity. They appear especially to protect against stomach and pancreatic cancer. Citrus juices are antiviral and the pulp in citrus fruits contains a unique pectin that may reverse atherosclerosis (clogged arteries).

Tips: • Use organically grown citrus and eat some of the well-washed skin and white pulp, which are not in their juices.
   • Eat one citrus fruit daily and squeeze one lemon into your drinking water each day. The lemon's beneficial antimicrobial

and mucous-eliminating properties eliminate parasites from your body.

10. SEA VEGETABLES Nova Scotia dulse, chlorella, spirulina (blue-green algae), Irish moss, kombu, nori, wakame, and dunaliella salina (South Pacific algae) are full of rare trace minerals. Sea vegetables are alkaline-forming to buffer the acid ashes of proteins and grains. They remove from the body toxic chemicals and heavy metals like mercury. They are antibacterial and antiviral and combat the herpes virus that causes cold sores on the lips or mouth area.

Tip: Because of their iodine content, soybeans or soy products should always be accompanied by some form of sea vegetables to counteract soy's thyroid-suppression tendency.

11. GRASSES Grasses, including alfalfa, barley, and wheat grass, provide the body with an enormous amount of chlorophyll and alkalinity. Chlorophyll deodorizes bad breath and kills bacteria in the mouth and colon.

Tip: Grow grasses, such as wheat grass, and juice them yourself. Grasses should be harvested young, while they contain no allergy-causing gluten. You can also purchase them as dry powders, which you mix with water and drink.

12. COLORFUL FRUITS, VEGETABLES, AND MUSHROOMS These foods, with which I include olives, contain huge varieties of antioxidants and phytochemicals. Leafy greens, yellows, reds, and purples are all natural cancer inhibitors. Their enzymes aid digestion if some are eaten raw at each meal.

Tips: • Use one tablespoon daily of organic, extra-virgin, expeller-pressed olive oil (always unheated) on your salad.

- Consume bitter green vegetables like escarole, rapini, endive, dandelions, or natural sauerkraut three times a week.
- Ferment or culture vegetables at home, and use once a week.
- Fresh vegetables and fruits can be juiced. Fruit juices should be mixed with water and sipped. You require only about four ounces of fruit juice daily because of the high sugar content. When juicing vegetables, use only two carrots per serving and use all other vegetables like watercress, cucumbers, and so on, to keep the sugar (calorie) count down. Two carrots provide 25,000 IU of beta-carotene. Each fresh fruit and vegetable is a potent source of live enzymes and organic, easily absorbed food-sourced vitamins and minerals.

ANTIOXIDANTS AND PHYTOCHEMICALS IN SUPERFOODS

Active Element	Superfoods	Protective Action
Genistein and daidzein	Legumes, soybean sprouts	Inhibits estrogen and receptor enzymes
Protease Inhibitor	Fermented soy products, rice	Destroys enzymes involved in spread of cancer cells
Flavonoids	All herbs, fruits, veggies	Blocks cancer enzyme receptors
Indole-3-carbinols	Cruciferous vegetables, kale, broccoli, cauliflower, mustard greens, cabbage, brussels sprouts	Breaks down estrogen; inhibits cancer growth; quickly detoxifies xenobiotics
Isothicyanates	Mustard, horseradish, acerola berries, all herbs, chili peppers	Detoxifies carcinogens; removes them from the body
Sulphoraphane	Broccoli	Extremely powerful antioxidant
Sulfur	Garlic, onions, bee pollen	Inhibits cancer, detoxifies; promotes glutathione production
Catechins (tannins)	Bilberry, Japanese green tea	Very powerful antioxidants
Fiber	Whole grains, vegetables, fruits, nuts, seeds, legumes (sprouted), hemp seeds, apple fiber, whole brown rice, bran	Absorbs bile and cancer-causing substances: improves healthy colon bacteria; may improve estrogen balance; reduces serum cholesterol
Lignans	Flaxseed, walnuts, pure soy lecithin, milk thistle	Inhibits estrogen; protects against breast and colon cancer; inhibits prostaglandins that spread cancer; modulates PMS
Glutathione	Lean beef, potatoes, avocados	Immune-enhancing; protects liver from toxins; antioxidant
Eleutheroside E	Siberian E. ginseng	Anti-fatigue, anti-stress
Omega-6 fatty acids	Leafy vegetables and seeds, evening primrose, sunflower, borage, and black-currant oils	Regulates prostaglandins; maximizes immunity; reduces cholesterol
Omega-3 fatty acids	Flaxseed oil, fish oil, hemp oil	Anticancer; antitumor; reduces cholesterol
"Friendly Bacteria" (GI flora)	Active culture yogurt, dairy-free probiotic cultures, fermented veggies, FOS (fructo-oligosaccharides)	Enhances immunity; decreases level of carcinogens; detoxifies; deactivates enzymes that may prompt agents turning into cancer; protects intestines; activates phytoestrogens

ANTIOXIDANTS AND PHYTOCHEMICALS IN SUPERFOODS

Active Element	Superfoods	Protective Action
Triterpenoids	Licorice root	Inhibits estrogens and prostaglandins; slows down rapidly dividing cancer cells
Polyacetylene	Parsley, curry, turmeric	Inhibits prostaglandins; destroys cancer-causing benzopyrene
Terpenes	Citrus fruit, pulp and skins	Increases helpful enzymes to destroy carcinogens; decreases cholesterol
Carotene (vitamin A precursor)	Barley and alfalfa grass, carrots, sweet potato, squash, yams, all red, orange, and yellows	Antioxidant; normalizes precancerous cells (alpha, beta, and many more carotenes combined)
Retinoids (vitamin A analog)	Red, orange, and yellow produce, spirulina and chlorella	Protects epithelial tissue; anticancer
Vitamin A	Orange, yellow, and green vegetables; liver, milk, cantaloupe	Antioxidant; anticancer agent
Vitamin C	Acerola berries, fruits, vegetables, supplements, edible flowers	Antioxidant cell protection; immune support; inhibits nitrosamines in stomach
Vitamin D	Fish, moderate sunlight exposure	May have anticancer effects for breast and colon
Vitamin E (tocopherol)	Wheat germ, nuts, seeds, whole grains, plant oils and supplements	Antioxidant; immune support; inhibits tumor growth
Selenium	Garlic, onion, whole grains, tuna, cabbage, nutritional yeast	Antioxidant; immune support; cancer inhibitors
Plant Sterols	Cucumber, cabbage, tomato, squash, whole grains, broccoli	Reduces cholesterol and differentiation agents
Lycopene	Red grapefruit, tomato	Antioxidant; combats cancer cells
Dipolar molecule	Pure soy lecithin	Emulsifies and removes cholesterol
Chlorophyll	Chlorella, wheat grass	Antibacterial; antiviral
Resveratrol	Grape seed and skin (extracts)	Powerful anticancer inhibitor
Flavonglycosides	Ginkgo biloba	Inhibitor of lipid peroxidation in the brain
Silymarin	Milk thistle	Supports liver enzymes and liver cleansing

Making Superfoods a Part of Your Life

Superfoods are a legal, free labor force that greatly benefit your health and longevity. These foods are not expensive and are readily available year-round in North America in your local, organically grown farmers' produce stand; local farmers' markets; in grocery-store produce sections; in specialty-produce stores; in ethnic markets; in frozen-food sections; as seeds, nuts, peas, and legumes in bins at dry bulk-food stores; in quality health food stores everywhere as herbs, organic produce, frozen vegetables, seeds, nuts, peas, legumes, organic whole grains, organic rice, and seasonal produce; in your own or a neighbor's orchard, vegetable garden, berry patch, herb garden, balcony container garden, window herb garden, and right on your kitchen countertop where you can easily watch red clover or sunflower seeds sprout, bursting full of antioxidants and phytochemicals.

A plant-based diet protects your body from a host of chemicals and pathogens that bombards you daily, whether you are sleeping, exercising, driving the children to school, operating a computer, plowing a field, walking with your loved one through a park, meditating, or dancing up a storm with some good friends.

Superfoods act as natural chemical collectors, or toxic-garbage collectors, roaming your blood vessels and 100 trillion cells, to help neutralize and eliminate the thousands of various chemicals that we breathe, eat, or swallow each day. Your cells have been age-proofed by nature, and by consuming Superfoods you have eliminated toxic residues, wastes, and chemicals before they seriously hurt you. Foods have come to the rescue and all along helped you to repel the oxygen-free-radical storm and chemicals zeroing in to destroy your natural beauty and strength.

If you ate broccoli (full of sulforaphane) at lunch, tomatoes (high in lycopene) at supper, a yam (full of beta-carotene) at lunch, low-fat tofu (full of genistein) at supper, oatmeal (full of plant sterols and fiber) at breakfast, an organic apple (full of malic and tartaric acids and pectin) for a midmorning snack or a "green drink" (see Chapter 4) of condensed Superfoods midafternoon, you would have methodically reinforced your body's ability to isolate, hold, and drag chemical intruders from your body before they can do any harm.

The next chapter will tell you how you can make Superfoods a part of your life.

5 POINT SUMMARY

- The human immune system developed to combat "living threats" such as viruses, bacteria, parasites, dirt, and dangerous substances that could initiate cancer or degenerative disease.
- Nature provides the human body and its immune system with an incredible array of anticancer, antibacterial, antiviral, antidisease supports called phytochemicals and antioxidants, which are found in many common foods.
- Foods that are extremely potent sources of these powerful phytochemicals and antioxidants I call Superfoods. They are toxic-waste collectors patrolling your body.
- Some examples of Superfoods are: apples, pears, oranges, lemons, lettuce, tomatoes, soy sprouts, all herbs, yams, whole grains, garlic, grapes, yogurt, legumes, seeds and nuts, sea vegetables, and ALL fruits and vegetables.
- You need Superfoods daily to protect your cells and bloodstream from the ever-growing and unsuspecting chemical threats in our environment.

5 POINT ACTION PLAN

- Beginning today, eat more fresh, seasonal fruits, vegetables, and also herbs as garnishes to age-proof your cells.
- Consume 2 to 3 pieces of whole, organic fruit each day. Make one fruit selection a citrus fruit and eat some of the skin and/or pulp.
- When cooking vegetables, try to leave them crunchy-tender. Eat some vegetables uncooked, such as parsley, shredded carrots, celery sticks, red-pepper slices, tomatoes, salads, and herbal garnishes at two meals each day. High-quality frozen vegetables can replace fresh vegetables on occasions that necessitate their use.
- Go out of your way to use a wide variety of colors in your fresh fruit and vegetable selection. To add color to dishes, grate or shred carrots, beets, celery, radicchio, and turnips; or chop herbs such as parsley, watercress, rosemary, basil, thyme, and ginger—unheated—to your final plate.
- Use in moderation some combination of whole-grain sourdough, spelt, quinoa, rye, millet, amaranth, hemp seed, and kamut breads. Chew these well, as they begin digestion in the mouth.

Use Superfoods Daily

HEALTH REFLECTION

Superfood antioxidants and phytochemicals give your cells layer upon layer of protection and accelerated healing. Fuel your body wisely.

Sickness is not what the body is for.
Dr. David Schweitzer, Ph.D., M.D.

The significant problems we have today ... cannot be solved at the same level of thinking with which we created them.
Albert Einstein

This chapter explains how you can incorporate Superfoods into your daily diet. In doing so you will not be giving up anything; rather, you will be adding life-giving, life-sustaining whole foods: fruits, vegetables, whole grains, water, sea vegetables (algae), herbs, legumes, nuts, lean protein, fiber, vitamins, minerals, food enzymes, and essential fatty acids (EFAs). These foods are stockpiled with antioxidants and phytochemicals that block the function of and protect the body against the initiation of cancer cells.

Your family, friends, and co-workers may challenge your choice for change. Many of them will not hesitate to voice their pessimism. "You think that stuff is going to make you live longer?" "Gee, why do you have to be so different? You're getting weird." However, once the results of your new lifestyle habits begin to show in the sparkle of your eyes, the sheen in your hair, the clarity of your thinking, and a more positive attitude towards yourself and life, those pessimists may be the first to compliment you and, who knows, they may opt for change also!

Fueling Your Body

Cells in your body are being replaced constantly. If each cell is replaced exactly, this indicates that your body's biochemical interactions continue to work optimally. Within six months, most cells in your body will be replaced. The body you have today is built almost entirely of what you ate over the past six months. If the proteins, fats, and carbohydrates you consumed were of high quality, chances are, your bones, teeth, muscles, blood, and nervous system are in tip-top shape.

In their comprehensive book *Prescription for Nutritional Healing*, Dr. James F. Balch, and his wife, Phyllis A. Balch, compare the body's cells to millions of tiny engines that are on call 24 hours a day, seven days a week. These tiny motors require "high-octane fuels" to run smoothly. When you fuel your body with low-octane fuels that don't give it the proper amount of energy and leave a lot of "sticky" cellular debris that is toxic or harmful to the engine's continued performance, your body malfunctions and stops repairing itself.

This extraordinary body nature so graciously and skillfully designed for your benefit has an amazing ability to heal itself. Consider what happens when you cut your finger or nick your face shaving. Your body automatically coordinates complex systems to coagulate the blood and stop the bleeding. Lymphocytes are couriered via immuglobulins to counter infection. A scab is formed over the wound as a protective barrier, allowing new skin to generate beneath its mantle, as ruptured blood vessels heal. Eventually the scar heals as well. If you could watch this process under a microscope, you would be absolutely amazed at the "magic" taking place. Medicine has no simple answer for this complex feat. Nature does not do this using guesswork. It accomplishes the process with orderly and incredible precision. There is no command station or organ specific for repair. The body intrinsically knows how to heal the impaired function.

The complexity of this accomplishment is enormous. Most people just consider it normal until their system malfunctions. Then they turn to harsh reactive "antis"—antidepressants, antihistamines, antidiarrheals, antidiuretics, anti-inflammatories, anxiolytics, antibiotics, and antibacterials. These drugs are all strangers to the body and have complicated side effects.

We have lost our trust in the body's ability for self-diagnosis and spontaneous self-repair. Therefore, we have also lost our natural balance. It is essential to the body's healing capacity that we take the time to follow a Superfood dietary strategy.

THE DIET/DISEASE LINK

Although heart disease is still the leading cause of death in North America, the mortality rate from heart disease is declining, thanks to better education and treatment. Although cancer continues to be the second leading cause of death in North America, the prognosis for certain forms of the disease has vastly improved since 1980. Each of us owes a debt of gratitude to the researchers, health professionals, physicians, and scientists who have taken us this far. Researchers have shown a direct link between diet and cancer by studying ethnic groups in their respective countries, compared to those who have migrated to North America.

Take a look at these facts:

- Japanese women on a very low-fat diet seldom contract breast cancer. Japanese women who move to North America and change their diets experience much higher rates of breast cancer.

- Africans who eat a high-fiber diet seldom contract bowel cancer. Africans who move to North America and change their diets have much higher rates of colon cancer.

Common Superfood Support

Let's look at the different groups of foods that can fuel your body with high-octane fuels and examine when they should be eaten.

Fruits and Vegetables

Our grandmothers and mothers were in perfect balance with nature when they encouraged us to eat our vegetables. I hear my mother's voice even now: "Eat your greens." As we saw in the previous chapter, fruits and vegetables offer the body a huge array of antioxidants and phytochemicals, as well as organic water, cell salts, fiber, vitamins, minerals, high-quality carbohydrates for energy, and a small amount of protein. They offer significant protection from cancer, heart disease, and degenerative diseases, and allow the immune system to function well. They are necessary for good cell reproduction. They support the body's ability to self-repair as it finds necessary.

Be Daring—Invite Some New Veggies Home for Supper Tonight

- Eat ten servings daily of fruits and vegetables—a minimum of five full cups of veggies and salad each day from a variety of colors and textures. One serving of a fruit, vegetable, or salad is equal to half a cup.
- Vary your fruits and vegetables by color, flavor, texture and shape, and growing style.

GO ORGANIC

One of the most encouraging, positive changes I see happening in society is the rapid growth and availability of organic fruits, vegetables, herbs, grains, dairy and animal foods. This has happened as a response to consumer demand for chemical-free food. Organic foods are free of pesticides, fungicides, ripening agents, fumigants, and other unhealthy toxic, manmade chemicals. The residues of these toxic chemicals in our food chain are major health hazards for everyone. Try to purchase organically grown foods. Support the stores that stock them and demand organic foods from the ones that don't include them in their produce section.

Organic farmers enrich and rebuild soil naturally by the use of compost and manure. They do not use chemicals to extend the life of the produce after it is picked, nor do they put wax on the food to give it a shiny appearance. Since organic produce does not have the wax coating or insecticide or fungicide residues on the surface, you do not have to peel or scrub organic produce before you eat it. All you have to do is wash it well. Because you can eat the peel and skin, organic produce provides more fiber and nutrition. The *Journal of Applied Nutrition* indicates that organic apples, pears, potatoes, and wheat had over 90 percent more minerals than conventionally grown food.

Organically grown food can cost more, but the extra price is well worth the saving to your health. Besides, if enough consumers buy organically grown produce, the price will come down.

If you do use commercially grown produce, give your fruits and veggies a cleansing bath before you eat them. Solutions are available in whole-food stores and supermarkets. Made from naturally derived citrus fruits and coconut extracts, these products remove surface pesticides, enhance the removal of dirt from hard-to-clean fruits and vegetables, and kill bacteria. They have been clinically proven to remove E.coli, salmonella, shigella, and other bacteria.

Designate one scrub brush to wash all fruits and vegetables. Rinse it well and often. Each evening sprinkle a little hydrogen peroxide on the brush head, let sit for 20 seconds, and rinse off. This keeps the brush germ free.

By color: Choose fruits and vegetables of every color: green, red, yellow, orange, white, purple, brown.

By flavor: Try bland in lettuce, pungent in garlic, sweet in beets, or sharp in cilantro;

By texture and shape: Incorporate tender sunflower sprouts, hearty squashes, irregular roots, and various leaves.

By growing style: One day eat vegetables that grow upwards (broccoli, rapini, cauliflower); the next day choose veggies that grow downwards (roots such as carrots, yams, parsnips, and turnips); the next, eat ones that hang (pole beans, broad beans, zucchini, eggplant, yellow summer squash); and then choose ones that grow sideways (squash, pumpkins).

- Eat some raw veggies daily for their enzymes: at two meals a day, have salad, celery sticks, or shredded veggies. Add a small portion of protein to your daily salad—such as pinto beans, fava beans, fat-free dry cottage cheese, white water-packed solid albacore tuna, chicken pieces, baked tofu, whole freshly ground seeds or nuts or tempeh.

- Two to five times a week consume small amounts of sea vegetables: Nova Scotia dulse, hiziki, nori, wakame, chlorella, Irish moss, or spirulina. Chop or sprinkle them on salads, in stews, on top of lightly steamed vegetables. They are available in health food stores and Asian food markets. Roll your own sushi at home, in nori seaweed squares. Make soups with seaweed stock or miso. Use Nova Scotia dulse daily, as it contains a moderate amount of iodine. Only use kelp under health-professional care, as it contains too much iodine that may cause an imbalance in your body's homeostasis (balance) if used daily.

- Firm tofu, soybeans, and soy products contain a thyroid-depressing element. To counterbalance it, eat these foods with a sea vegetable rich in iodine. Consume dulse, wakame, or agar regularly if you are vegetarian. Choose tamari, which contains more protective phytochemicals, rather than soy sauce. Bragg Aminos, a condiment made from soybeans, contains natural sodium. If you prefer less sodium, dilute either a wheat-free tamari or a wheat-free Bragg Aminos with one-third water. Both products are available at health food stores.

- Exchange fat for fiber: do what the Japanese do—make complex carbohydrates your staple. Eat 40 to 50 grams of insoluble fiber a day (250 percent more than the average North American) from fruits, vegetables, sprouted and cooked beans, and sprouted seeds.

- Eat three pieces of fruit daily: eat the whole organic fruit with the skin. Chew fruit well. Consume one citrus fruit a day, and fresh berries and melons in season. Fruit juices are high in calories and lack the fiber of whole fruits. When you drink fruit juices, sip four ounces or mix the juice with water.

- Never, never, never combine raw fruit with other foods. Celery juice (99.9 percent water) is the only exception: it can be combined with fruit juices. Never combine honey or fruit with yogurt or it may feed an overgrowth of the yeast candida in the small intestine. Eat fruits whole, one at a time. Fruits were meant to digest easily, give you energy, and leave your stomach in about half an hour. If you mix them with proteins, they may sit in your stomach for 1.5 to 3 hours, where they languish. They then ferment, forming sugars and alcohol that feed yeast called candida albicans. Candida overgrowth is a problem for a majority of North Americans. Eat fruit 30 minutes before other foods or in between meals, at least two hours after any other food.

- Cook vegetables crunchy-tender to preserve their heat-sensitive nutrients such as vitamins and enzymes.

- Eat healing herbs daily: add culinary herbs such as cumin, basil, poppy seeds, oregano, parsley, dill, rosemary, and marjoram to salads or as garnishes on entrées. Drink herbal teas such as chamomile to replace coffee and tea. Try them plain without honey, milk, or rice milk. Alternate your herbal-tea choices.

GAS ALERT

If you increase your consumption of fruits and vegetables, especially the cruciferous vegetables (broccoli, brussels sprouts, cabbage, and cauliflower) and experience flatulence, bloating, or a "rumblin-tumblin" stomach, you may not have enough of the enzyme alpha-galactosidase in your digestive system. Commercial products like Beano, which contain alpha-galactosidase, are available in pharmacies, health food stores, or supermarkets. Use a few capsules or five drops of liquid in or on the first mouthful of any of the above foods. Beano is also extremely effective for those who experience gas, indigestion, or bloating after eating whole grains, tofu, beans, peas, seeds, or nuts. Do not avoid these Superfoods because they give you gas or digestive difficulties. Simply overcome the condition quickly with alpha-galactosidase.

Fiber

Fiber is the indigestible residue in the plants we eat. Made up of cellulose, gum, pectin, mucilages, lignins, hemicellulose, and polysaccharides, dietary fiber is necessary daily for good digestive health, quality inner hygiene of the intestines, and efficient bowel movements. Populations that have a low fiber intake have higher incidences of colon cancer.

- Choose a variety of fiber sources daily: fruits, vegetables, and whole grains. (See Chapter 9.)
- Insoluble fiber, like cellulose in grains, is a good bulking agent that helps to eliminate cholesterol. Soluble fibers like pectin in apples or celery helps to clean the bowel and keeps the body regular.

Whole Grains

There are good reasons for the popularity of grains. Together with beans, they are the only foods that contain all the major nutrient groups needed by the body: carbohydrates, protein, fats, vitamins, minerals, and fiber. Animal foods contain protein but no carbohydrates; sugar is pure carbohydrates without protein; and fruits and vegetables are high in vitamins and minerals but too low in protein and fats.

- Use whole grains as condiments or a side dish, not as the primary source of your complex-carbohydrate intake. (See Chapter 9.)
- Choose whole grains, those with the germ and bran left on. Because of processing, refined white flour has lost up to 97 percent of the vitamin

B complex, zinc, chromium, magnesium, potassium, and fiber, plus 25 percent of the protein.

- Saliva contains a digestive enzyme called ptyalin, which initiates the breakdown of starches. Whole-grain products must be chewed well to be properly digested.
- Grains such as amaranth, barley, and triticale are high in lysine, an essential building block of protein missing in most grains. Quinoa and spelt supply all eight essential amino acids and can be used as meat and dairy substitutes.
- Try non-dairy grain and legume milks. These are made from rice, soy, or nuts, and are available in health food stores and supermarkets. Drink the low-fat unsweetened varieties. Do not give soy milk to children, as it may disrupt mineral absorption in their gut.
- Boil grains like bulgur or rolled oats as breakfast cereals.
- Bake bread, buns, waffles, and pancakes with whole grains.
- Bake whole grains pilaf style or steam them, like couscous.
- Avoid puffed wheat, puffed rice, or rice cakes, as the heating breaks down cell walls and these grains become high-glycemic foods that force a sharp rise in insulin production, as their sugars are absorbed by the intestines too quickly and cause a hormonal imbalance in the body.
- Combine grains with buckwheat groats, beaten egg white, firm tofu, or rice milk, herbs, and vegetables, and bake as a veggie burger. You can add a few seeds and nuts to this delicious dish.
- People with wheat allergies or intolerance to wheat or corn can try one of the other grains or some combination of sourdough spelt, rye, amaranth, kamut, and quinoa.
- Try unleavened breads that contain no flour, yeast, sugars, or oils, but that include all the fiber and germ of the whole grain. They are made from sprouted grains, slightly chopped, molded to a loaf and either sun-dried or baked at a very low temperature. The grains are usually some combination of sprouted spelt, millet, flax, oats, kamut, amaranth, or quinoa. These breads were made in the desert by the Essenes, about the time of Christ.

Fats

Fats, or lipids, are the most concentrated source of energy in the body, and provide approximately 60 percent of the body's energy requirements in a resting state. Fats contain nearly twice the calories per gram as carbohydrates or proteins. Fat is vital but consuming too much leads to health problems.

The body stores fat as glycogen in the muscles and the liver. Enzymes can break down the glycogen to glucose to burn as energy. The body can also accumulate an unlimited amount of fat and store it just under the skin, anywhere in the body.

Most people consume too much of the wrong type of fat. The body synthesizes all the fatty acids (the organic acids from which fats and oils are made) it needs from proteins, carbohydrates, and fats, except for two essential fatty acids (EFAs) which you must eat: linoleic and linolenic acids. These EFAs should be consumed in a ratio of 5 or 6 to 1 of linoleic (omega-6 EFAs) to linolenic (omega-3 EFAs). Most people consume an imbalanced ratio of 24 to 1. (See Chapter 10.)

Depression has steadily been on the rise while our intake of omega-3 EFAs has sharply decreased. While studying the effects of fish oil on cholesterol, researchers at the National Institute of Health, Washington, D.C., noticed that subjects with the lowest levels of omega-3 EFAs reported the highest levels of depression. Omega-3 EFAs control hormonal distribution, body temperature, and brain stability.

- Linolenic acid (omega-3 fatty acid) is found primarily in fish, or the oils of flaxseeds, hemp seeds, or pumpkin seeds. It keeps the skin and other tissues youthful and healthy by preventing dryness. Eat salmon, herring, mackerel, and sardines three times a week. If you do not eat fish, take EPA-DHA fish oil capsules daily. If you do not eat animal foods, consume one or two tablespoons of organic flaxseed oil daily. Most people are severely deficient in omega-3 EFAs. These oils should never be heated or used for frying.

- Linoleic acid (omega-6 EFAs) is necessary for the transport and breakdown of cholesterol. It is plentiful in vegetable fats such as sunflower, corn, olive, and soybean oil. We consume too many omega-6 EFAs and not enough omega-3 EFAs, and this imbalance is very dangerous. North Americans consumed 35 million gallons of olive oil in 1996, which is a good oil, an omega-6 EFA, but only $1\frac{1}{2}$ million gallons of equally necessary omega-3 EFAs from flax oil or fish oils.

- Unsalted butter is acceptable in small amounts. It is a saturated fat (an unhealthy fat associated with increased incidence of heart disease and high levels of LDL cholesterol) and should be used sparingly for taste. (The body does not need saturated fats, so consume only a minimum amount.)

- Avoid margarine, vegetable shortening, grocery-store liquid vegetable oils, palm or palm kernel oils. All are high in saturated fats and trans-fatty acids. Saturated fats come from animal sources and eating large amounts is associated with heart disease and arthritis.
- Use one tablespoon of expeller-pressed extra-virgin, "green" organic olive oil—a good source of linoleic acid—daily on your salad. Use 1 to 2 tablespoons (depending on body size) of organic, expeller-pressed flax oil, or better still, a combination of flax, borage, sunflower, sesame and pumpkin oils—a great source of omega-3 EFAs—pressed without light or oxygen. Check the date of pressing on all bottles of oil. Use them within three months of the pressing date. Buy small opaque bottles that prevent light from breaking down the oil. Replace them often with bottles of fresh oils. These bottles have been flushed and sealed with an inert gas like nitrogen or argon, which prevent oxygen from causing the oils to oxidize or go rancid. To ensure freshness, squeeze a vitamin E capsule into each newly opened bottle of oil, along with a capsule of alpha lipoic acid. These oils are available in health food stores and grocery stores. Once opened, refrigerate to maintain the product's freshness.
- Avoid fried foods, as the oils may go rancid in cooking.
- If you want to lightly sauté or stir-fry with olive oil, use garlic and onions, as their antioxidants help prevent the oil from oxidizing and forming oxygen-free radicals. I sauté vegetables lightly in pure water to a crunchy-tender consistency. Only after removing the veggies from the heat do I add the organic olive oil, so it does not go rancid and maintains its full lovely aroma and flavor.
- Avoid excess levels of arachidonic acid (fat) by limiting your consumption of fatty red meats, egg yolks, and organ meats.
- Avoid foods made with new synthetic fat substitutes.

Protein

Next to water, protein is the most plentiful substance in the body. Protein sources are eggs, animal meats, fish, legumes (beans), nuts, seeds, dairy, grains, nutritional yeast, bee pollen, and sea vegetables (chlorella, spirulina).

Vegetable proteins (beans, nuts, seeds, legumes, nutritional yeast, chlorella, spirulina, and grains) are less concentrated sources of protein than animal proteins (meat, poultry, fish, milk and milk products). Vegetable protein sources have higher concentrations of fiber and starches (carbohydrates) and more of them per volume must be consumed, to match the protein in animal foods. You do not need to eat a complete protein at each meal. The body will store amino acids from sesame seeds and combine it with those from soybeans to make its own complete amino-acid requirement for protein synthesis.

- You cannot absorb more than about 30 grams of protein at a meal. If you eat too much protein at one meal, it turns to fat! Make sure you distribute your protein requirements throughout your three meals and two snacks, to maintain a good protein-fat-fiber-carbohydrate balance.
- To keep your blood sugar (energy) balanced, never go more than four hours without eating.
- Since meat is a major source of saturated fat, try to eat less of it. Animal saturated fat accumulates environmental toxins. If you do eat meats, choose lean cuts. Try to replace red animal protein with turkey, chicken, fish, and white solid water-packed albacore tuna. Once you have done this, try an alternative vegetable source of protein, rather than an animal source, at one or two meals a day. (Refer to Chapter 9 for daily protein requirements.)
- Remove all visible excess fat from the meats you consume. Take the skin off chicken before broiling.
- Cook meat well to eliminate any pathogenic viruses or bacteria.
- Buy meat that is organically fed, free-range, and free of antibiotics and growth hormones.
- Choose only fat-free cottage cheese, quark, or organic yogurt with "live cultures." No other dairy is necessary. If you do not consume dairy at all, substitute yogurt with fat-free soy yogurt. If you do drink milk, choose fat-free, lactose-reduced milk, and make sure no rBGH has been used in the cows. This bioengineered growth hormone is used to force cows to produce more milk. Ask the store to find out from their supplier if the milk contains rBGH. This substance does not have to be marked on the food label.
- Sprout and cook beans or legumes. Sprouting nuts and seeds greatly enhances their nutrient value and digestibility. (See Chapter 7.)
- Eat nuts, seeds, and nut butters (almond butter, pumpkin butter, or cashew butter) in moderation. Only use organic peanut butter, certified free of the potentially harmful carcinogenic mold afloxin. They are high in fat. Most people do not chew nuts and seeds sufficiently to digest them and absorb their nutrients. Grind nuts and seeds in a coffee grinder to break them down, then add uncooked or unheated to prepared oatmeal or use as toppings on salad or veggies.

- Tofu has no fiber and can be a surprising 40 percent fat. Choose low-fat, firm tofu. Include fermented soy by-products such as miso, texturized vegetable protein (no MSG), soy yogurt, and tempeh. In Japan, only small amounts of homemade tofu are eaten. Do not depend on it as your major protein source. Firm or extra-firm tofu is fermented longer and has a greatly reduced fat content and more condensed protein.

- Eat egg whites from free-range chickens raised without drugs and hormones. The yolks contain too much arachidonic acid, which makes destructive series 2 prostaglandins. If you want to eat the yolk, compromise, and for every three eggs eaten, use three egg whites and one yolk. Do not fry or scramble eggs; they oxidize when exposed to air and heat. It may be best to poach, soft-boil, or hard-boil eggs. Eggs are an excellent source of sulfur-bearing amino acids that are needed to protect the body from viral and bacterial infections. Commercial eggs may contain toxin residues of drugs and hormones. Eggs do contain cholesterol (fat), but also sufficient lecithin to emulsify the cholesterol. If you do eat yolks, limit them to two a week. If you suffer from high cholesterol or arthritis, eat only high-protein egg whites.

- Try lactose-free ion-exchanged whey protein, cross-flow microfiltered whey protein, or hydrolyzed soy protein powders in shakes. Don't forget to chew them before swallowing. They are food and you must engage ptyalin, the enzyme secreted in the mouth, for good digestion.

- High-quality nutritional yeasts and primary grown brewers yeast (not a by-product of beer brewing) can be 55 to 60 percent biologically complete protein. Make sure these yeasts are unbleached and not chemically treated. Chlorella and spirulina (both sea vegetables) are 60 percent biologically complete protein sources.

- Buy local, in-season fish or fresh frozen fish. If fish stinks, avoid it since it has started to produce dangerous tri-methylamine, which produces the bad smell.

- Eat protein lower on the food chain. Animals high on the protein chain accumulate environmental toxins because they live longer and are exposed to more antibiotics, growth hormones, and antifungal sprays.

- Refer to Chapter 10 for information on how to combine a sweet or a dessert with protein to minimize those "sugar blues."

Superfoods and Nothing Less

In addition to vegetables and fruits, Superfoods include lean proteins, "good" fats, fiber, and complex carbohydrates for a health-giving nutritional program. Superfoods means that in any classification, you choose the very best food source almost all the time; if you don't, you will never reach optimum health and peak performance, let alone wellness. Eat wisely and be healthy.

5 POINT SUMMARY

- Be determined to add more Superfoods to your daily diet.
- Consider just how remarkable your body is.
- Your body can self-repair and restore itself if you feed it high-quality Superfoods (high-octane fuels).
- Every six months most of your cells replace themselves. You are today what you have eaten for the last six months. It only takes the next six months to dynamically renew yourself. Be determined!
- There exists a direct link between diet and disease. Do not be one of its negative statistics.

6 POINT ACTION PLAN

- Smile at the pessimists who do not support your move to a health-giving diet. Let them see the results.
- Stop several times a day to be grateful to your body and thank it with sincere appreciation.
- Eat more fruits, vegetables, high-quality fiber, a few whole grains, and lean protein. Try sourdough wheat alternatives. Do you need Beano?
- Avoid saturated fats in red meats, butter, bakery items, margarine, fried foods, and full-fat dairy. Use fat-free, plain white organic yogurt with "live cultures" instead of mayonnaise. Use unsalted butter in small amounts occasionally, but never margarine. Replace butter, at times, with quality olive oil, but never exceed your daily quota of one tablespoon of organic, extra-virgin olive oil and 1 to 2 tablespoons of flax or a flax-sunflower-borage-sesame-pumpkin-seed oil if you are a vegetarian. If you eat fish, choose salmon, herring, mackerel, and sardines (which are a potent source of EFAs) two to three times a week and eat no flax oil, only one tablespoon of organic, extra-virgin olive oil daily on your salad.
- Do not hesitate to make some radical changes in your idea of proper nutrition by incorporating more Superfoods into your daily diet.
- The above recommendations are practical, sensible, and probably very familiar. But repeating them is important as they are the bare essentials to a healthy Superfood dietary strategy. Most important, my knowledge and experience can assure you that choosing Superfoods will accelerate your healing and fortify your optimum health.

Green Drinks: Nutritional Life Insurance

HEALTH REFLECTION

Each cell in your body knows exactly what to do with every antioxidant and phytochemical it finds in whole foods.

The body is always seeking its own perfection.
Harvey Diamond, *Fit for Life*

Optimal health is the birthright of us all.
Linus Pauling, Ph.D.

To explain green drinks, I need to go back to 1972, when I was the head of guidance services for a vocational high school in Niagara Falls, Ontario. The students in this school achieved at a much lower level than average students. They came from dysfunctional families and many had not experienced any loving parenting in their 14 to 18 years of life. They were emotional, sensual, sensuous, curious, physical, loud, ill-informed about the world, and generally in poor health. Often I had to rush young teens suffering from heroin or LSD overdoses to hospital or because a nose had been broken in a fight. I spent many evenings trying to bring peace and balance to raging families.

I learned a lot from these experiences and began to observe and take note of these students' diets. A typical diet was:

Breakfast: 2 cups of coffee with Coffee-mate and 2 to 3 teaspoons of sugar, maybe a doughnut.
Lunch: French fries, gravy, and a carbonated soda.
Supper: macaroni dinner from a box.

I began to suspect that poor nutrition was one of the main reasons these students experienced a high rate of attention deficit disorders, general learning disabilities, severe behavioral problems, and hyperactivity. They had all been classified as "learning disabled." Many were on methylphenidate (Ritalin), a very potent drug.

In 1978 I worked with a young lady who was diagnosed with Down's syndrome, a congenital defect, usually caused by the presence of an extra No. 21 chromosome and characterized by an IQ averaging 50 to 60, short stature, a small head flattened at the back, and poor motor skills. My job was to help her develop social skills so she could interact better with her peers.

A young, highly dedicated orthomolecular physician in Toronto, Dr. Zoltan Rona, agreed, with parental consent, to do a full range of blood-gas testing on her. The results showed a high imbalance in minerals: too little magnesium, calcium, zinc, potassium; too few vitamins; and abnormal hormone levels. After one year of a revised nutritional program, exercising at the local Boys and Girls Club, and self-esteem training, she was a different person. She now had more energy and a longer attention span; she was more alert and she felt healthier. Since she felt better, she had more energy with which to greet other teens cheerfully, and they responded much more favorably and enthusiastically to her. In her case, both her IQ and her grades increased about 20 percent. My conclusions remain unremittingly positive. Unquestionably, a proper dietary strategy that incorporates sufficient exercise can improve anyone's daily performance and optimum health.

This experience led me to two men who became my mentors: Dr. Abram Hoffer, a psychiatrist practicing in Saskatchewan, whose suspicions that many of the people under his care were also nutritionally malnourished led him to a distinguished career diagnosing and upgrading the nutritional deficiencies of his patients; and Linus Pauling, the vitamin C pioneer who helped me understand the role of nutrition in human health.

I was so excited by my new awareness that foods could dramatically affect health for better or worse, that nutritional research became my focus. I began to make vitamin and mineral formulations for orthomolecular physicians. Then, in 1984, I began the intensive study of the composition of organically grown whole foods. I was fascinated with the breakdown of biologically complex forms found in foods, such as the various fats, fibers, vitamins, minerals, water, carbohydrates, protein, antioxidants, and phytochemicals. I traveled to Asia, Europe, North Africa, the

Caribbean, and throughout North America studying basic foods, local diets, the use of indigenous herbs, foods grown without pesticides in properly nourished soils, and sea vegetables grown in the pristine oceans of the world.

I was also inspired by the work of Dr. Lee Wattenberg, a researcher at the University of Minnesota. In the 1960s, he began studying enzymes that ward off cancer in animals. His first hypothesis was that animals naturally produce high levels of these enzymes. When he switched their diets from commercial animal-feed pellets to green pellet feed, the amount of protective enzymes rose in the test animals. Ultimately he realized alfalfa meal was responsible for the heightened enzyme production. In 1978, his research group found that indoles—compounds in broccoli and cruciferous vegetables—helped keep lab animals from forming breast and stomach tumors. "That was the prototype," Wattenberg said. "You could add constituents to an animal's diet and essentially protect against the development of cancer." This was medicine's first safe preventive step for stopping cancer.

One by one, other researchers isolated other phytochemicals. In 1994, Dr. Paul Talalay and his colleagues at Johns Hopkins School of Medicine in Baltimore, isolated sulforaphane in broccoli. In 1992, Gladys Block and her colleagues at the University of California at Berkeley reviewed approximately 200 research studies and found that a diet high in fruits and vegetables almost always cut the risk of cancers of the lung, colon, pancreas, stomach, bladder, cervix, ovary, and endometrium. People who ate a lot of fruits and vegetables had half the cancer risk of people who ate the least amount of these foods. The news was stunning: eating a balanced diet of colorful fresh produce can prevent cancer—plain and simple.

GOOD HEALTH THE OLD-FASHIONED WAY

Many people would like a simple pill, jammed full of phytochemicals, targeted to fight cancer. Tempting as such a pill might be, human intervention into the Divine Blueprint has rarely proved successful. After all, we are the creators of fast foods and genetically engineered foods. As Dr. Wattenberg states, "Every vegetable, every fruit, has literally hundreds of constituents–any protection is likely due to a combination rather than a single chemical." Trying to make one chemical into a pill is counterproductive as a quick-fix formula. Do not look for someone to cram a garden full of phytochemicals into a pill. Get them the old-fashioned way, one meal at a time! Vitamin-mineral supplements have their place in this dietary strategy, but they can never take the place of nature's powerful bounty of nutrients found in Superfoods.

Super-Superfoods

After six years of study, I had isolated, with the help of other researchers, some Superfoods that are more nutrient-rich than any Superfoods I have discussed so far. As mentioned earlier, Superfoods support optimum health since they fuel the body in keeping with our genetic makeup.

These Superfoods are:

- Grasses: alfalfa, barley, and wheat grass grown organically.
- Soluble and insoluble fibers: high-pectin apple fiber, brown rice germ, and bran.
- Sprouts: hydroponically and organically sprouted soy sprouts.
- Sea vegetables: chlorella (a freshwater green microalgae); Hawaiian spirulina (most people call it a blue-green algae); Nova Scotia dulse (a purple sea veggie).
- Dairy-free probiotic cultures: grown on brown rice rather than dairy to avoid dairy intolerances, and consisting of L.acidophilus, L.rhamnosus type A, L.bifidus, L.plantarum, S.thermophilis, bifidobacterium bifidum, and longum.
- Fructo-oligosaccharides (FOS): high-molecular-weight sugars to feed "good" intestinal bacteria but not broken down to a sugar.
- Bee products: colorful bee pollen from pristine areas.
- Herbs and their extracts: milk thistle, Siberian E.ginseng, licorice root, ginkgo biloba, Japanese green tea, grape seeds (skins and their extract), European bilberry.
- Phosphatidyl choline (PC): improves memory, heart health, physical performance, and removes clogging cholesterol from the arteries and the liver. High-quality soy lecithin granules are the richest source of PC and contain 22 percent phosphatidyl choline.

Separately, each of these foods is a potent Superfood, but their synergistic combination enhances and gives the body a huge range of nutrients, antioxidants, phytochemicals, and pH balance. This gave Superfoods a whole new classification.

Further Research

In 1989, I combined the ingredients described above into a powerful concentrated formula comprising naturally occurring vitamins, minerals, amino acids, enzymes, chlorophyll, antioxidants, and phytochemicals. The main challenge was how to make these extraordinary Superfoods available to everyone. After years of extensive preliminary testing, my colleagues and I learned how to dry these foods quickly at very low temperatures so they could easily be cold-ground (a process called cryogenics) to a fine powder. To maintain freshness, the ingredients had to be properly blended and not mass-produced. They had to be made fresh on a monthly basis and oxygen removed from each bottle so these potent foods would not deteriorate. This process made Superfoods available, convenient, affordable, and naturally good-tasting. Green drink powder is stable because of its extremely low moisture content and large array of naturally occurring antioxidants.

What a breakthrough! These nutrient-rich foods, grown organically around the world in the oceans and on the earth's soils, were no longer available to a limited few but now could be made available universally.

Word spread and in 1990 I was encouraged to bring my "green drink" from the research lab out to the public as GREENS+. In 1996, GREENS+ was voted the Natural Nutritional Foods Association's People's Choice gold winner as Product of the Year in the United States in the category of nutritional drinks, beverages, and waters. In 1996, GREENS+ was also recognized by *Alive* magazine, in Canada, as the Beverage of the Year gold winner and also received the most prestigious award in Canada as Nutritional Supplement of the Year. In 1996, GREENS+ also won the International Hall of Fame award as Nutritional Product of the Year. This award was presented in Atlanta, Georgia, in May 1996. To me, however, the best awards are the countless individuals who have approached me daily, excited about their health restoration and the part GREENS+ has played in their personal wellness program.

Why Take a Green Drink?

Quality green drinks like GREENS+ are an economical, convenient way to ensure that every day you consume an entire range of unique Superfoods not available from your organic farmers' market, grocery-store produce section, or bins of whole grains. They do not replace these necessary foods; they simply allow you access to fascinating, extremely health-supportive groups of foods, herbs, and sea vegetables. They should be used daily with a diet that includes as many other Superfoods as possible.

Think of "green drinks" as SUPER-Superfoods or as nutritional life insurance. They are available in powder or capsule form. I suggest you use the powder form and ingest the capsules only if you find it difficult to use the powder. Both forms will give you wonderful results.

Green Drink Directions

On waking, drink 8 to 32 ounces of room-temperature or slightly heated water with 1 to 2 tablespoons of freshly squeezed lemon or lime juice. This helps to cleanse the GI tract after the anabolic processes have cleansed cells while you were sleeping. Next, wait 15 to 30 minutes. Then add a quality green drink powder like GREENS+ to 4 to 8 ounces of pure water, fresh vegetable juice, or unsweetened fruit juice such as orange, apple, cherry, grape, or a tropical blend. Shake in a tumbler for 5 to 10 seconds and sip. Fifteen minutes later you are ready to consume food.

It is best to take green drinks on an empty stomach 15 to 30 minutes before any meal. On an empty stomach they are absorbed quickly and do not mingle with other foods that would retard their absorption or be a hidden allergen. Green drinks are considered hypoallergenic (not allergy-causing).

If you use supplements, ingest them with your green drink so they get mixed in the natural matrix of the foods. Do not take supplements in tablet form, only in capsules or soft gels.

QUALITY GREEN DRINKS:

- are quickly and easily absorbed
- give you a natural pick-me-up without any caffeine or sugar
- are very low in carbohydrates and are a low-glycemic food
- contain no sugars
- contain no cholesterol
- are about 35 calories per serving
- are extremely low in natural sodium and phosphorus
- enhance mental acuity and overall well-being
- are full of natural antioxidants
- are full of natural phytochemicals
- contain no MSG, gluten, preservatives, flavors, or colorings
- contain no dairy products
- taste good naturally
- give you a steady level of robust energy and peak-performance nutrition without bloating your stomach

Green drinks require very little energy to digest and absorb. Therefore:

- they are a net energy gain to the body
- they do not use up the body's vital enzymes or energy, which is then free to be used in thinking, moving, cleansing, or maintaining optimal good health.

On days of extra demand, stress, PMS, travel, athletic performance, late work hours, exams, commuting, late meetings, or with a cold or flu, take a second green drink at 3:00 to 4:30 p.m.

When you purchase a green drink, check that three conscientious precautionary methods are used to maximize the quality. First, the green drink should be cold processed without heat to preserve living enzymes. Second, only cold-grinding, termed cryogenics, should be used to mill the green drink to a fine powder. This keeps the temperature of the process cold, preserving complete vitality and nutritional value since many of the foods are highly sensitive and destroyed if exposed to heat. Third, each bottle must be nitrogen flushed and contain both an oxygen absorber and a moisture-absorber packet to ensure the highest possible freshness. Nitrogen flushing forces corrosive oxygen out of the bottle and replaces it with inert nitrogen. Nitrogen is an odorless gas that makes up 78.9 percent of the air you breathe. Nitrogen is heavier than oxygen and replaces it in the bottle. Oxygen can rapidly depreciate the nutritional value of food. In this oxygen-free environment, the green drink remains fresh, potent, and does not oxidize. These three procedures protect the potency, quality, and integrity of your green drink.

20 Unique Superfoods in Green Drinks

1. ACEROLA BERRIES This bright red berry contains a potent source of highly bioavailable, natural vitamin C.
2. ALFALFA, BARLEY, and WHEAT GRASS Organically grown young grasses are free of the gluten or allergens found in mature wheat or barley. Each is high in chlorophyll, a well-documented colon cleanser, deodorizer, and detoxifier of chemicals in the body.
3. APPLE PECTIN Pectin, a necessary fiber in apples, helps maintain intestinal balance. It helps prevent absorption of toxic heavy metals in the intestinal tract and carries them safely out of the body. (Destructive heavy metals such as mercury, cadmium, aluminum, iron, and lead routinely enter our food and water supplies.)
4. PHOSPHATIDYL CHOLINE (PC) This dipolar molecule can hold on to fat and water at the same time. It emulsifies extra cholesterol that clogs the arteries or liver, and pulls it through the watery blood to the liver for processing and excretion. PC is vital to good memory, proper cell signaling, and a healthy heart. Soy lecithin is the most nutrient-rich source of PC and contains about 22 percent PC.

5. BEE POLLEN This substance contains a high amount of vitamins, phytochemicals, minerals, and enzymes. It is a potent source of a vital anti-aging antioxidant called superoxide dismutase (SOD). Bee pollen is collected by honey bees from flowers. Use bee pollen only from pristine areas not affected by urban pollution.

6. BILBERRY This herb contains anthocyanidin pigments, potent phytochemicals that strengthen capillary walls and assist the eyes to adapt from dark to light or light to dark. Bilberry supports superior vision.

7. BROWN RICE GERM and BRAN These are sources of both soluble and insoluble fibers and naturally occurring vitamin E.

8. CHLORELLA Chlorella pyrenoidosa is a freshwater green microalgae. It chelates (holds on to) heavy metals and chemical toxins and eliminates them from the body. Chlorella increases serum albumin levels, necessary for optimal health. Higher albumin levels are a necessary biomarker for a long and healthy life.

9. DAIRY-FREE PROBIOTIC CULTURES Yogurt is a fermented dairy product containing necessary "good bacteria" that humans need in their intestines. Dairy-free probiotic (meaning in-favor-of-life) cultures are various "good bacteria" grown on vegetables for those who have difficulty digesting dairy products.

10. ROYAL JELLY A well-known supporter of immune functions, royal jelly is rich in protein, vitamins, and enzymes. Premium-quality royal jelly is 5 to 5.5 percent 10-HDA, a super-nutrient containing vitamins A, C, D, and E, as well as nine B-complex vitamins. Royal jelly contains 22 amino acids and notable quantities of the minerals calcium, copper, iron, potassium, magnesium, silicon, and sulfur.

11. GINKGO BILOBA Ginkgo comes from an ancient family of Japanese trees that live, on average, more than 2,500 years. It increase the cholinergic (nerve impulses) mechanism linked to memory and makes for a stronger immune system.

12. GRAPE SEED and SKINS Grapes contain a powerful antioxidant group called polyphenols, which protect the brain and connective tissue from aging. Grape skins contain resveratrol, a powerful cancer-inhibiting phytochemical shown to block the development of precancerous and cancerous growths.

13. JAPANESE GREEN TEA Green tea contains antioxidants and phytochemicals called polyphenols and a subgroup called catechins. They are very strong antiviral, antibacterial, and anticarcinogenic components.

14. HAWAIIAN SPIRULINA PACIFICA Generally known as a blue-green microalgae, spirulina is actually a cyanobacteria. A potent source of available iron, vitamin B_{12}, beta-carotene, vitamins, and minerals, spirulina is 60 percent protein. Hawaiian- or Californian-cultivated spirulinas are scientifically grown, and the algae (bacteria) are monitored constantly to ensure their nutritional safety and potency.

15. LICORICE ROOT Licorice root boasts strong antiviral activities and prevents the suppression of immunity by stress. It improves immune competence. Combined with the proper vegetables that give a low-sodium to high-potassium ratio, licorice is reported to lower high blood pressure.

16. MILK THISTLE A potent antioxidant and liver detoxifier, milk thistle (silybum marianum) enhances liver function.

17. NOVA SCOTIA DULSE This purple-red algae, or sea vegetable, is a source of rare trace minerals and especially organic iodine. Iodine is necessary for the thyroid gland to function—determining a human's weight, mood, and energy level. If you rely on soy products such as tofu for your main protein source, use Nova Scotia dulse daily.

18. SIBERIAN E. GINSENG This herb helps to detoxify the body. It is an anti-fatigue, anti-stress, and adaptagenic herb. Adaptagens help to balance physical, mental, or biochemical stresses in the body.

19. SOY SPROUTS Soy sprouts are hydroponically and organically grown. They contain the potent anticancer phytochemicals genistein and daidzein. Sprouting eliminates phytic acid, that makes minerals difficult for the body to absorb.

20. RED BEET JUICE POWDER Organically grown red beet juice facilitates digestion as well as stimulates both the kidneys and lymphatic system. Red beets contain large amounts of potassium, phosphorus, magnesium, calcium, fiber, phytochemicals, antioxidants, and a rich red pigment.

Do You Need a Green Drink?

To determine if you need to take a green drink daily, answer yes or no to the questions on the following page.

SEVEN OR MORE "YESes": You are probably getting 6 to 10 servings of vegetables daily and 2 to 3 of fruit. Bravo! Make sure you are using a mixed diet with a large array of colors each day.

SIX OR FEWER "YESes": You may be phytochemically deprived. You may not be getting enough antioxidants from food. You may need nutritional life insurance.

	Yes	No
I eat a large colorful salad every day.	❏	❏
I eat something raw at each meal, every day.	❏	❏
I eat celery or carrot sticks, an apple or orange at two snacks every day.	❏	❏
I eat at least four kinds of colorful veggies every day.	❏	❏
I eat 2 to 3 pieces of organic, whole fruit each day.	❏	❏
When I have a sandwich at lunch, I have veggie sticks with it.	❏	❏
I eat some form of sea vegetable, in a salad or main dish, 2 to 3 times a week.	❏	❏
There is always some herbal garnishing at two meals each day.	❏	❏
I drink a glass of fresh vegetable juice 2 to 3 times a week.	❏	❏
Total number of Yes answers _____		

If you score six or lower, try the suggestions below to give your diet a turbo-boost.

8 Ways to Boost Your Diet

1. Every day have a quality green drink such as GREENS+ mixed in water, vegetable juice, or unsweetened fruit juice. One serving (one tablespoon of powder, or 12 capsules) is approximately equal to 5 to 6 servings of organic salad or veggies.
2. Perk up your meals with garlic, chives, and various colored onions. Their sulfur compounds help your body break down cancer-causing carcinogens. Their selenium content is a great antioxidant.
3. Munch on crunchies from the garden rather than chips or dips from a package. Snack on sticks of celery, carrots, orange yams, red peppers, turnips, or crisp sugar snap peas—even at work.

4. Take a fruit break twice a day. Eat berries and melons in season.
5. Garnish your plates with parsley, ginger, watercress, basil, sage, dill, rosemary, thyme, oregano; or shred raw carrots, onions, red cabbage, tomatoes, celery, beets, daikon, or zucchini as a color burst.
6. Be daring: invite some new, colorful vegetables home for supper.
7. Bye-bye, iceberg lettuce. Hello, luscious spinach, arugula, endive, leaf lettuce, oak lettuce, romaine lettuce, mesclun, mezuna, mustard greens, bibb, endive, kale, chard, dandelion greens, watercress, and parsley in salads. Put colorful, edible flowers like nasturtium in salads.
8. Use fresh vegetables and small portions of fruits as low-calorie finger foods.

Superfoods, ADD, and Learning Disabilities

Superfoods are necessary for a child's complete development. Green drinks are a convenient way to ensure your child obtains superior nutritional support. Children and adults who have trouble concentrating or who are hyperactive will benefit from a Superfood dietary strategy and supplements that can calm and focus them naturally. Most children or adults classified as having Attention Deficit Disorder (ADD), Attention Deficit Hyperactivity Disorder (ADHD), or as being learning disabled have a lack of centralized nervous-system control caused by a neurochemical imbalance. (See Chapter 6.) Theories about the causes of ADD and ADHD include a congenital predisposition set at conception or birth; a brain allergy to certain foods, aluminum, or heavy metal toxicity; or nutritional imbalances such as low blood sugar or a deficiency in essential amino acids or fats.

Many practitioners believe that more than half of all ADD children go undiagnosed. More common in boys than girls, ADD manifests in three main behavior patterns: impulsivity, distractibility, and hyperactivity. Although ADHD and ADD are similar disorders, ADD isn't necessarily accompanied by hyperactivity.

The conventional treatment for these conditions is a protocol of behavior modification and medication. The drugs are stimulants, to enhance the flow of dopamine in the brain, which can increase impulse control and attention span. This class of prescription drugs include Ritalin and Cylert. Antidepressants are also used to treat depression and decrease hyperactivity and aggression. For pronounced mental and emotional problems, doctors may prescribe a variety of drugs including Lithium. According to a December 1996 study published in the journal *Pediatrics*, the use of

Ritalin has increased 250 percent from 1990 to 1995. Today, approximately 1.8 million children in North America—2.8 percent of all schoolchildren—are on Ritalin.

Many parents of ADD children don't realize there are less invasive alternatives. The first option is to alter a child's diet. Food can be psychoactive, especially for children, since their brains demand almost 50 percent of total calorie intake. Approximately 20 percent of an adult's calorie intake goes to brain function.

A proper alkalizing Superfood dietary strategy is essential to children who undergo massive cell expansion as they grow. (See Chapter 5 on alkaline-acid–producing foods and diet.) Children already have extraordinary metabolic needs, and if they do not get the basic requirements for cell growth, it is impossible for them to meet the requirements needed for external functioning such as attention span, proper behavior, and mood. They should avoid potential allergy-producing foods such as milk, chocolate, wheat, corn, peanuts, pork, cold cuts, sausage, fried foods, soft drinks, sugar, and NutraSweet. The following strategies must be included in their superior daily diet:

- an alkalizing diet (See Chapter 5)
- sufficient water (avoid excess fruit juice) (See Chapter 6)
- low- or moderate-glycemic diet (See Chapter 11)
- Superfood dietary strategy of sufficient protein, colorful vegetables, fats, and complex, low-glycemic carbohydrates
- a green drink, minimum once a day or preferably twice a day
- DMAE (2-dimethyl amino-ethanol) that normalizes behavior by stimulating the central nervous system
- the amino acids GABA, glutamine, and glycine
- B-complex vitamins
- magnesium, potassium, and chromium
- herbal teas of chamomile, passion flower, lemon balm, and valerian that have a calming effect
- organic flaxseed oil or salmon fish-oil capsules daily for the essential fatty acids

Always make sure children are properly diagnosed by a qualified health-care practitioner. Show him or her this section and feed your children wisely.

For more information, contact Children and Adults With Attention Deficit Disorders, in Canada at (604) 222-4043, and in the United States at (954) 587-3700, or toll free at 800-233-4050.

My favorite support group is the Center for New Discoveries in Learning, located in Windsor, California. Call them at (707) 837-8180, and ask for their wonderful book *What's Food Got To Do With It*. Two highly dedicated women at the center, Dr. Sandra Hills and Pat Wyman, are the powerhouses in developing diets, videos, cassettes, and literature designed to help you work with your child naturally, with great success.

3 POINT SUMMARY

- Super-Superfoods have been discovered that offer nutritional life insurance.
- If you are not eating ten servings of vegetables and 2 to 3 pieces of fruit every day, you will require the enormous nutritional support of a green drink.
- Learning disabilities, ADD, and ADHD have a nutritional deficit as the major problem.

4 POINT ACTION PLAN

- To ensure maximum protection, eat a diet of mixed colors of fresh fruit and vegetables.
- Include a green drink daily in your diet for superior nutrition and optimal cell performance.
- If you scored 6 or lower on the questionnaire above, turbo-charge your diet with all eight suggestions that follow the questionnaire.
- A Superfood dietary strategy with additional supplements must be incorporated daily for your children's physical and emotional health and learning ability.

5

The Acid-Alkaline Balance
Part 1: Acid Runs Batteries, Not Your Body

HEALTH REFLECTION

pH indicates acidity or alkalinity and the overall state of your health.

*The average 20th century diet, lifestyle and environment
produces far more acid than is healthy.*
Sam Queen, *Health Realities Newsletter*

*Diets that over-emphasize one kind of food and ignore the necessary balance
of the acid-alkaline system rarely succeed. How can they?*
Dr. Christiane May-Ropers, *Never Again Acidic*

When I was studying the Asian diet and food-growing techniques in China, Japan, Korea, and Hong Kong in 1985, I had an experience that gave me an entirely new perspective on how foods dramatically affect the balance, or homeostasis, in our bodies.

I had gone for a wonderful run through the Chinese countryside, just outside the seaport city of Shanghai. I was walking down a street, "cooling down," when an elderly Tai Chi master politely approached me and initiated a conversation. He explained that my strenuous physical exercise had created an enormous amount of acids in my body, most of which I expelled as carbon dioxide through each of my exhalations.

"It is imperative that you consume sea vegetables, fresh vegetables, and ripe fruit in sufficient quantities to help buffer all the acids you are creating," he said. He explained that my heavy breathing was the result of the body working hard to expel carbon dioxide, not as most think, to bring oxygen in.

"Do you have a flavor on your tongue?" he asked.

"Yes, a sort of sticky-sour taste," I replied.

"Imbalance, too much acid," he said. He also suggested that after a run I engage in a few steady, slow-breathing exercises to establish proper rhythm of oxygen in and carbon dioxide out, to remove acid and alkalize the system. "Meditation," he told me, "is a good counterbalance to running and, as a complementary exercise, calms the body and makes it alkaline."

A week later I was eating a dish of tofu, rice, herbs, and vegetables at a small roadside café. On top of this dish was a piece of thick brown seaweed. I did my best to eat it, but eventually, frustrated in my attempt to chew it, I moved it to the side of the plate with the chopsticks. An amused university professor introduced himself. He asked if he could explain why the sea vegetable on the plate should be eaten with the meal.

I was fascinated at his explanation of the yin-yang (acid-alkaline) classification of foods. He said that this topic was not understood by Western nutritional science, but it was critical to keeping the body in balance. The sea vegetable, he explained, contained highly absorbable minerals that added to my alkaline reserve and were necessary to balance (buffer or neutralize) the acidifying ashes left from the digestion of the rice. The tofu and vegetables, along with the wild green herbs, added more alkalizing foods, allowing for necessary digestive enzymes to eventually buffer the acid ashes left from the digestion of the rice.

An Introduction to Acid and Alkaline

The average human body is filled with fluids both inside (intracellular) and outside (extracellular) the cells in the muscles, the brain, bones, the bloodstream, the spine, saliva, and in urine. Average adults carry approximately 10 gallons of fluid in their bodies.

All fluids have a certain level of acidity or alkalinity. This level is measured by the pH value. The pH scale runs from zero to 14. A pH of 7 is considered neutral, at the midpoint, while a pH higher than 7 is considered alkaline and a pH lower than 7 is considered acidic. The higher the number, the more alkaline the solution; the lower the number, the more acidic the solution.

A strong acid like hydrochloric acid can burn your hand. Bicarbonate of soda, as sodium bicarbonate, is a strong alkali and can neutralize (buffer) the burning, corrosive effects of hydrochloric acid. Alkaline solutions like ammonia can also cause damage. Vinegar is an acid and can neutralize the caustic effect of a strong alkaline solution like ammonia.

Most fluids in the body are, or should be, alkaline with a pH of 7 or more, except for the fluid in the stomach. Stomach fluids are called gastric juices and have an acidic pH of 1.0 to 3.5 so they can break up and digest foods in the stomach.

Generally the pH of body fluids is not measured in whole numbers but in tenths ($1/10$), as 6.5, or in hundredths ($1/100$), as 7.43. With pH numbers there is a vast difference between two consecutive whole numbers like 6.0 and 7.0, or 7.0 and 8.0. In this example, 6.0 is ten times more acid than 7.0 but 100 times more acid than 8.0. Small changes in pH can therefore dramatically affect the way your body operates.

For metabolic functions to operate optimally, the acid-alkaline levels have to maintain a good balance. Arterial blood, as an example, has a narrow range of pH. It balances between 7.35 and 7.45, with the ideal reading being pH 7.4. If your arterial blood drops below 7.35 to even 7.34, this spells trouble and health-compromising acidemia will ensue. If the pH of arterial blood goes above 7.45 to even 7.5, this also spells health-compromising trouble. If the pH of arterial blood goes below 7.3, the body goes into tetanic convulsions and eventually death results.

What Is pH?

Acid-Alkaline Scale

ACID		NEUTRAL		ALKALINE	
stomach acids	white vinegar	balanced water	arterial blood	ocean water	baking soda
0.0 1.0	3.5		7.4	8.0	10.0 14.0

7.0

Balanced functioning cell

The abbreviation pH stands for potenz (power) and hydrogen (H is the symbol for hydrogen) and refers to hydrogen ion activity in a one-liter solution. Acids contain a large portion of hydrogen ions (H+), which have a positive electrical charge. Hydrogen atoms have one proton in their nucleus and one electron spinning around it. The chemistry of hydrogen depends on one of three processes: loss of electron to form H+; gain of electron to form H-; sharing of electron by covalent bond formation as in H_2. Hydrogen ions (H+) have an insatiable appetite and are always trying to replace their missing electron.

Bases or alkalis, contain a large proportion of hydroxyl ions (OH-). Unlike the ever-hungry H+ ion, the OH- carries an extra electron and is

Hydrogen Atom and Hydrogen Ion

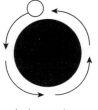
hydrogen atom

hydrogen ion (no electron)

always looking to donate it. So when H+ meets an OH-, they bond, neutralize each other by forming H_2O (water) and a salt. Because of equal H+ and OH-, water is neutral with a pH of 7.0.

Acids have a higher proportion of H+. So the more H+ ions, the more acidic is a solution. Generally, every solution contains a certain amount of hydrogen cations (H+) and hydroxyl-anions (OH-). The amount of H+ determines the acidity of the solution, while the amount of OH- determines its alkalinity. In the case of water at 25° Celsius, if H+ and OH- ions are present in equal numbers, the pH would be 7, neutral. Even within the body, different tissues have varying extracellular pH levels that the body constantly monitors and regulates. The consistency of pH in your urine is maintained by buffers, exhalation, and kidney excretions of acids and bases. The kidneys secrete hydrogen ions (H+), either few (to make a solution more alkaline) or many (to make a solution more acidic).

- venous blood: 7.30–7.5 (7.35 is ideal for first morning plasma)
- arterial blood: 7.35–7.45 (7.4 is ideal)
- muscle: 6.9–7.0
- connective tissue: 7.09–7.29
- urine: 4.5–8.0 (6.8 is ideal for first morning urine)
- saliva: 6.0–7.0 (6.5 is ideal for first morning saliva)
- gastric juices: 1.0–3.5
- feces: 3.0–8.3
- pancreatic juices 8.0–8.3

Water is not necessarily neutral. You can have acid water or alkaline water, according to the amount of oxygen. To explain, pure water is H_2O. H_2O has no pH value because it is not yet ionized. Ionization requires a trace of metal, such as copper (Cu_2+); that is, ionized water looks like this: H+, OH- + H_2O. pH is the negative log of the concentration of hydrogen ions versus OH- ions. If the two are equal in number then the pH is 7.0. If a fish is dropped into the water and it consumes some of the oxygen in the

OH-, the water becomes more acid, such as pH 6.5. If air is bubbled back through the water and the oxygen gets restored, you might have pH 7.0 again, or possibly pH 7.2, and so on. Acid water coming into your home is bad because it indicates a higher level of metal ions that are likely unwanted. Metals that alkalinize the water include magnesium. High-magnesium water is also known as "hard" water, and it is in areas of hard water that chronic disease is lowest. High copper water, on the other hand, causes very acidic water, such as pH 6.0. It is in areas of such "soft," acidic water that chronic disease is most prevalent.

Iron, as an example, can be an alkaline-promoting heavy metal (as found naturally in organic whole foods) when present in just the right amounts to make healthy red blood cells. An iron overload results in a number of acidic conditions such as arthritis, and is easily oxidized to form many corrosive oxygen-free radicals. Do not use supplements with iron in them unless you are using them under, and being monitored by, a knowledgeable health-care professional.

Arterial Blood Acid-Base Balance

When I Run I Create Acids

When I run, lactic acid, pyruvic acid, and ammonia build up in my legs. This causes a burning sensation leading to fatigue, and the muscles slow down.

As I fatigue, the lowering of pH in my muscles can lead to decreased membrane permeability in which necessary nutrients do not easily enter the fatiguing cell. Toxic residue from cellular metabolism is not fully removed from the cells through normal detoxification pathways, and cellular dysfunction begins. Toxins are stored rather than excreted and the body becomes a breeding ground for microbial, as well as viral, infections, which results in illness. The liver, connective tissue, and the lymphatic systems accumulate toxic debris that accelerate molecular and tissue aging.

The result is that less energy is produced in the cells. Production of adenosine triphosphate (ATP)—a compound involved in the storage and transfer of energy in muscle cells—declines as there is a progressive functional decline in oxidative phosphorylation (phosphorus is needed for ATP synthesis and either becomes deficient from having to work too hard getting rid of hydrogen ions in the kidneys, or the extended exercise brings about insufficient electrons for the synthesis of reduced phosphorus, which is required to make ATP). The result is less ATP production and consequently less energy.

As a result of the acid overload, cellular metabolic dynamics are disrupted. (One hundred trillion cells operate at less than optimal levels.) This is the beginning of premature aging and degenerative diseases.

When Your Body Is Too Acidic

What happens when your body is too acidic? Many researchers believe that health can be impaired as a result of the following effects:

- Free radical oxidation occurs with greater ease, while antioxidant activity is impaired. You age faster.
- Vitamins and minerals from foods or supplements are not absorbed. Cell-wall permeability decreases.
- Friendly bacteria in the small intestines die and the immune system is impaired as the gradient (the ability of the intestinal wall to absorb) in the small intestine is altered.
- Connective tissue becomes weakened, causing skin and hair to lose tone and texture.
- Sleep patterns are disturbed.
- Colds, infections, headaches, and flus become more common as cells are biologically "stressed" with the toxins that are building up and not being removed efficiently.
- Physical and mental energy is depleted, affecting stamina and moods as ATP production declines.
- Athletic performance is decreased because more ammonia is produced, as well as lactic acid, limiting muscle contraction and expansion. Less oxygen is available to cells. Hemoglobin, with lower blood pH, has decreased oxygen affinity, which reduces the amount of oxygen it can bind to, and therefore less is brought to the cells.

How The Body Buffers Acids

As you read this, your body is creating acids. But don't worry. It's just business as usual—a by-product of natural cell function. The acids your body produces are relatively weak and usually do not cause any problems. The bicarbonate (HCO_3) buffering system neutralizes the weak acids your body is continually making as exhaled carbon dioxide (CO_2). This causes no metabolic stress on the body. The hydrogen ions (H+) are being neutralized (buffered) and their numbers decreased. When H+ (hydrogen ions) are decreased, the alkalinity of a solution increases.

Acidity and Alkalinity

0 ⟵⟵⟵ more H+ / more acidity ⟵⟵⟵ ⟶⟶⟶ less H+ / more alkalinity ⟶⟶⟶ 14

To counter these acids, the body has a six-layer buffering system.

Layer 1 involves the lungs. Carbon dioxide, an acid, is exhaled by the lungs.

Layer 2 involves protein and hemoglobin. When you don't have sufficient red blood cells and hemoglobin to carry oxygen, causing anemia, your body becomes acidic. Similarly, when your diet lacks adequate protein, you will lack the protein you need to bind to toxins that might otherwise bring about acidemia.

Layer 3 involves a series of alkaline buffers required in the so-called Krebs, or citric acid, cycle that produces the most efficient source of energy (from fat). These alkaline buffers include citrate (from lemons and limes), malate (from apples and apple cider), lactate (from cultured dairy foods), phosphate (from seeds and free-range eggs and soy lecithin sources) and acetate (from apple cider vinegar).

Layer 4 involves the kidneys, where bicarbonate is either made from the amino acid glutamine, or the complete oxidation of the alkaline buffers discussed above, returned to the bloodstream, or excreted along with hydrogen ions.

Layer 5 is the emergency buffering system that involves the parathyroid hormone (PTH) and bone phosphate. When all else fails, and/or when the phosphate level of the blood gets too low to make ATP energy, PTH is called upon to pull phosphate from the bone. Along with the phosphate comes free calcium, leading to other problems like osteoporosis.

Layer 6 involves minerals such as sodium, calcium, magnesium, potassium, which are abundant in organically grown, colorful fruits, vegetables, sprouts, grasses, herbs, and sea vegetables neutralizing or buffering strong corrosive acids. A Superfood diet allows the body to replenish the supply of neutralizing minerals—referred to as the alkaline reserve.

Part 2: How Foods Affect Your Acid-Alkaline Balance

HEALTH REFLECTION

The limit of homeostasis, or balance in the body, is the limit of adaptations in molecular dynamics to the acid-alkaline balance.

*Life is a struggle, not against money, power
or malicious animal magnetism, but against hydrogen ions.*
−H.L. Mencken

What Foods You Should Eat To Be Alkaline

The chart below lists acidifying foods and alkalizing foods. Most people should proportion their diet to consume 75 percent of foods, by volume, from the alkalizing foods, and 25 percent, by volume, from the acidifying foods. We have reversed the proportions so that the modern diet in developed countries comprise a majority of acidifying foods and a minority of alkalizing foods. It is easy to understand why degenerative diseases like cancers, osteoporosis, fibromyalgia, arthritis, chronic fatigue syndrome (CFS), immune dysfunction, and irritable, inflamed bowels are so rampant today.

The body needs more alkalizing food than acidifying foods. It really is as simple as that.

Buyer Beware

Want proof that our modern-day diet is composed of too many acidifying foods? Just walk around any supermarket and you will notice that the fresh fruit and vegetable section is, at a maximum, 5 to 10 percent of the total size of the store.

ACIDIFYING AND ALKALIZING FOODS

A Recipe For Life

This chart provides information that shows the contribution of various food substances to the acidifying or alkalizing of body fluids and, ultimately, to the urine, saliva, and venous blood.

The kidneys help to maintain the neutrality of body fluids by excreting the excess acid or alkali in the urine.

In general, it is important to eat a diet that contains foods from both sides of the chart.

Allergic reactions and other forms of stress tend to produce acids in the body. The presence of high acidity indicates that more of your foods should be selected from the alkalizing group.

You may find it useful to check your urine pH using pHydrion paper in order to find out if your food selection is providing the desired balance. Check urine pH three times a day.

A urine pH of between 6.8 in the morning and 7.4 in the afternoon is ideal, but it will vary over the day depending upon the foods you eat as well as allergic reactions and other stress factors. Your urine pH should average 7.0.

People vary, but for most, the ideal diet is 75 percent alkalizing and 25 percent acidifying foods by volume.

Alkalizing Foods

Vegetables
Garlic
Asparagus
Fermented Veggies
Watercress
Beets
Broccoli
Brussels Sprouts
Cabbage
Carrot
Cauliflower
Celery
Chard
Chlorella (algae)
Collard Greens
Cucumber
* Eggplant
Kale
Kohlrabi
Lettuces (all types)
Mushrooms
Mustard Greens
Nova Scotia Dulse
Dandelions
Edible Flowers
Onions
Parsnips (high-glycemic)
Peas
* Peppers
Pumpkin
Rutabaga
Sea Veggies
Spirulina (algae)
Sprouts (all types)
Squashes
Alfalfa Grass
Barley Grass
Wheat Grass
Wild Greens
* nightshade veggies

Note: Use organically grown whenever possible

Fruits
Apple
Apricot
Avocado
Banana (high-glycemic)
Blackberry
Blueberry
Cantaloupe
Cherries, Currants
Dates, Figs
Grapes
Grapefruit, Lime
Honeydew
Nectarine
Orange, Lemon
Peach, Pear
Pineapple
Raspberry (all berries)
Strawberry
Tangerine
* Tomato
Tropical Fruits
Watermelon

Protein
Free-range eggs
Whey protein powder
Fat-free cottage cheese
Lean chicken breast
Organic yogurt
Almonds
Chestnuts
Tofu (fermented)
Flax Seeds
Pumpkin Seeds
Tempeh (fermented)
Squash Seeds
Sunflower Seeds
Millet
Sprouted Seeds, Nuts

Other
Apple cider vinegar

Bee Pollen
Lecithin Granules
Dairy-Free Probiotic Cultures

Beverages
GREENS+
Veggie Juices
Fresh Fruit Juice (unsweetened)
Organic Milk (unpasteurized)
Mineral Water (non-carbonated)
Quality Water

Teas
Green Tea
Herbal Tea
Dandelion Tea
Ginseng
Bancha Tea
Kombucha

Sweeteners
Stevia

Spices & Seasonings
Cinnamon
Curry
Ginger
Mustard
Chili Peppers
Salt (Sea, Celtic)
Miso
Tamari
All Herbs

Oriental Vegetables
Maitake
Daikon
Dandelion Root
Shiitake
Kombu
Reishi
Nori
Umeboshi
Wakame
Sea Veggies

Acidifying Foods

Fats & Oils
Avocado Oil
Canola Oil
Corn Oil
Hemp Seed Oil
Flax Oil
Grape Seed Oil
Lard
Olive Oil
Safflower Oil
Sesame Oil
Sunflower Oil

Fruits
Cranberries

Grains
Rice Cakes
Wheat Cakes
Amaranth
Barley
Buckwheat
Corn
Oats (rolled)
Quinoa
Rice (Brown, Basmati)
Rye
Spelt
Kamut
Wheat
Hemp Seed Flour

Dairy, Milk & Hard Cheeses
Cheese, Cow
Cheese, Goat
Cheese, Processed
Cheese, Sheep
Milk (avoid BGH)
Butter

Nuts & Butters
Cashews
Filberts
Brazil Nuts
Peanuts
Peanut Butter
Pecans
Tahini
Walnuts

Animal Protein
Beef
Carp
Clams
Duck
Fish, White Meat
Lamb
Lobster
Mussels
Oyster
Pork
Rabbit
Salmon
Shrimp
Scallops
Tuna
Turkey
Venison

Pasta (White)
Noodles
Macaroni
Spaghetti

Other
Distilled Vinegar
Brewers Yeast
Wheat Germ
*Potatoes

Drugs & Chemicals
Chemicals
Drugs, Medicinal
Drugs, Psychedelics
Pesticides
Herbicides

Sweets & Sweeteners
Molasses
Candy
Honey
Maple Syrup
Saccharin
Soft Drinks
Sugar
Aspartame
Fruit-Flavored Drinks

Alcoholic Beverages
Beer
Spirits
Hard Liquor
Wine

Beans & Legumes
Black Beans
Chick Peas
Green Peas
Kidney Beans
Lentils
Lima Beans
Pinto Beans
Red Beans
Soybeans
Soy Milk
White Beans
Rice Milk
Almond Milk

When you shop, stay on the perimeter, where you will find fruits, herbs, fresh sprouts, vegetables, plain fat-free yogurt, fat-free dry cottage cheese, fat-free milk, lean meats or fish, whole-grain breads, and bins of legumes, seeds or nuts. Once you enter the aisles, you encounter an expensive array of modified, processed, highly packaged, acid-forming foods. Buyer beware!

Vegetarians Beware

It is not only animal protein, grains, dairy, or sugar that cause an acidifying influence. Many vegans or vegetarians are far too acidic. Let us look at the hypothetical daily food consumption of a vegan or vegetarian.

Breakfast Organic rolled oats boiled with organic rye, topped with whole peanuts and a few unsalted cashews, and rice or soy milk. This is an acidifying meal. Plain organic yogurt and exchanging the peanuts and cashews with pumpkin seeds and sunflower seeds would balance this meal.

Lunch Veggie burger of Brazil nuts and grains, on a 12-grain sprouted bun garnished with tomatoes, sprouts, and unsalted baked blue corn chips. This is an acidifying lunch. More raw veggie slices on a bed of lettuce would balance this meal.

Supper Organic brown rice and black beans or adzuki beans. This is an acidifying meal. A green garden salad, shredded carrots, yams, turnips, and beets, plus a fresh herb on the black beans, would balance this meal.

The vegan or vegetarian made a conscientious effort to eat organic foods and nutritious foods full of enzymes. The dilemma is that this day's food resulted in a net gain of acid influences on the body. Continually eating in this fashion leads to illness. It is not just by eating too much meat or dairy that you can become too acidic.

Vegetarians or meat eaters can both equally become severely toxic (acidemia) if their diets do not contain sufficient amounts of alkalizing foods.

Some Surprises

Not all foods are easy to classify. Many foods that taste "acidic"—strawberries, grapes, lemons, limes, apple cider vinegar, yogurt, for example—are considered alkalizing. Extrinsically (outside the body) they are acidic but intrinsically (inside the body) they are alkalizing. The organic acids that make them taste "acidic" stimulate the pancreas to dump alkaline buffers into the body. Later, as they pass through the liver or kidneys, the esters of these acids are completely metabolized to form the major bicarbonate buffer and water. They are not metabolized to carbon dioxide and the minerals that are "left behind" are not the only reason for their adding to the body's alkalinity.

The alkalizing quality of lemon or lime juice can be used to your advantage. Three times a day add two tablespoons of lemon or lime juice to water and drink. The lemon or lime is acidic for the first 1 to $1\frac{1}{2}$ hours of digestion, but after metabolizing, it leaves an alkalizing effect on the body. You may want to rinse your mouth with one mouthful of water after drinking the lemon or lime juice to remove the citric acid from your teeth. Swallow this mouthful of water after rinsing.

In addition, some foods thought by health professionals to be acidifying are actually alkalizing, and vice versa.

Alkalizing Surprises

- All vegetables, sea vegetables, herbs, sprouts, green drinks, fruits (except cranberries), fermented soy products like miso, firm tofu and tempeh, fat-free organic yogurt, fat-free dry cottage cheese, lean white meat of poultry, hydrolyzed whey or soy protein powders, some seeds, nuts, legumes, apple cider vinegar, bee pollen, dairy-free probiotic cultures, grasses, and soy lecithin granules are alkalizing foods.
- Raw, unpasteurized cow or goat milk and some of the soft, cultured cheeses (cottage cheese, blue cheese) made from them are alkalizing because of their high calcium levels. Kefir is acceptable, but because of its high sugar content, is not recommended. Yogurt's lactic acid stimulates the pancreas to release bicarbonate (alkali buffer) into the small intestine, which can raise the urine and saliva pH.
- Celtic sea salt, not iodized sodium chloride, is an alkalizing agent because of its sodium content.
- Surprisingly, coffee is also alkalizing, but only if it is not decaffeinated and is drunk black, following a meal. The caffeine is an alkaloid, causing an alkalizing effect. The remaining components of coffee are highly acidifying. I am not promoting coffee drinking, but if you do occasionally drink coffee, have it black, nondecaffeinated, and only following a meal. If you drink coffee on an empty stomach, it is acidifying since it is a stimulant of serum chloride. (See Chapter 7 for a discussion of the negative habitual use of coffee in your diet.)

Acidifying Surprises

- All fats and oils, sugars, grains, regular milk as well as skim, hard cheese, alcohol, most meats, eggs, fried foods, hydrogenated fats, white flour, mass-produced bakery items, pesticides on any foods, processed foods with sugar (any sweeteners), monosodium glutamate (MSG), heavy metals or any chemicals, chronic stress, and excess free radical oxidation are acidifying.
- Cranberries are the only acidifying fruit. They do not stimulate the pancreas. They carry an antibiotic that works only in an acidic environment, which is rare among fruits.
- The popular high-protein diets recommended for losing weight are acidifying. They allow only a minimum amount of alkalizing vegetables and forbid acidifying carbohydrates like grains. Green drinks, low in phosphorus, are necessary and vital on these diets. Green drinks contain, on average, four grams of carbohydrates and zero grams of sugar per serving.
- Macrobiotic diets are high in whole grains such as rice, which are acid-forming. These diets do promote acid-alkaline balance with the liberal use of sea vegetables (alkaline-forming) like kombu, dulse, wakame, hiziki, nori (used in sushi making), and agar, a sea vegetable that acts like gelatin.
- All pesticides and herbicides are acid-forming.

Reaching the Right Proportion

To measure volume sizes by sight, cup one hand and imagine how much food would fit in that palm. As you proportion your foods according to the acidifying-alkalizing chart above, pretend they are in your palm. For each three palmfuls of food from the alkalizing side, have one palmful from the acidifying side. Remember, both sides contain good foods. You

NATURAL BALANCE

Somehow or other your body's inner guidance system seeks out balance. Indeed, it is miraculous what the body does to try to keep balance at all costs. When people drink margaritas (acidifying), they instinctively use salt and lime (alkalizing). When people consume a meal of cooked red meat (acidifying), they like coffee (alkalizing, with a meal) and salt (alkalizing). What a wonderful body you have–just remarkable! Your dog will eat grass, an alkalizing food, to try to neutralize (buffer) the excessive acidity of a high-protein diet. Mix 1 teaspoon of a green drink into 4 ounces of water and feed this to your dog, cat, or birds. They will lick the bowl clean enjoying the alkalizing food.

need both the acidifying and alkalizing food groups. They complement each other. What is important is to keep the proportions correct.

My Meal

While I was writing the last chapter, my wife, Elvira, called me to supper. Let me describe that supper so that you can see how we eat and how we combine Superfoods for an eye-appealing, colorful, delicious meal.

All our foods are from organically grown sources.

Vegetable Dish Yellow summer squash was sliced thin and steamed for less than a minute. Small red tomatoes, quartered, were added raw. Parsley was chopped fine and mixed in, and flax-borage-sunflower-sesame-pumpkin-seed oil was drizzled on top (1 tablespoon per person) with a little apple cider vinegar.

Protein Dish Soaked and slightly sprouted lentils were well cooked so they remained whole, a little firm but easily digested. They were then added to a miso (fermented soy) broth that was not cooked but gained heat from the lentils. A sea vegetable, Nova Scotia dulse, orange yams, onions, garlic, and rosemary were added in the last ten minutes of the 30-minute cooking time. The vegetables were crunchy-firm rather than mushy-soft. Cilantro, a Mexican herb used in traditional dishes of Mexico, was broken by hand, and along with sesame seeds, sprinkled generously over the cooked lentils.

Whole-Grain Dish Elvira cooked whole-grain brown rice for 40 minutes. She added liberal amounts of raw ginger, thyme, oregano, basil, and sage in the last five minutes of cooking. She topped the final cooked rice with chopped green onions and red peppers.

Nutritional Analysis of This Meal

- There were raw herbs and colorful vegetables for enzymes.
- There were omega-3 and omega-6 essential fatty acids.
- This was a phytochemical- and antioxidant-rich meal providing large amounts of alpha- and beta-carotene, chlorophyll, soluble and insoluble fibers, flavonoids, genistein, daidzein, lycopene, monoterpenes, phenolic compounds, plant sterols, polyacetylene, quinones, allyic sulfides, retinoids, vitamins, minerals, and lean protein.
- The whole brown rice and lentils are both medium- to low-glycemic foods and give off their sugars slowly so the blood maintains homeostasis, or normal and balanced blood sugar levels for constant energy.

- This meal was approximately 75 percent alkaline and 25 percent acidic ash by volume.
- The lentils are over 20 percent protein and an ideal 15 percent fat. The rice and lentils made a complete protein.
- This meal reflects a perfect profile of calories from carbohydrates (rice and vegetables), protein (lentils, sesame seeds, miso, and rice) and fat (flax-borage-sunflower-sesame-pumpkin-seed oil). The proportion of calories are: carbohydrates—55 percent; protein—25 percent; fat—20 percent
(Note: This meal cost about $4.40.)

For more suggestions on Super Meals see the recipes and meal plans in Chapter 18.

How You Will Feel

When you adjust your food consumption to a 75 percent alkalizing and 25 percent acidifying proportion, your body fluids should gain their proper acid-alkaline balance (homeostasis) within 4 to 6 weeks. Once you build up your alkaline reserves, you will:
- have deeper, more restful sleep patterns;
- notice that your hair and nails grow faster and thicker;
- experience abundant energy both midmorning and midafternoon;
- enjoy increased mental acuity that gives you better cognitive retention, better recall, and better mental alertness;
- suffer from fewer colds, headaches, infections, and flus;
- notice a reduction in candida (yeast) overgrowth (very often, yeast infection and mercury/heavy-metal exposure occur in the same individual), chronic fatigue syndrome (CFS), arthritis, and fibromyalgia.

Your pH Level and Your Mental State

Your mental state can have an impact on your pH levels. Prayer, quiet meditation, Tai Chi, reflexology, massage therapy, shiatsu, acupuncture, breathing exercises, therapeutic touch, calming music, hatha yoga, walking in nature, deeply appreciating nature, reaching out to others with love and sincere compassion—all these activities help to promote a calm, alkaline body.

Similarly, your body's pH level may affect your mental state. Researchers at the John Radcliffe Hospital in Oxford, England, believe intelligence may be directly linked to pH levels in the cortex part of the brain. Using an electromagnetic scanner, the team measured the pH in the cortexes of 42 teens. The teens then completed a widely used IQ test. The results showed that those whose pH readings of 7.0 or more had significantly higher IQ levels. This is the first time that intelligence was linked to a pH biochemical marker in the brain.

As I described in Chapter 4, when I was head of guidance services for that vocational high school in Niagara Falls, I carefully monitored the diets of several students. When they consumed a diet that was 90 to 100 percent acidifying foods, they were angry, uptight, argumentative, and violent. In contrast, alkalizing diets are calming.

Violence of all types is escalating partly because people, in general, are too acidic. Drivers commit violent crimes on the freeway because they get "ticked off" at someone else's driving. Imagine if prisons, halfway houses, and rehabilitation centers employed an alkalizing food diet.

Generally, the telltale signs of hyper-irritability are common to acidosis. There is a marked difference between the behavior patterns of an alkalizing and an acidifying diet. I believe that Attention Deficit Disorder (ADD), over-irritability, hyperactivity, mood swings, violent tempers, a high degree of agitation, learning disabilities, and "brain allergies" may be heightened by an acidifying diet.

How to Monitor Your pH

The pH level of fluids in your body fluctuates according to your food choices and your stress load.

When your diet contains sufficient alkalizing foods, your internal environment is alkaline. When your internal environment is alkaline, your urine and saliva are a "healthy alkaline."

You can easily assess your pH levels by monitoring your urine, saliva, or venous blood. Monitoring the urine is a simple process that requires pH paper with a range of 5.5 to 8.5 with small gradient changes such as 6.0, 6.2, 6.4, and so on. Venous blood gives the most accurate reading.

Quality pH papers like pHydrion papers and nitrazene paper are readily available in health food stores or pharmacies. (Check the Appendix for sources.)

How To Do It:

1. Tear off a small piece of pH paper from the roll, about 1 inch.

2. Place the pH paper in contact with urine, collected midstream in a paper cup. Collect first morning urine upon rising before you drink water or eat anything, or two hours after a meal. Collect urine after six hours of uninterrupted sleep. If you plan to get up at 6:00 a.m. but get up at 5:00 a.m. to pass water, check your urine pH reading at 5:00 a.m.
3. Once the urine makes contact with the pH paper, immediately compare the paper's color to the color chart on the dispensing box.
4. To get an accurate measure of your state of health, pH levels should be recorded three times a day—morning, afternoon and night—for 30 days.

Interpreting Your pH Readings

An ideal range for first morning urine pH should be 6.8. Your healthy pH readings typically fluctuate as follows:
- 6.6 to 7.0 at 7:00 a.m.
- 6.8 to 7.2 at 3:00 p.m.
- 7.0 to 7.4 at 9:00 p.m.

A pH level that ranges between 4.5 and 6.0 is termed "acidosis." In initial stages of acidosis, energy may still be excellent. However, over time, the body will go into "burn-out" mode as the aging process accelerates.

The opposite end of the pH spectrum results in "alkalosis," levels constantly between 7.5 and 8.0 or more. In this state, sluggishness and lethargy are common; the "fires of life" are cooling down. If your pH is 7.5 to 8.0 or more at each testing and you aren't a vegan who is consuming insufficient protein, your kidneys may be secreting ammonia into your system to try to counterbalance the effects of an acid-producing diet or a potential bacterial infection. This situation is serious and should be addressed immediately by following the ten remedial actions listed below.

A dramatically fluctuating pH level, from high acid to high alkaline, could be responsible for mood swings and sudden energy drops.

Saliva Readings

Although urine pH readings allow you a precise method of determining overall body-fluid pH levels, you may also record your saliva pH readings.

Saliva pH changes slowly and indicates the alkalizing or acidifying effect of foods you have eaten and your stress load over the past five days. In contrast, urine pH changes rapidly depending on your life stresses and on the foods you have eaten over the past 12 hours.

If you do test your saliva pH, never put the paper in your mouth as it contains chemicals. Simply swallow several times to clear your mouth of saliva, then discharge a large portion of saliva into a clean spoon. Put the pH paper into the spoon for five to ten seconds, then compare its color to the pH color chart on the dispensing box.

An ideal first morning saliva pH reading, before you drink water or brush your teeth, is 6.5.

Remedial Action

If your pH is consistently below 6.4, take remedial action immediately. To alkalize your body in five days to 2 weeks, do the following:

- Eat 75 percent alkalizing food and 25 percent acidifying foods, by volume, daily. Use organic produce when possible, especially yams, turnip greens, mustard greens, broccoli, collards, rapini, dandelions, and spinach.
- Drink one or two quality green drinks such as GREENS+ daily—one in the morning and one midafternoon.
- Drink 8 to 12, 8-ounce glasses of pure water, depending on your body size and water needs, through a straw. (When you drink water through a straw, you consume 95 percent water, not air, and you can drink four times as much water before you feel full.) Three times a day add two tablespoons of freshly squeezed lemon or lime juice to the water. Avoid coffee, tea, or soft drinks.
- Eat plain white yogurt or soy yogurt daily—half a cupful midmorning and half a cupful midafternoon.
- Use a magnesium-potassium L-aspartate or citrate supplement daily. Avoid the use of supplements in tablet form as they contain binders, fillers, excipients, and food shellacs that make them difficult to digest, and many people may be allergic to these non-nutritive ingredients. Manufacturers produce tablets, as they are the least expensive way to produce a supplement. Only use supplements in capsules, soft gels, or as powders you mix with a liquid of choice.
- Use 2 tablespoons of organic apple cider vinegar (not in cases of candida) on salads daily, or in 6 ounces of water sipped 10 minutes before a protein meal to aid digestion.
- Moderate exercise tends to counter free calcium excess by promoting the flow of calcium to the bone rather than away from it.
- Eat 1 to 2 tablespoons of raw, unprocessed pumpkin seeds or sunflower seeds daily. Chew them well.

30-Day pH Test Journal

Day	pH reading		
	Morning	Midday	Evening
1			
2			
3			
4			
5			
6			
7			
8			
9			
10			
11			
12			
13			
14			
15			
16			
17			
18			
19			
20			
21			
22			
23			
24			
25			
26			
27			
28			
29			
30			

An ideal range for urine pH should be 6.2 to 7.4, typically fluctuating as follows:
- 6.2 to 7.0 at 7:00 a.m.
- 6.6 to 7.0 at 3:00 p.m.
- 7.0 to 7.4 at 9:00 p.m.

Be energized, by being alkaline!

Use this 30-day pH Test Journal to record your daily urine pH readings. Add each column for a 30-day reading and divide by 30 to get an average, referred to as a baseline urinalysis assessment. Your monthly average pH should be 7.0. Urine tested in the early morning, upon awakening, is the result of anabolic metabolism while you were sleeping. Urine tested two hours after any daily meal is the result of catabolic metabolism (cell functioning while you are awake). You want the results of both.

- Use cultured soy products such as tofu, miso, and tempeh, three times a week. Always cook these foods with some form of sea vegetable to add balancing iodine.
- If dietary means are not sufficient to lower pH levels, consult a certified nutritionist or health professional and use potassium-magnesium supplementation (magnesium raises pH independently of alkaline buffers). Concord grape juice, salmon, live-cultured yogurt, apricots, peaches, lima beans, yams, Swiss chard, blackstrap molasses, soybeans, sunflower seeds, squashes, moderate use of whole grains, and lean meats are excellent sources of potassium and magnesium. Bananas are a source of potassium but they are a high-glycemic food that actually cause acidemia. Their high amount of simple sugar tends to kill the friendly bacteria in the small intestine, allowing the E.coli to take over. The Superfood dietary strategy eliminates bananas or recommends they be consumed occasionally in very small amounts. Note also that commercial bananas are subject to heavy spraying of pesticides and ripening gases.

Recovery Eating With Superfoods

Many athletes like to "flush" or "detoxify" their systems after major competitions that created an increase in body acids. Generally they will only drink green drinks, eat raw salads, fresh fruits, put fresh lemon or lime juice in their drinking water, eat steamed or thinly sliced raw vegetables, fat-free yogurt, or fresh vegetable or fruit juices they make in a home juicer. Concord grape juice with its high potassium content and apple juice with its alkalizing malic acid are most popular. Athletes follow this regime for 1 to 3 days. This diet is 90 percent raw, full of food enzymes, high-quality fibers, and is very alkalizing to the body. It builds up alkaline reserves of minerals and reestablishes the proper acid-base balance after strenuous exercise. It also detoxifies the body of cellular and colon wastes. The large amount of dietary fibers ensure good colon cleansing.

Other athletes like to "carbo-load" by consuming from 40 percent for two days, then to 80 percent for one day, and back to 75 percent for two days, of all their daily calories from complex carbohydrates for five days before an endurance event. Carbo-loading cycles like this are designed to load muscle glycogen (energy) stores for better endurance, not for strength or power, in muscle tissue intensely exercised.

If the carbo-loading uses ripe fruit, a green drink, fresh vegetables, salads, sea vegetables, grasses, lemon or lime juice in drinking water, and fat-free yogurt, then the alkaline reserve (alkalizing minerals in foods) is built up. This "stacked deck" of alkalizing foods will not only supply stored carbohydrates as glycogen in well-exercised muscles but let you perform longer and harder as the alkaline reserve neutralizes (buffers) the acids produced from strenuous muscle exertion. If you perform to exhaustion, eventually the acids win out, but you will have performed longer because you cushioned the corrosive acid buildup.

Carbo-load only under professional supervision since it often results in an acidic condition, because excessive carbohydrate intake causes a loss of urinary phosphate and magnesium (important alkaline buffers). It also promotes weight gain by slowing the activity of the thyroid. Reversing this trend requires exercise first thing in the morning followed by a protein breakfast milkshake using fat-free rice or soy milk, fat-free yogurt, soy lecithin granules, and hydrolyzed whey protein powder.

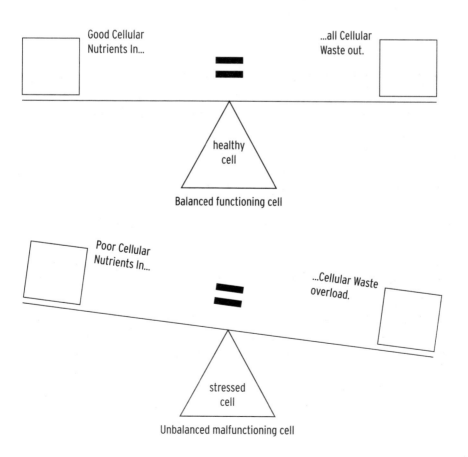

Good Cellular Nutrients In... ...all Cellular Waste out.

healthy cell

Balanced functioning cell

Poor Cellular Nutrients In... ...Cellular Waste overload.

stressed cell

Unbalanced malfunctioning cell

Your Detox Day

You can benefit from the "tricks of the trade" of serious athletes. Designate one day a week as a "detox day." Once in the morning before any food, and again in the afternoon about 3:30 to 4:00 p.m., take two servings of a strong alkalizing green drink such as GREENS+ that is low in phosphorus, mixed in pure water, vegetable or unsweetened fruit juice. The remainder of your food on this day should be 2 to 3 pieces of ripe fruit (but not bananas); a large colorful salad; fresh, homemade vegetable or fruit juices; some sunflower or red clover sprouts; a few vegetables steamed crunchy-tender; and unsweetened herbal teas like chamomile, stinging nettle, or dandelion. Drink 8 to 12, 8-ounce glasses of quality water. Complete the day with a walk in nature concentrating on some rejuvenating slow-breathing exercises. End your day with a sauna, steam bath, infrared sauna, or warm bath in which you use natural sponges to rub your skin of toxins and debris, excreted as a result of the "detox day." You can incorporate Harvey Diamond's mono-diet on this day. (See Chapter 8.)

3 POINT SUMMARY

- Your body is naturally and continually producing acids, whether it is moving or at rest. Stress, pollution, and exercise increase acid production in your body.
- The weak acids created by cellular metabolism and by eating fruits (except cranberries) are exhaled routinely as carbon dioxide. They cause no stress on the body.
- The strong acidifying residues of most proteins, grains, fried foods, most dairy, alcohol, and sugar must be neutralized (buffered) by the 6-layered buffering system discussed above. These alkalizing supports are plentiful in green drinks, herbs, fresh vegetables, ripe fruit (except bananas or cranberries), apple cider vinegar (maximum 2 tablespoons a day), lemon or lime juice (maximum 6 tablespoons a day), fermented soy products, sprouts, sea vegetables (seaweed, algae), grasses (alfalfa, barley, wheat grass), fermented organic dairy such as fat-free, plain yogurt, fat-free cottage cheese, whey (lactose-reduced) protein powder, lean white meat of poultry, some seeds and nuts, and soy lecithin granules.

3 POINT ACTION PLAN

- Eat a diet that is 75 percent alkalizing foods by proportion of volume and 25 percent acidifying foods by proportion of volume. This suggestion applies if you are a meat eater, vegan, or vegetarian.

- Record your urine pH readings for 30 days. Calculate your baseline pH reading (average of 30 days). You should average an ideal 6.8 to 7.2.

- Vegetarians and vegans should check the composition of their diets very carefully to ensure that they are including sufficient amounts of alkalizing foods in their diet.

6

The High-Performance Superdrink – Yes, Water!

HEALTH REFLECTION

Water, water everywhere, and hardly a drop above suspicion.

*Drink far more water than you're currently drinking—up
to 8-12, 8-ounce glasses a day.*
Dr. Julian Whitaker, M.D., Shed 10 Years in 10 Weeks

Even if you're on the right track, you'll get run over if you just sit there.
Joe Graci, Jr.

In this chapter I hope to change radically and permanently the way you think about water. No matter how wonderful a dietary strategy is, no matter how convincing the argument to follow it is, if it does not show you the importance of drinking water, it is doomed to fail. Simply put, superior performance demands superior water intake.

Whenever I fly across the Pacific Ocean, the Atlantic Ocean, or the Indian Ocean, I am amazed. Water covers 70 to 75 percent of the earth's surface. What is equally amazing is that each of us is also a "body of water." Your body is mostly water—between 60 to 70 percent. Your brain, which you trust to navigate you through life, is 74 percent water. The muscles that propel you are 70 to 75 percent water. Your efficient courier system—your blood—is 83 percent water. Even the bones that so faithfully support you are 22 percent water. Plain and simple, water is the most important component of your body.

Only oxygen is more essential to sustaining life. You can live for 35 to 50 days without protein, carbohydrates, and fats. You can live only five days without water in a moderate climate and only three days without

What the Human Body is Made Of

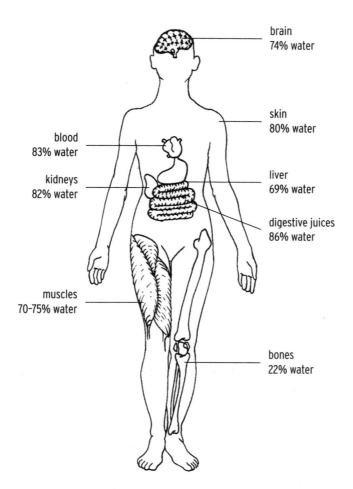

brain
74% water

skin
80% water

blood
83% water

kidneys
82% water

liver
69% water

digestive juices
86% water

muscles
70-75% water

bones
22% water

Water makes up approximately 60 to 70 percent of your body composition. The average body contains 95 to 96 pints of water, 65 pints inside your cells and the remainder outside your cells.

What is your body made of

water	60-67%
proteins	15-19%
fat	12-15%
minerals	3%
carbohydrates	2%
vitamins	1%

water in a very hot climate. When you lose 5 percent of your water supply, your mental and physical performance declines by a hefty 30 percent. Once you lose 20 percent of your water supply, you perish.

Water is present as the major element in every cell and tissue of your body. Every single bodily function is monitored by and depends on the efficient flow of water to vital organs and each of your 100 trillion cells. Your body's water supply is responsible for and involved in regulating every biological process including:

- controlling body temperature through 2 million sweat glands that act as the body's air conditioner and that remove heat via perspiration (which is 99 percent water); the heat of the blood evaporates the sweat, cooling the body
- maintaining blood pressure, digestion, absorption, and circulation
- flushing out the body's metabolic waste products through the kidneys as watery, pH-balanced urine or through the colon as solid waste
- maintaining youthful skin with proper elasticity and flexibility
- developing muscle tissue
- forming the foundation of blood and the body's extensive lymphatic system fluids (the garbage-collection system of the body)
- lubricating every joint, as well as every organ to keep them moving well
- being the primary waterway transport system of bioelectric minerals, hormones, and nutrients carried by the blood's protein albumen, water carries energy and information
- supplying energy to a fatigued body, since fatigue is most often only a water deficit, not a food deficit

How Do We Lose Water?

Whether you're hoeing the garden, negotiating a pay increase, driving children to a school outing, sleeping, recovering from a cold or flu, struggling with a stressful day, or powering your way through a serious workout, your body is losing water and your performance is sagging. In fact, everybody is losing water every minute of the day.

Water is lost through sweat and elimination. Most of it is removed by the kidneys, through which the entire blood supply is filtered 15 times an hour. A small but constant amount of water is eliminated through evaporation. You lose small amounts of water when breathing and tearing. Tear ducts lubricate your eyes 30 times every minute. Those tears then drain down the nose and evaporate. You exhale moisture from the water-lined lungs and nasal passages.

All combined, under normal circumstances, you lose almost 6, 8-ounce glasses of water, naturally, every day. Excess salt, high climatic temperatures, strenuous activity, intense exercise, and drinking caffeinated beverages such as coffee, tea, or soft drinks cause you to lose more water. Dry climates draw out more water from you than humid air does.

The Signs of Dehydration

Despite a constant need for fresh water, many people do not consume enough of it for good health and long life. The lack of sufficient water in your body is called dehydration. When you are dehydrated, your temperature rises. Then, you not only lose more water but also valuable electrolytes such as the essential minerals sodium and potassium, which are dissolved in the water.

When you become dehydrated, the body responds with its own warning signals:

- blurred vision
- dizziness
- dry mouth ("cotton mouth"), which is a sign of serious dehydration
- fatigue
- flushing skin (as the body heats up), then dry, hot skin
- headaches
- heaviness of the head
- overall weakness and unsteady gait
- rapid pulse
- shortness of breath

The body employs very sophisticated thirst signals, but most often people ignore them or interpret them as hunger signals. Society and advertising encourages us to regard the above signs of dehydration as signs of hunger. Moreover, since we are not taught to drink water when we are young, we mistakenly eat food rather than drink water.

Harvey Diamond compares thirst signals to the flashing red light on a car's dashboard that signals the need for an oil change. Wise people see this signal as helpful; others consider it downright annoying. But, like that signal, the body's early-warning signals should not be ignored.

More often than we realize, we all experience mild dehydration. It can easily result from airplane travel, not consuming enough fruits and vegetables (which are 90 percent water), a change in climate, working in dry air, skipping a meal "on the run," or aerobic exercise, drinking coffee, tea, or other caffeinated beverages. How often has flying left you exhausted or irritable? A three-hour flight in a pressurized airplane pulls about 3, 8-ounce glasses of water from your body, and the longer the flight the greater the fluid loss. If you skipped a meal in the hectic rush to catch a flight, then consumed coffee or alcohol to make up for the exhausting rush you were in, you compounded dehydration, promoting even greater fluid loss than just the flight itself would.

Caffeinated and alcoholic beverages alter your fluid needs. Caffeine, which acts as a diuretic, increases urine production. Caffeine stimulates kidney action that excretes fluids, while alcohol inhibits vasopressin (an antidiuretic hormone) secretion in the brain. An 8-ounce glass of water along with your morning cup of coffee or tea will help compensate for this effect. Similarly, if you drink alcoholic beverages, top them off with two glasses of water to help replenish lost fluids.

Water and Aging

At birth we are composed of 77 percent water. As adults, women tend to be 60 to 62 percent water and men 65 to 67 percent water. As we become seniors, most of us become severely dehydrated. The elderly actually have a built-in decreased sense of thirst. Since nature wants a renewal of the species, it naturally reduces our thirst sensation so we become gradually and increasingly dehydrated with age. Most seniors live on the "threshold of dehydration." Since water regulates all bodily functions, and once depleted has no reserves to draw upon, bodily functions steadily decline. Don't let this happen to you!

To quote Joe Graci, Jr., my older brother: "Even if you're on the right track, you'll get run over if you just sit there." If you do not drink enough water daily, chronic dehydration will affect the operation of the majority of your cells and become a cumulative disease producer, regardless of your age.

The Body's Response to Dehydration

Your brain understands the crisis management of water, and it demands priority service. The brain is only one-fiftieth of your total body weight but receives 20 percent of all blood circulation. When brain cells become dehydrated, they shrink. This causes biochemical stress, depending upon how rapidly fluid loss occurred. The body goes into "drought manage-ment," according to F. Batmanghelidj's *Your Body's Many Cries For Water*. A rationing and distribution system assures that some cells will get water, while others will suffer and malfunction. As it increasingly loses water, the body closes down some capillary beds, causing circulation problems. The body has no alternative: the vital "priority" organs must get water to function.

When some capillary beds shut down, there is less space for the cir-culating blood, creating an increase in pressure called elevated blood pressure or hypertension. Many health professionals prescribe a diuretic to expel water, but that only aggravates the condition. Water itself is the best diuretic.

Drinking sufficient amounts of water turns off a posterior pituitary hormone called vasopressin. Vasopressin is an antidiuretic hormone. An antidiuretic holds water in the body and does not let it be excreted. When you drink fewer than 3, 8-ounce glasses of water a day, your body goes into dehydration. To preserve what water it can, the brain secretes the hor-mone vasopressin. Vasopressin causes you to bloat. Overweight individ-uals who begin to consume 6 or more 8-ounce glasses of water a day, turn off vasopressin, recycle their water more efficiently and, to their surprise, can lose up to ten pounds in three weeks. Vasopressin is the chief cause of water bloat among women who suffer from premenstrual syndrome. If you suffer from PMS, cut your salt intake, start drinking much more water, eat Superfoods high in natural sodium and potassium, and forget the diuretic. You'll be glad you did!

Smart Water Replacement

Your basic fluid needs vary each day, depending on the climate, stress, and situations you face. The best guide for optimal water intake is the color and odor of your urine. Kidneys produce urine to clean out waste residue from tissues and blood. Besides checking your morning urine for a pH reading (see Chapter 5), also examine its color and odor. If your urine is a dark yellow, your kidneys did not have enough water. They were forced to concentrate the waste residue in a smaller volume of urine. Yes, your urine color should be slightly darker upon rising since you drank no water all night, but it should be a pale color with no odor all day and evening. (Supplementing with large amounts of the vitamin B family will color urine bright yellow.) Cloudy urine or strong odor in your urine is a sign of water deficit. Your urine color may be the easiest checkpoint to determine if you are drinking enough water.

Optimally your body should void five to six bladderfuls of pale-colored urine each day, unless you have kidney problems, in which case you must carefully monitor your water intake and voiding, and report it to your health professional.

I encourage you to drink 6, 8-ounce glasses of water daily for basic good health. If you really want to prehydrate, in self-defense, drink 8 to 12, 8-ounce glasses of water daily, for superior good health. If you engage in strenuous exercise, work outside in hot weather, if you have hypertension or are a frequent flyer, your eventual goal will be to drink 10 to 14, 8-ounce glasses of water daily.

Athletes must think of water as prime self-defense. Running, kayaking, swimming, power walking, cliff climbing or biking, treadmill running, stationary biking, StairMasters, rowing machines, aerobics, and weight-resistance training in a gym will cost you about 4, 8-ounce glasses of water an hour. In hot weather, this amount doubles. As you lose water, your blood becomes saltier, making you thirsty. Unfortunately, your thirst can be blunted after strenuous exercise or hard work.

How To Do It

1. As soon as you wake up, drink 1 to 4, 8-ounce glasses of room-temperature or slightly heated water, through a straw. If you drink water from a glass or bottle, you consume mostly air—"gulp, gulp, gulp"—and feel bloated from all the air in your stomach. When you drink through a straw, you consume 95 percent water and you can drink four times as much water before you feel full.

2. Add two teaspoons of freshly squeezed lemon or lime juice to your water three times a day, upon rising, midafternoon, and in your final water intake in the evening. The juice will help alkalize your body and neutralize (buffer) acids created from digesting certain foods or normal cellular metabolism.

3. One-half hour before each of your three meals and two snacks, drink 1 to to 1 1/2, 8-ounce glasses of water through a straw. If you do not have enough water in your stomach, digestion is impaired. Also, if the blood becomes too thick after eating because of a lack of water, the blood will try to draw water from the cells. Water intake should precede food intake by half an hour. Unfortunately, coffee, soft drinks, beer, and regular tea do not count as daily water needs. Fruit and veggie juices do!

4. If you exercise or work hard and sweat in hot weather, add 4, 8-ounce glasses of water per hour of strenuous exercise or work.

5. Never drink while you are eating, as the liquid flushes through the stomach quickly into the small intestine. It will dilute and drain some of the digestive juices out of the stomach. This spells stress, as the body must secrete more digestive enzymes. If you continue to consume liquid while you eat, your body's signals get confused as the stomach says, "Quick, there are no enzymes. Secrete more," and the body says, "What's wrong? Just sent some!" We all know in economics what happens with a big demand and a small supply—economic upheaval. The body experiences a similar upheaval, of the digestive kind.

6. Wait at least two hours after any meal, especially supper, to consume your last water of the evening. Fresh fruit juices or vegetable juices count as a glass of water, as do unsweetened herbal teas.

7. Wherever you go, carry a full water container with a secure lid and straw. Get into the habit of continually drinking from your container throughout the day to stay prehydrated.

8. If you consume lots of water-rich fresh fruits and vegetables, they will easily provide you with 2 or 3, 8-ounce glasses of water daily, as they are 90 percent water. Even bread is 35 percent water.

DAILY WATER INTAKE

1. Consume water upon rising	1 to 4, 8-ounce glasses
2. Water before three meals and two snacks	5 to 7 ½, 8-ounce half glasses
3. Water consumed two hours after supper	1 to 2, 8-ounce glasses

DAILY TOTALS: 7 to 13 ½ half glasses daily.

Increase your water intake gradually, by adding only 1, 8-ounce glass of water on each successive or second day. Increasing water intake too quickly can overwork your kidneys and digestive system. Increase by gradual increments to reach full hydration.

If you have kidney disease, congestive heart disease, or use a diuretic, consult a health-care professional before increasing your water intake. Please show your health-care professional this chapter.

If you have been ill or chronically dehydrated, do not rush out and immediately drink 12, 8-ounce glasses of water. The cells in your body are like sponges and will slowly reabsorb water at a limited rate. It may take 5 to 14 days for your body to adapt to a new level of water intake and become fully hydrated. The practical law here is to rehydrate gradually. Let the body get back to homeostasis.

Salt Supplements for Hot Weather?

Definitely not! Sweat may taste salty but it is a lot less salty than the rest of you. Serum sodium levels stay pretty stable in the body. Sodium, potassium, and chloride are the three main electrolytes (an ion or atom that conducts electricity in the body). Every living cell requires some sodium to function properly. It regulates the body's water balance and blood volume, aids digestion by assisting in the production of hydrochloric acid in the stomach, and controls the volume of extracellular (water outside the cell) fluid in the body. Electrolytes have an electrical charge and are the electrical system of each cell. Sodium is the main cation (positively charged electrolyte) and is more concentrated on the outside of the cells than the inside. The inside of the cell is negatively charged. Because opposites attract, sodium moves from the outside of a cell to the inside, creating electrical potential.

While moving into the cell, sodium interacts in an electrochemical exchange process with potassium. Potassium is another positively charged cation. Because both potassium and sodium are positively charged cations, they are in constant competition to enter negatively charged cells. This shifting of sodium and potassium across the cell membrane is an "ionic dance" that creates an electrical potential. The electricity this action produces is the driving force of your muscles. Excess sodium and insufficient potassium disrupts what is called the sodium-potassium pump and your energy supply diminishes.

Get Your Sodium from Food

Most people do not realize how much salt they eat every day. The average North American consumes 5,000 mg (5 g) daily of sodium. Many North Americans consume up to 15,000 mg (15 g) of sodium daily. Most government guidelines suggest 2,400 mg a day. Most nutritional researchers suggest only 1,000 to 2,000 mg (1 to 2 g) daily, and these should be naturally occurring sodium in whole foods. Superfood sources of sodium are seafood, all fruits and vegetables, especially celery, yogurt, and non-fat cottage cheese, Nova Scotia dulse, spirulina, chlorella, and all other sea vegetables.

All natural Superfoods contain a perfect balance of sodium and potassium. Processed foods dangerously tip the scale in favor of sodium. Restaurants are notorious for serving food loaded with sodium. Of the 5,000 mg a day the average North American consumes, 80 percent or 4,000 mg of dietary sodium comes from processed foods such as cheeses, crackers, luncheon meats, soups, and soy sauces.

Years of high-sodium intake can throw off the body's critical balance of sodium and potassium. Your body naturally contains more potassium than sodium, at a ratio of about 2 to 1. You may require additional potassium, in supplements of 100 to 150 mg a day, to reset the sodium-potassium imbalance. Superfoods high in potassium that naturally reset this imbalance are beet greens, acorn squash, avocado, apricots, blackstrap molasses, yams, whole grains, soybeans, lima beans, Swiss chard, sunflower seeds, lean meats, salmon, tomatoes, spinach, and ripe cantaloupes.

The simplest way to reduce sodium intake, says Assa Weinberg in *How To Live 365 Days a Year the Salt-Free Way*, is to eliminate the use of table salt. If you do use salt, consider a shaker of Nova Scotia dulse, or a 20 percent Celtic sea salt mixed with 80 percent of a herbal mixture.

Instead of taking salt pills when you sweat heavily in warm weather, prehydrate by drinking water and consuming a large variety of sodium- and potassium-rich foods. That's all! This will give you about 800 to 2,000 mg of organic sodium and 1,600 to 4,000 mg of organic potassium daily. Remember, your Superfoods, if properly chosen, will give you sufficient amounts of both nutrients, and in the ideal proportion nature intended.

Water, Water Everywhere

You don't always get what you think you're getting when you turn on the tap. In fact, you might not be getting what you think you are getting out of a bottle of water, either. Despite repeated warnings, 86 percent of all North Americans still use faucet water to drink and cook with.

An article in *The New York Times* stated: "More than one in five Americans unknowingly drink tap water polluted with feces, radiation or other contaminants." Pathogens including bacteria, viruses, and protozoa contaminate ground and surface water through animal feedlot runoff, human sewage, and septic-tank overflow. Lead can leach into water from pipes in older homes or in newer homes that use copper pipes with lead soldering. Cadmium, a heavy metal, can leach out of pipes, especially in areas of acidic water. Cadmium enters the water supply from electroplating and the manufacturing of nickel/cadmium batteries or from leaky landfills.

Synthetic organic chemicals (SOCs), human-made chemicals such as pesticides and fungicides, including industrial chemicals such as dioxins and PCBs, enter your water supply through agriculture runoff, pesticide use, the treatment of wood for homes and the leakage of above- and below-ground storage tanks. Volatile organic chemicals (VOCs), including solvents such as benzene, formaldehyde, and carbon tetrachloride, can enter ground water from factory disposal and run into downstream areas.

Water-treatment authorities treat water to minimum standards and in potentially hazardous ways. City water is heavily chlorinated to kill germs and fluoridated to prevent tooth decay. Since some city waters are very acidic, calcium hydroxide, an alkali, is added to change the pH so the water doesn't corrode the pipes.

Bottled Water

Justifiably alarmed at the hazards of using tap water, many people purchase bottled water. Although bottled water is a good transitional fix, it is not a solution. In fact, both the containers and the water itself might be doing more harm than good. The very soft bottles that hold the water are made of polycarbonate resins that get absorbed into the water. And often the water itself is not adequately tested.

If you do use bottled water, only purchase it in very hard plastic bottles. And always call the bottler's 800 number and ask the following: where is the source of the water and how does it get to the bottling site; and what contaminants it is tested for and what are the results of the testing. Ask for a recent independent lab analysis of their water for biological, inorganic, radioactive, and synthetic contaminants, as discussed below.

Water-Treatment Systems

The best way to maintain the quality of your drinking water is to invest in a home water-treatment system. It may seem like an expensive solution, but filtering your own water is far cheaper than buying bottled water.

COMPARATIVE COSTS

tap water...less than $.01 per gallon
bottled water ....about $1.20 per gallon
double carbon filter with UV light ....about $.05 per gallon
reverse osmosis...about $.20 per gallon
fractional steam distillation ....about $.25 per gallon
acid-alkaline electrolysis ....about $.30 per gallon

Most important, water-treatment systems offer the best way to deal with complex contamination, such as trace chemicals in municipal supplies or wells in the vicinity of leaching waste dumps. There are four main high-quality systems to choose from. They are:

1. *GAC Units* These granular-activated carbon systems come in countertop or undersink units with one or more carbon filters and with or without ultraviolet (UV) lights.

2. *Acid-Alkaline Water Units* These units are water ionizers. They come in countertop units with a UV light, carbon filters, and an electrolysis chamber containing positive and negative electrodes. They split water into acid water and alkaline water, and reduce the water-molecule size by one-half.

3. *Distillation Water Units* Fractional distillation units are generally made of stainless steel with or without a post carbon filter. Distillers boil water and lift it from the contaminants. Vented distillers allow the removal of organic chemicals.

4. *RO systems* Reverse osmosis is a multistage filtration system. Water passes through a synthetic semipermeable membrane under pressure. The membrane lets treated water pass through, but contaminants are washed down the drain. These units come with prefilters, postfilters, UV lights, or colloidal silver ionizers.

Choosing Well

Before you purchase any unit, have your water tested. (Any water-filter supply store will direct you to local agencies.) Then check to see that your particular water contaminants are removed by the system you chose. Check the unit's ability to remove contaminants from these four categories:

- biological contaminants (bacteria, viruses, parasites)
- inorganic contaminants (lead, chlorine, asbestos)
- radioactive contaminants (radium, strontium 90)
- organic (synthetic) contaminants (pesticides, industrial solvents)

WATER-TREATMENT TERMS

- *Ultraviolet lights* (UV lights) kill viruses, bacteria, protozoa, and parasites in the water. The water runs under the light. These lights must be replaced every 12 months.

- *Colloidal silver ionizers* give off small amounts of silver that kill viruses, bacteria, protozoa, and parasites in the water. UV lights and colloidal silver ionizers kill bacteria that build up and grow on any filter that is repeatedly used.

- *Prefilters* take out large particle-size contaminants before they can clog your treatment system.

- *Postfilters* are used after the main treatment to remove any final contaminants. Replace pre- and postfilters annually

- A *chlorine reduction cartridge* must be used to filter municipal water that runs through a TFC (thin film composite) RO (reverse osmosis) system. It is not needed on a CTA (cellulose triacetate) RO system.

- A *silifos softening filter* is necessary to make hard well water soft before it can go through any RO system.

Don't be discouraged by the cost of water-treatment units, which may run from $250 to $2,000. They may seem expensive, but no more so than other major appliances like refrigerators, stoves, television sets, CD units, and washers and dryers. And I have yet to find a television set that gives crystal-clear water. Don't hesitate to purchase a proper water-treatment system.

Thumbs Up and Down

Each water-treatment system has some thumbs-up features and some thumbs-down features. Do not accept a unit that delivers its final treated water with more than 30 ppm (parts per million) of contaminants. Let's look at some aspects of each unit.

GRANULAR ACTIVATED CARBON

Thumbs Up
- water at 30 ppm contaminants
- $250 to $700
- above or below sink
- easy to replace filters
- if it has a UV light that is replaced annually
- if it has two long granulated carbon cartridges through which water can slowly drip

Thumbs Down

- may not remove asbestos or lead
- if it has no UV light
- if it does not have two long carbon cartridges

ACID-ALKALINE WATER

Thumbs Up

- good oxidation reduction potential (antioxidant)
- high 8-9, pH ionized alkaline water to drink
- acidic water is astringent, wash your face with it to restore skin pH
- leaves all minerals in water
- if it has a double carbon filter and a UV light

Thumbs Down

- $1,300 to $2,000
- mainly a filtration system; high-quality Japanese units have a double carbon filter and a UV light that filter to a one micron size, but that may not be sufficient if you have heavy metals like lead in your water

VENTED FRACTIONAL WATER DISTILLERS

Thumbs Up

- whistle-clean water at 3-10 ppm contaminants
- no plumbing necessary
- stainless steel
- vented to let volatile gases escape
- if a carbon filter is used as a postfilter, or if a colloidal silver ionizer is used as a postfilter

Thumbs Down

- $1,100 to $1,500
- uses electricity
- must be cleaned every 2 to 4 weeks
- should add 2 tablespoons of liquid minerals to every five gallons of treated water, to replace lost minerals. "Concentrate," from Trace Minerals, is a good product for this purpose. Do this with RO water also.

REVERSE OSMOSIS SYSTEM

Thumbs Up

- very clean water at 10-20 ppm contaminants, only if a TFC filter is used and maintained well
- if a colloidal silver ionizer is used as a prefilter
- if a UV light is used as a postfilter
- only if the unit has a built-in 5-filter system

Thumbs Down
- $900 (installation under sink necessary)
- minerals are removed as in distillation (but can be replaced)
- cartridges replaced every 6 months
- hard well water needs a silifos softener
- TFC units need a chlorine reduction cartridge if you receive municipal water or they will be destroyed
- CTA units do not need a chlorine reduction cartridge but are not as effective as the TFC units in removing contaminants

Other Options

You may want to invest in a water-treatment system that treats all the water entering your home, providing clean water for drinking, cooking, bathing, brushing your teeth, and clothes washing.

If you do not treat all the water entering your home, and use municipal water treated with chlorine, purchase a good dechlorination filter. It quickly attaches to your showerhead, can cost from $35 to $50, lasts one full year, and is effective at removing 99.9 percent of all chlorine.

Water Is Your Best Liquid Asset

Crystal-clean water is one of the sweetest things imaginable. You cannot do a lot about the air you breathe outside your dwelling, but you can do an enormous amount about the quality of water entering your home. It will pay off in more vigorous and healthy years for your life, and enable you to maintain peak performance, both physically and mentally.

6 POINT SUMMARY

- You are mainly a "body of water," composed of 60 to 70 percent water.
- The power of water is the chemistry that powers life.
- You may be chronically dehydrated. The majority of senior citizens are dehydrated.
- When you lose 5 percent of your water supply, your mental and physical performance declines by a hefty 30 percent. Once you lose 20 percent of your water supply, you perish.
- Most people interpret their thirst signals as hunger signals.
- Water, water everywhere, and hardly a drop above suspicion. Your tap water may be contaminated.

6 POINT ACTION PLAN

- Try to drink a minimum of 6, 8-ounce glasses of pure water through a straw each day. Soon you will be able to drink 8 to 12, 8-ounce glasses of pure water through a straw. Add a total of six tablespoons of fresh lemon or lime juice to your daily water consumption.

- If you engage in long, strenuous exercise or perspire profusely in a hot-weather work environment, drink more water. If you are a frequent flyer or a flight-crew member, prehydrate before your flight and rehydrate while flying.

- Carry a water container with a secure lid and attached straw wherever you go and drink from your container throughout the day.

- Learn the signs of dehydration and at these times drink water rather than eat food.

- Eat your ten servings of colorful vegetables and two to three servings of ripe, seasonal fruit daily. These natural Superfoods are 90 percent water and supply you with all the sodium and potassium you require, in the proper ratio.

- Have your tap water or well water tested for contaminants. This will cost about $35. If your water needs to be cleaned up, consider one of the options discussed above. Remember, water is your best liquid asset.

Color Your Plate With Superfoods

Everyone loves to eat.

Most health problems begin right in our kitchen.
Dr. Carolyn DeMarco, M.D.

Health is a matter of choice, build it, one meal at a time.
Steve Meyerowitz, The Sproutman

Congratulations! Your good sense, curiosity, and maybe even inspiration have brought you this far. If you apply all or even some of the health principles mentioned, you will feel better, look better, think better, and even sleep better. You will also feel more fully the magnificence and natural wisdom your body possesses. The precision with which a healthy body operates is extraordinary.

The Wonder of Food

We all share one thing—we all love to eat. Every culture, every nationality loves to eat. The wandering Bedouins in the Moroccan desert, the Bajans of Barbados, the macrobiotics of Japan, remote villagers in China, the Cajuns of Louisiana, the Québécois of Montreal, the hearty fishing people of the Canary Islands, the independent tribal people of India's Himalaya Mountains, Vancouver vegans, or ranch hands in Montana—all live by eating and love to eat.

We like to nourish our family, friends, and neighbors with healthy food, and to experience the nourishing effects that the rituals surrounding food and eating can have. Food preparation itself is a universal ritual, and we all enjoy sharing the kitchen atmosphere where foods are prepared.

Traditionally, prior to eating, people of all cultures express gratitude and pay respect to the food, to God, to Mother Nature the sustainer, to the "bread earners," to the food preparers, and to the honored guests. Whatever the ritual—a prayer, a chant, a silent meditation, a song, a poem, a reading, a dance, the holding of hands or a supportive embrace—the effect is always the same. The ritual helps us appreciate the earth that gave us the food, the nourishment the food gives our bodies, and the bonding that eating gives the participants. This ritual of grace or thanksgiving, followed by sharing, generates a feeling of healthy cohesiveness that goes beyond the meal to encompass the rest of the day. Food combines science and spirituality, philosophy and technology. If we prepare, share, or eat food unconsciously, we might easily ignore the many benefits of the ritual itself. We might not properly nourish ourselves, or truly nourish those people with whom we have the opportunity of sharing the meal. In doing so, we are led into an unhealthy relationship with food.

Superfoods bless us when we eat them. Shouldn't we thank or bless them first? Preparing food properly is a conscious process. Our attitude and mental outlook unquestionably influence the preparation, taste, aroma, texture, and presentation of a meal.

This chapter introduces you to some colorful, fun, alternative Superfoods that are so outrageously delicious they will easily add zest and flare to your meal preparations. These foods also promote the simple art of conscious food preparation. Maybe I should warn you about the success your new food preparations will bring. There is an old saying: "Success is relative—the more success, the more relatives." Conscientious eating has great merit, but its value increases a hundredfold when the food has been conscientiously prepared, blessed, shared, and then eaten.

Gourmet Greens

Lettuce is North America's favorite green. Lettuce is green because it contains the potent antioxidant and phytochemical chlorophyll. But that beautiful vibrant green color isn't the only good news. Lettuce is a source of healing organic water, fibers, beta- and alpha-carotene, B-complex vitamins, vitamins A, C, and E, calcium, iron, potassium, magnesium, manganese, and the dark green varieties contain co-enzyme Q_{10}, necessary for a strong heart. The darker the leaf the more abundant the vitamin A content. The tips of a lettuce generally contain more of these nutrients than the fibrous rib.

Remember when I said, "Bye-bye, iceberg lettuce—hello, luscious spinach, arugula, endive, leaf lettuce, oak lettuce, romaine lettuce, mesclun, mizuna, mustard greens, bibb, endive, kale, chard, dandelion greens, watercress, and parsley"? All the lettuces mentioned are full of vitamins that contribute to the growth and vibrant health of nails, hair, and skin. Mustard greens have 600 percent more vitamin C and 500 percent more calcium than iceberg lettuce. Dandelion greens have 20 percent more beta-carotene, 600 percent more iron, 400 percent more vitamin B$_2$ and 300 percent more vitamin C than iceberg lettuce. Watercress is high in sulfur (responsible for the vegetable's strong flavor), which cleans the bloodstream and supports pancreatic health. Iceberg has none.

Whenever possible, buy organically grown produce. Greens should be served at room temperature, immediately after tossing. The younger the green leaf, the tastier it is. Store all greens loosely wrapped in a cotton cloth in the vegetable crisper. Do not store apples with tender greens, as the ethylene produced by apples will cause leaf browning. Environmentally safe storage bags called Ever-Fresh bags also keep fruits and vegetables in the refrigerator fresher and more flavorful, three to ten times longer than conventional storage methods.

Lettuce Get Acquainted

- ARUGULA The emerald-green leaves have a delicate texture and a sharp, peppery flavor.
- BIBB Medium green leaves with a velvety texture and a mild flavor. The heads are small with curved flat, delicate leaves.
- CURLY ENDIVE This frilly-leafed lettuce has a bittersweet taste and pale green color.
- GREEN or RED LOOSELEAF Large fan-shaped heads are either light green or tipped in reddish-purple with a mild-sweet flavor.
- MESCLUN This lettuce is a widely available but pricey mixture of young tender greens and colorful herbs of many flavors containing red looseleaf, arugula, mizuna, pansy heads, and curly endive.
- MIZUNA The lettuce has long, dark green jagged leaves with a mild mustard-like taste.
- WATERCRESS Often mixed with mild-flavored greens like leaf lettuce and bibb, watercress has a distinct peppery flavor, crunchy stems, and deep green, round leaves.

When you toss your next salad, experiment with these various green lettuces. Eating colorful salads is a wonderful way to include raw "live foods" in your daily diet. Living foods have live enzymes. Enzymes are proteins that initiate biochemical reactions such as digestion in the same way a spark plug initiates combustion. Pull the spark plugs from your car's engine, and your car won't start. Without the enzymes in raw foods, the body lacks the digestive "spark plugs" to easily break down foods.

Plant and animal food products have plenty of enzymes in their natural state. Unfortunately, food enzymes are destroyed at 122 degrees Fahrenheit. That is the reason I suggest you eat some raw food at each meal. Have seeds and nuts on your oatmeal at breakfast; tomatoes, onions, red peppers, herbs, sunflower-seed sprouts, and grated carrots on your sandwich at lunch; or a colorful salad or shredded beets and herbs to garnish your supper protein entrée. All these "live foods" provide those essential enzymes. Remember, presentation is everything. Present your food with a multitude of colors from a wide range of unheated lettuces in salads or as garnishes.

Festive Mushrooms

There are 700 kinds of edible mushrooms, each with a unique flavor. Europeans have always appreciated the gastronomic value of mushrooms, and Asians have used mushrooms for thousands of years to maintain health and promote longevity. Mushrooms are renowned for their ability to slow or stop pathological processes by turning on beneficial killer T-cells. They especially enhance superior immune system functions involved in inhibiting cancer development.

In North America, mushrooms are underrated and even regarded with suspicion by many people. Only recently have some of the more exotic varieties appeared in North American produce markets and are now popular gourmet-cuisine ingredients. Maitake (my-TAH-kay), reishi (rai-SHI), shiitake (shi-TAK-ke), morel, chanterelle, enoki, wood ear, oyster, porcini, and large portabella mushrooms are now available in regular produce markets, health food stores, organic farmers' markets, and Asian specialty shops. Mushroom-growing kits are available in gourmet produce departments and in many health food stores. They make great gifts! Until recently, these mushrooms grew only in the wild and were very expensive. Thanks to cultivation techniques developed in the last ten years, they are now accessible and affordable.

Many people consider mushrooms to be treasures of the earth. In China and Japan, shiitake, maitake, and reishi mushroom broth is savored by itself or as a base to soups, sauces, or stir-frys. The cook coarsely chops 3 cups of mushrooms, 10 cloves of garlic, 2 large onions. These, along with

3 tablespoons of chopped ginger root and 1 cup of chopped daikon (large white-fleshed radish with a sweet-spicy flavor) are placed in 10 cups of water and brought to a boil, then simmered for 30 minutes. In the last 5 minutes of cooking, cayenne and white or black pepper are added to taste.

Mushrooms can also be added to stir-frys, roasted vegetables, or a steamed vegetable medley. Or they can be broiled on top of either a marinated piece of tofu or a fresh catch of salmon. The possibilities are endless.

Mother Nature's Healing Herbs

Herbs pack a lot of power in a small quantity. Not only do they flavor our food, they provide nutritional and medicinal value as the mediators of many metabolic processes. Culinary herbs are Superfoods with gentle medicinal properties. Gingko biloba is an example of a herb that accelerates the delivery of oxygen to the brain so that the brain can function at full capacity.

Herbs should be used sparingly to enhance the flavor of foods and never to dominate them. As a rule, in a dish of four servings, use 2 tablespoons of coarsely chopped fresh herbs; or 1/2 teaspoon of powdered dry herbs; or 2/3 teaspoon of dried, chopped herbal flakes.

Some of the best flavors and aromas of herbs come from the aromatic oils contained in them, but in time the ingredients in these oils dissipate. Leafy green herbs have the most aromatic oils and are the most flavorful when they are fresh. When you increase your seasoning repertoire, try to use fresh herbs. They are found in almost every market produce section. Or grow a small home-herb garden. It's easy, requires little space, and is well worth the effort. Chives, basil, parsley, dill, oregano, and rosemary comprise a good starter garden.

Use fresh green herbs in salads, soups, stews, sauces, and stir-frys, and to garnish entrées. The most common fresh herbs are cilantro, parsley, watercress, bay leaves, sage, rosemary, basil, oregano, fennel, dill, chervil, marjoram, thyme, chives, and tarragon. You can safely eat several flavorful flowers and herbs such as nasturtium, violets, lemon balm, sorrel, savory, and scented geraniums. Use fresh garlic and ginger root daily in your cooking.

Herbal Tea-Healing Effects

Herbal teas are a great addition to any pantry. Here are some particularly good choices:
ALFALFA treats bladder disorders and both low and high blood sugar levels.

ALOE VERA soothes an acidic stomach or inflamed intestines.

ANGELICA, BLACK COHOSH, CHASTE TREE BERRY, DONG QUAI, and LICORICE normalize menstruation.

BILBERRY improves vision and mental clarity.

BLACK COHOSH relieves PMS, menstrual cramps, and the symptoms of menopause.

CAYENNE (red pepper) improves circulation and relieves arthritis.

CHAMOMILE relieves constipation and stress (use for only short periods of time).

DANDELION LEAF detoxifies and cleans the liver.

GINGKO BILOBA aids mental acuity.

ECHINACEA (ek-i-NAY-sha) stimulates the immune system as a treatment for colds, flus, and infections.

GOLDEN SEAL (an endangered species; Oregon grape can be used in its place) slows bacterial growth and reduces inflammation.

GREEN TEA acts as an antioxidant and potent cancer inhibitor in the intestinal tract.

SIBERIAN GINSENG relieves stress, fatigue, and frazzled nerves.

HAWTHORNE helps those with stage II (more advanced) heart problems.

KAVA KAVA relieves nervousness, agitation, and anxiety.

PYGEUM AND SAW PALMETTO protects the prostate against benign prostatic hyperplasia (BPH)—enlargement of the prostate gland.

FEVERFEW relieves migraines and arthritis.

GINGER acts as an antinausea and antimicrobial medicine, and cleanses the colon.

Purchase these herbal teas singly or in combinations. Purchase them in bulk, as herbal powders, and experiment with your own combination.

Superfoods from the Sea

The benefits of sea vegetables (seaweeds) in the human diet are well known to cultures that evolved by the sea. They are a dietary staple to coastal people in Hawaii, Asia, Ireland, Iceland, South America, Canada's West Coast and Atlantic provinces, Scotland, and Iceland. These green foods are fantastic sources of vitamins, digestive enzymes, minerals, proteins, and trace minerals like chromium and selenium, rarely found in modern-day soils. Sea vegetables are rich in fiber, vitamins, including A, B, C, and the entire B-complex, especially B_{12}, minerals including calcium, iodine, sodium, potassium, magnesium, absorbable organic iron, and trace minerals. Most varieties of sea vegetables contain from 15 to 60 percent protein. According to Dr. Rosalie Bertell, president of the International Institute of Concern for Public Health, in Toronto, seaweed can bind to and eliminate heavy metals from the body. In the 1960s and 1970s, researchers at McGill University, in Montreal, showed that sodium alginate, a derivative of sea vegetables, binds to nuclear radiation molecules like strontium 90 (a dangerous compound of atomic fallout) and helps eliminate it and other nuclear radiation from the body.

Clearly, sea vegetables are some of the most beneficial foods you can eat. They are virtually fat free and low in calories. By eating sea vegetables, you return to the ancestral source of life—the oceans—and replenish yourself with the vast reservoir of essential and sometimes hard-to-find nutrients.

In North America, sea vegetables, which range in color from purplish-red to greenish-black, are grown and harvested in the clean, deep ocean waters off Maine, Nova Scotia, and California. They are washed with springwater and air-dried. Sea vegetables are available in bulk form or prepackaged at most natural food stores. They are also available as condiments and in shaker bottles, to be used as spices and for salt substitution. Dried sea vegetables will keep indefinitely if stored in a jar in a cool, dark place.

You might have to acquire a taste for sea vegetables, but once you include them in your diet, especially if you consume tofu, you will be hooked. Before you use them, rinse the dried leaves in cold water and soak them in cold water for 3 to 10 minutes until just soft. You can then dry-roast them for 5 to 10 minutes in a frying pan, then crush into powder to be added to bean dishes, rice dishes, soups, casseroles, salads, breads, vegetables, miso soups, or lean animal protein. Contact The Mendocino Sea Vegetable Company (707-934-1037) for their wonderful *The Sea Vegetable Gourmet Cookbook*.

A Glossary of Sea Vegetables

AGAR Agar has a very mild taste and may come as a light yellow powder or translucent flakes. Use as a gelling agent or thickener in fruits, sauces, and vegetable dishes.

ARAME Arame has a mild and delicately sweet flavor. Dry-roast then sprinkle it on tofu, beans, salads, or vegetables.

JAPANESE CHLORELLA A green single-celled algae that is a powerhouse of nutrients, chlorella is included in high-quality green drinks.

KELP (brown or laminara) Since kelp has a strong salty flavor and an extremely high iodine content, you should use dulse instead, which is not as iodine intense.

NOVA SCOTIA DULSE Dulse has a salty flavor. Soak it for 3 minutes then dry-roast it in a fry pan for 5 minutes. Crumple and add to any dish. Use it as a salt substitute!

KOMBU Kombu has a natural mild flavor. Soak it for 3 minutes in cold water then cook it for 35 to 40 minutes. Use it as a base or stock. Added to soy or other beans, kombu aids in digestion.

NORI Nori has a mild, sweet taste. It is most commonly available in dried sheets which are used to roll rice, vegetables, meats or seafoods, called nori rolls.

HAWAIIAN SPIRULINA Available as a fine green powder, this multi-celled blue-green algae is absolutely a treasure chest of nutrients. Drink it daily as part of a good-quality green drink.

WAKAME A potent and flavorful sea vegetable, wakame should be soaked for 15 minutes in cold water then diced to use in miso soup, salads, rice dishes, stews, bean dishes, or as a condiment.

Smoothies: Return to Blender

Busy people have rediscovered smoothies—fruit drinks that can replace a fruit snack and power you through a morning or afternoon with lots of zip. The best news is that the only hardware you need is a blender, and the entire process may take only two minutes. Don't overindulge in fruit smoothies though. Small amounts of these colorful, fiber-rich foods are sufficient at one time.

There is one law that governs the taste of smoothies: the riper the fruit, the sweeter the smoothie. Otherwise, your choices are unlimited. Fruit smoothies can include pears, grapes, and pineapple as bases. Use one or more of the base fruits frozen, then add the other fruit and a little water, if necessary. Buy frozen fruit for your base or freeze your own. For a wider variety of colors and nutrients, add dark orange fruits like apricots, peaches, papaya, mangoes, and cantaloupe. Orange fruits are powerhouses of vitamin A and beta-carotene. A rainbow of colors and nutrients unfold when you use strawberries, blueberries, blackberries, raspberries, black currants, red currants, kiwi, fresh figs, oranges, and grapefruit. Experiment until you find the perfect one for you.

You can quickly adapt this idea to make a protein shake with a great flavor and smooth texture. Use 6 ounces of fat-free rice milk, soy milk, oat milk, or skim milk as the base. Add 2 heaping tablespoons of a fat-free plain "active culture" yogurt for those excellent bacterial cultures and as a thickening agent. Add 2 tablespoons of oil-free soy lecithin granules that super-clean your arteries, make your skin and hair shine, and smooth out the protein shake. Finally, add a large scoop of one of these low-fat protein powders: ion-exchanged whey protein or cross-flow whey protein; soy protein powder; milk and egg white protein powder. Soy lecithin granules and low-fat protein powders are available at every whole food store. You must chew each mouthful before swallowing a protein drink, since the food needs to be salivated well. This drink will deliver 25 to 30 grams of complete protein and makes a great protein meal. It can be properly balanced with a half or a whole slice of sour-dough, whole-grain bread topped with 1/2 teaspoon of salt-free butter or 1 teaspoon of either pumpkin butter, almond butter, or cashew butter.

Sprout Superfoods in Your Indoor Garden

Sprouting seeds provides a great opportunity to grow our own food. It is simple to sprout seeds or grains indoors, 12 months of the year, even in limited space.

Choose alfalfa, clover, radish, kale, buckwheat, sunflower, red pea, broccoli, and chia seeds. Use organic seeds or grains that have not been pretreated for agricultural purposes. Place them in tight bamboo baskets, flax cloth bags, or in jars. Water them in the morning and again in the late evening. And then in 5 to 14 days remove them and they are ready to eat.

For more information and detailed instructions, consult *Sprouts, The Miracle Food* by Steve Meyerowitz, affectionately called the Sproutman (see Appendix for source).

Reasons to Sprout

- Sprouts are partially predigested and therefore very easy to digest;
- Live enzymes readily available in sprouts add to the stomach's digestive enzymes;
- Sprouts are an easy, inexpensive way of raising organic foods and reducing food costs; and
- Sprouts are extremely nutritious and the richest food source of vitamins and minerals.

Kombucha or Mushroom Tea

Kombucha "mushroom" tea is another homegrown Superfood. It has been used in Asia for centuries to restore health and as a detoxifier of body wastes. The "mushroom" is a large, flat, pancake-shaped fungus-like

SPROUTS REDEEMED

Many popular authors have warned people not to eat sprouts, especially alfalfa sprouts. The concern came from an article written by Dr. Bruce Ames, a prestigious biochemist at the University of California at Berkeley, who was reviewing another researcher's work. Alfalfa beans contain a toxin called L-canavanine. Canavanine is an analog of the amino acid arginine that is incorporated into protein in place of argine. Monkeys fed alfalfa tablets containing L-canavanine sulfate developed symptoms similar to lupus in humans. None of this research included alfalfa sprouts as they are typically consumed by humans. The alfalfa used in the research was one- to three-day-old non-green seedlings which were then oven-dried to reduce their bulk. No tests were done with mature, green alfalfa sprouts.

Recent research shows that L-canavanine rapidly decreases in plants as they mature during germination. L-canavanine in a mature alfalfa sprout represents a 0.00075 percent concentration.

Dr. Ames told me that there is no concern with eating sprouts, even alfalfa sprouts. If you are still cautious, eat fewer alfalfa sprouts. L-canavanine is also present in onions, garlic, and soybean seeds. It is their protection from insects. Mature plants contain very little and are not a concern.

growth. It is not really a mushroom but part lichen, part bacterium xylinum, and part yeast culture. Cigarette smoke will kill it, even second-hand smoke.

The "mushroom" itself is not eaten. Rather, a tea is made by fermenting the mushroom for about a week in a mixture of pure water, sugar, green, or black tea, with apple cider vinegar or a small portion of previously made tea. The mushroom produces smaller daughter "mushrooms" that can be used to produce more tea. Use only glass cookware to make the tea and keep it in sterile condition.

To get started you need a daughter mushroom from a friend's main crop. Ask around. So many people are growing (fermenting) kombucha mushroom tea, that you may find you receive your start-up daughter mushroom from a co-worker, your banker, your neighbor, a retired grandfather, or your auto mechanic. Most growers like to give a daughter mushroom to other first-time users as a gift, so they can propagate their own homegrown crops, which are surprisingly easy and inexpensive to make. Use it in moderation!

Soy Lecithin Granules: The "Fat-Fighter"

I am delighted to introduce you to, or perhaps reacquaint you with, the single most important Superfood—soy lecithin granules that are not dried on whey powder.

High-quality soybean lecithin granules are nutty-flavored little golden nuggets that are increasingly finding their way into kitchens. The biochemical name for lecithin is phosphatidyl choline (PC). The very highest-quality soy lecithin granules include 22 percent phosphatidyl choline. A tablespoon of soy lecithin granules weighs 7.5 grams and contains about 1,723 mg of phosphatidyl choline. It takes 2,000 pounds of soybeans to make one pound of this high-quality lecithin. Lecithin from animal sources such as eggs is predominantly saturated; lecithin in plants is basically unsaturated. Use 2 tablespoons or 15 grams daily in your food preparation.

The highest concentrations of lecithin are located in the vital organs: the brain, heart, liver, and the kidneys. The brain shows a dry composition (a measure without liquid) of 30 percent lecithin. The outer layers of the nerve fibers are 60 percent lecithin. Soy lecithin emulsifies and removes the "bad" cholesterol called low-density lipoproteins (LDL), and increases the "good" high-density lipoproteins (HDL) your body needs. LDL is devastating, as it clogs the arteries and increases the chances of heart or coronary disease.

Including high-quality soy lecithin granules in your daily diet will:

- lower "bad" LDL cholesterol, especially excessive plasma cholesterol; lower LDL that causes type II arteriosclerosis;
- reduce high blood pressure;
- dramatically increase fat-soluble vitamins A, D, and E absorption by as much as 100 percent;
- give hair added texture and sheen;
- help to convert dangerous homocysteine (a food by-product) to nontoxic compounds;
- allow the skin to retain more moisture and remain elastic;
- act as a "fat fighter," thus being a positive aid to all slimmers.

The spring 1997 edition of the *Technical Review*, a publication of the Israel Institute of Technology, confirms the discovery of an ingredient in the root of the licorice plant that, like lecithin, also prevents the buildup of cholesterol in the arteries. The ingredient, glabridin, delays the oxidation of "bad" LDL cholesterol, a major contributing factor to increased cholesterol on arterial walls that lead to arteriosclerosis, or narrowing of the arteries. "LDL, oxidized to a significant degree, has been found in patients who are at high risk for arteriosclerosis," said Professor Michael Aviram, of the Faculty of Medicine and head of the research team. He explained that arteriosclerosis can result in heart attack or stroke and is a primary cause of death in the Western world.

High-quality green drinks are a convenient way of daily consuming both soy lecithin granules and licorice root in well-balanced proportions. The high-end green drinks include large amounts of phosphatidyl choline. They are an alkalizing food.

Soy lecithin granules (not liquid, tablets, or capsules which may be rancid or oxidized) are readily available at all whole food stores. Store them in your refrigerator. Sprinkle 2 tablespoons on cooked oatmeal, sprinkle them over salads or vegetables, put them as toppings in soup, and use them in protein shakes.

I cannot say enough about the enormous support soy lecithin granules add to human life and longevity. Try it, and see for yourself.

3 POINT SUMMARY

- Food preparation is a universal ritual. Prior to eating, all cultures extend the ritual by expressing gratitude and respect to God, Mother Nature the sustainer, and to all humanity. Sharing food creates a feeling of healthy cohesiveness that can encompass the rest of the day.
- Superfoods can be colorful, outrageously delicious, and fun to work with.
- Color your plate with gourmet greens, festive mushrooms, fresh herbs, sea vegetables, sprouts, kombucha tea, and soy lecithin granules.

4 POINT ACTION PLAN

- Presentation is everything. Present your food with natural colors.
- Before you plan your weekly or daily meals, think of all the Superfoods that will add color and flair to your final preparations.
- Since you have to eat to live, include some quick blender meals on days when you are on the run.
- Golden soy lecithin granules (nuggets) are "fat fighters" that you need to get acquainted with and use daily! They are a wonderful alkalizing food.

The Clean Machine– Periodic Mono-Dieting

by Harvey Diamond, Co-author, *Fit For Life*

HEALTH REFLECTION

Mono-dieting is a gift, a blessing, and once experienced, you'll thank the day it became part of your life.

To have a renewed body, you must be willing to have
new perceptions that give rise to new solutions
Dr. Deepak Chopra, *Ageless Body, Timeless Mind*

Making one day a week a detox day and incorporating mono-dieting
into the Superfood dietary strategy is a surefire way to achieve
permanent supercharged health.
Dr. Ruth-Anne Baron, N.D., practitioner and lecturer

Periodic mono-dieting, if practiced intelligently, will cleanse and strengthen your cells, lymphatic system, and digestive tract more than any other action you could take besides fasting. There is no health routine that is more thorough, effective, or beneficial than a properly conducted fast, and no other area of healing that is more neglected, misunderstood, or maligned. Those who call fasting and starvation the same thing are sorely ignorant of human physiology. Equating the two is like equating swimming and drowning.

More than any other factor, periodic mono-dieting is responsible for my recaptured health and continued well-being. I have benefited immeasurably from the practice for more than 25 years and continue to reap the rewards of its effectiveness in helping me maintain the level of health I enjoy. The beauty of periodic mono-dieting is its simplicity. Anyone can use this tool to bring about an immediate improvement in health and to ensure their long-term health.

Periodic mono-dieting involves eating fresh, ripe fruits, and/or colorful vegetables and their juices, *uncooked*, for a length of time that can range from one day to several weeks.

Mono-diets take a number of forms. Here are three:

1. Drinking only fresh fruit and vegetable juice for 1 to 3 days.
2. Drinking only fresh fruit and vegetable juices and eating whole ripe fruits and colorful vegetables for 3 to 5 days.
3. Drinking only ripe fruit and vegetable juices and eating only fresh fruits and vegetables and salads for one day, to 7 to 10 days.

The first purpose of mono-dieting is to use as little energy as possible on digestion so energy can be freed up and directed toward the cleansing and rejuvenation of the lymphatic system, the human body's garbage collector, and the mechanism central in keeping you well. The second purpose of mono-dieting is to obtain the maximum amount of fuel and nutrients from the food being eaten.

Raw food fulfills these purposes better than cooked or processed food. Raw food requires less energy to digest and provides the most nutrients because it is in its purest state, its natural state. Cooking removes or denatures some nutrients. Human beings are the only species that eats cooked food, and humans lead all species in degenerative diseases. Obviously our superior thinking and reasoning abilities have not served us in this area.

Periodic mono-dieting should not be used as a diet in a crisis to empty out a swollen lymph gland or to deal with an existing cancer, although in both instances the approach can be beneficial. To gain the greatest benefit from periodic mono-dieting, make it a regular part of your lifestyle; use it as a means of long-term prevention and long-term wellness.

The extent to which you use mono-dieting is up to you; there is an unlimited number of ways to use periodic mono-dieting, and there are no specifically prescribed regimens. Some people have an all-juice or all-fruit day once a week. Some eat only raw food one day a week. Some have three straight raw days every month. Author and lecturer Dr. Gabriel Cousens suggests that every six months you drink only fresh juices for a week.

The object of mono-dieting is, of course, to do it! If you must discipline yourself by marking on your calendar exactly when you are going to mono-diet for a day or three days or five days or a week, then do it. Or if you wake up one morning and feel like having only juice that day, then that's your day. Mono-dieting is a flexible tool; it's regimented only if you function better that way.

If I seem to be harping on this one aspect it's because whenever food is discussed, people tend to look for restrictive rules they must follow as punishment for past dietary indiscretions. Cultivate a different viewpoint. See periodic mono-dieting as a dynamic part of your lifestyle that will inhibit early aging, cancer, and other degenerative illnesses.

With mono-dieting, the eating experience also becomes much more liberating. One of the most rewarding results of mono-dieting is the surge of energy and well-being it produces. Once you incorporate mono-dieting into your lifestyle, you never abandon it, even if you mono-diet only three days a year. You never get it out of your mind, once you see the tremendously positive impact it has on your life. You will look forward to mono-dieting with great anticipation. Indeed, periodic mono-dieting is not a punishment, it is a joy.

When I embarked on my journey down the path to optimum health, mono-dieting proved to be invaluable. It gave me my first glimpse of how good I could feel. After starting with short mono-diets of one, two, and three days—as my health steadily improved—I began increasing their duration until I was going ten days or two weeks, two or three times a year. My health problems dramatically improved, and I am convinced that periodic mono-dieting was the major reason. It remains my most important tool for health maintenance.

Energy

Let's face it, energy is everything. Without it, nothing is possible and nothing happens. A car without fuel goes nowhere; neither does a body without energy.

There is no way to discuss energy and energy levels without discussing digestion. When you consider the full extent of the digestive activities involved in taking in food, processing it, and extracting nutrients and delivering them to the cells, the elimination of wastes and all the interactions of the organs, stomach, intestines, pancreas, liver, and kidneys, and the metabolic processes that turn food into blood, muscle, and bone, it is no wonder that the digestive process takes such an enormous amount of energy.

There is precious little you can do that requires more energy than the digestion and assimilation of the approximately 70 tons of food the average

North American consumes in a lifetime. You likely have evidence of this. After eating a big meal of many kinds of foods, which do you look for, a mountain to climb or a sofa to climb into? Knowing the importance of energy to the cleansing process, what better place to free up some than from the vast amount required for digestion.

There are two ways to free up energy from the digestive process for use in other areas of activity. The first is to streamline digestion, have it work more efficiently. In some of my previous books I introduced the concept of food combining for just that purpose. The second way, the way that has the potential to free up huge amounts of energy, is to give the digestive tract less to do. With less work to do, energy that is routinely spent on digestion is automatically diverted to the lymphatic system and used by the body to cleanse itself of waste. The body always works on priorities, and removing impactions and silted-up waste that is interfering with the smooth operation of the system is at the top of the list. Lymph nodes in the breast, neck, underarm, or anywhere else in the body will not become swollen with waste if wastes in the body are kept to a minimum.

Thus, since it gives the digestive tract less to do, periodic mono-dieting is the most compelling and potent tool you can apply for optimum health. I know what a provocative statement that is. Indeed, many would immediately demand proof. Therefore, although the greatest proof is in the doing, let me offer a couple of exhibits, one scientific, the other observational.

Roy Walford is a medical doctor. He has been a UCLA professor since 1966 and is one of the world's eminent gerontologists. The director of a 16-member research laboratory at UCLA for the study of immunology and the aging process, he was also a member of the White House Conference on Aging, and the National Academy of Sciences Committee on Aging, as well as chairman of the National Institute on Aging Task Force in Immunology. He has written five books on immunology and aging and is a world-renowned expert in his field.

Dr. Walford has conducted numerous long-term experiments on aging. Based on the results of those experiments, he is convinced that he will live healthfully to age 120—in his opinion the life span within the reach of us all. His experiments have not focused on periodic mono-dieting. That is a term I have coined. But his experiments have studied the effect of less work for the digestive tract, over a long term, on health and longevity. His findings fully substantiate my premise that the less work the digestive tract has to do, the healthier you will be and the longer you will live.

Dr. Walford puts his experimental mice on what he refers to as "the restricted diet," which means they fast two days a week. Whereas most mice live about two years, Dr. Walford's mice live more than twice that long. They not only live much longer, they also show significantly lower rates of heart disease and cancer. Moreover, the small number of mice that do develop these diseases do so at a much later age than mice who are allowed to eat without restrictions. His experiments have consistently shown this improvement in health and longevity. Dr. Walford is seventy years old and vibrantly fit. He fasts two days a week.

Dr. Walford's experiments support what practitioners of natural hygiene have known for a long while: that during our lifetime, we will each consume approximately 70 tons of food, and the metabolic activities involved in processing that food, using what is needed and ridding itself of the rest, will take more energy from the body over a lifetime than any other activity. Learning to channel some of that energy toward cleansing is a gift of immeasurable value. This is the gift of periodic mono-dieting.

The practice of giving the digestive tract less work to do in order to free up energy for the healing process is common throughout nature. Anyone who has worked a farm or worked with animals has seen it over and over. A horse that is lame will "go off its food." It will hardly eat. Every stock-yard worker knows that when day after day a cow or horse or hog or sheep eats much less food than normal, there is something wrong with the animal. It has instinctively reduced its food intake so its body will have the energy to correct whatever is wrong. Pet owners know that when a dog or cat is sick or injured, the animal either refuses food altogether or hardly eats at all. Even when concerned owners entice their sick pets with the most tempting food, the animals will refuse to eat. They find a secluded spot and rest until the body completes its healing work.

A similar reaction can be seen in sick children who lose their appetite. Parents will frequently try to pressure them into eating by saying things like, "Eat this for Mommy," or, "The doctor says you won't get well if you don't eat." But having not been conditioned to believe that they have to eat when they are sick, they merely follow their instincts and refuse food. You have likely noticed a loss of appetite when you don't feel well. That loss of appetite is a natural tendency of the body to free up energy that is needed for other work. And although mono-dieting is a smart thing to do to speed recovery when you're not feeling well, the most intelligent use of periodic mono-dieting—indeed, its prime use and benefit—is as a normal and natural part of your lifestyle, as a means of preventing illness in the first place. It is an approach that helps you shift the focus from illness to wellness!

I do not recommend that mono-dieting be used as an emergency measure (the same way you would use a drug) once the effect of continued neglect has finally caught up to you. It should become a regular part of your healthy lifestyle, the same as anything else that you do on a regular basis. Would you ever seriously consider not dusting and cleaning your house periodically? Would you ever dream of not periodically changing the oil in your car? Then you mustn't consider not periodically mono-dieting to cleanse your inner body, because a clean inner body is easily as important—in fact infinitely more important—than a clean house or car. Why? Because a clean inner body is what ensures your success in maintaining abundant and robust good health.

Choosing a Mono-Diet

The type, length, and frequency of your mono-diet will vary according to your personal needs and wants. As you can see from the three options listed above, some mono-diets comprise only juices, some comprise juices, raw vegetables, and salads. Some will last one day, some will last a week or ten days. You may do one every week, every month, or every three months. Remember: There is no right or wrong involved in mono-dieting. This point cannot be made too frequently.

How can you find the mono-dieting option that is best for you? The only way to make an intelligent, informed decision is to experience the benefits. Only then can you decide how and when to mono-diet on a regular basis. While any amount of mono-dieting is beneficial, only on mono-diets of three days and more do you really start to see the power behind this practice. But even a one-day mono-diet will get you started.

The following three mono-diets—one day on juice; three days on juice, whole fruit, and smoothies; one week on only uncooked food—are examples only, not dictums. Follow them precisely or modify them to your likes and dislikes.

One Day on Juice

For one day, intermittently throughout the day, take in only juice, either fruit or vegetable or both. I have found that fruit juices work best for the first part of the day, with vegetable juice in the second part, and more fruit juice in the evening. But any way you want to do it is fine. You can have only fruit juice, only vegetable juice, or have fruit, then vegetable, up and back throughout the day and evening. As long as it's only juice you're taking in, it doesn't matter which you have or when. Also, when having only juice, it's best to consume approximately 10 to 14 ounces about every two hours. Again, this is only a guideline; feel free to alter it to fit your particular needs and desires. You may have a green drink once or twice a day in your juice.

It is important that you consume only fresh juice for 24 hours. Many books on juicing will give you an amazingly wide array of different juice mixes, both fruit and vegetable. Experiment. These drinks are fun and they're delicious. One of my favorites is apple-celery juice. "Ugh, apple-celery!" Right? Well, if you've never had it, you're in for a big surprise. Apple-celery juice is one of the most refreshing, delicious combinations I've ever had. There's something about that mixture that works. Just try it. You'll be hooked like so many other people I have turned on to it.

If you have read my book *Fit for Life*, you might be saying, "Hold on there, I thought it was a huge no-no to mix fruit with any other food." That is true, but as with everything in life, there are exceptions to the rule. Since it is very high in water content and has no complex starches, proteins, or fats, celery causes no problem when eaten with fruit. But, remember, celery juice is very potent; when mixing it with apple juice, make the mixture approximately three-quarters apple juice, one-quarter celery juice.

Three Days, Juice, Whole Fruit, and "Smoothies"

On this mono-diet, in addition to fresh juices, fruit and/or vegetables throughout the day, you also eat pieces of fresh fruit and fruit smoothies. Any fruit is okay as long as it is fresh. Smoothies are extremely easy to make. Put either apple or orange juice (fresh, of course) in a blender, add a frozen banana, and any other fruit you like, and presto, a fabulous smoothie. You can add frozen blueberries, strawberries, peaches, or other fruits to the juice and frozen banana. Have fun with these. There are an infinite variety, and they taste incredible. To freeze bananas, peel them and put them in the freezer in an airtight plastic container. Once again, you may use a green drink daily.

A Week on Only Uncooked Food

For a week, eat nothing but raw, uncooked food—all fruits and vegetables, their juices and salads. Have as much juice and as many whole fruits and vegetables as you like. In the evening, eat a large mixed salad, with a salad dressing of olive oil (which has been associated with a significant reduced risk of breast cancer), lemon juice, and your favorite herbs and spices. You can have other types of dressing, preferably with a minimum of chemical additives. After you consume the salad, refrain from eating fruit or fruit juice for three hours.

Remember, the above three mono-diets are examples only. You could do any of them for any length of time. Number one could be done for several days or a week, as could number two. Or number three could be done for one day or three. Or you could do number one for a day, number two for a day, and number three for a day. Anything goes when mono-dieting in terms of duration as long as the fruits and vegetables eaten are uncooked.

Tips and Tidbits for Periodic Mono-Dieting

For the most effective results, the juices you drink must be fresh, not pasteurized, canned, or made from concentrate. Drinking other than fresh, unheated juice almost entirely defeats the purpose of mono-dieting. Home juicers are readily available and inexpensive. When measured against the benefits you will reap, the cost of a home juicer is insignificant. You probably have at least one television set in your house. Well, a juicer is a whole lot less expensive and has the added enticement of making you healthy. Will your television do that for you? If you don't own a juicer, buy fresh-squeezed juice. That will do fine.

When drinking juice, it is best not to gulp it. Sip it instead. Drink it slowly so that all of it does not wind up in your stomach at once, which is hard on the body and can cause stomachaches. Swallow one mouthful at a time after the juice has had a chance to mix with your saliva.

Unlike other foods, fruit does not require a lot of time in the stomach for digestion. Most foods stay in the stomach about three hours. Fruit leaves the stomach in about 20 minutes to half an hour. Fruit juice leaves the stomach in less time than that. So, whether you are mono-dieting or not, you should not have fruit or fruit juice for about three hours after eating anything else.

If you have never eaten highly cleansing food exclusively for a few days, you may experience a side effect that is uncomfortable but quite valuable: diarrhea. A certain amount of waste accumulates in the digestive tract over time. When nothing but juice and fruit, which contain over 90 percent water, suddenly goes through your system for a few days, it is as though the digestive tract is being flushed and scrubbed. Diarrhea will rarely last more than 48 hours, and usually will last only 24 hours. After you consume only high-water, cleansing foods, a bout of diarrhea is not at all surprising. Of course, if you experience diarrhea for longer than 48 hours, for any reason, check with a health-care practitioner immediately. But to experience it because you're eating cleansing food is not something to be alarmed about.

Because their food intake is so restricted while mono-dieting, some people think that they might not have enough energy to work or do other things they need to do. Interestingly, the opposite is true. Your energy level will soar when you mono-diet. Remember that digestion requires huge amounts of energy. Since you are eating only uncooked food, you are eating the foods that require the least amount of energy to digest but that supply a great deal of energy. The one thing more people comment on when they mono-diet is their enormous increase in energy.

People who are prone to hypoglycemia (low blood sugar) get a little nervous when you talk about eating only fruit or eating very lightly. First, let's examine what low blood sugar is. The brain constantly monitors the bloodstream to make sure there is sufficient sugar and nutrients in the blood. If there is an insufficient supply, the brain sets off an alarm in the form of edginess, discomfort, and sluggishness. Fruit, whose sugar component of fructose turns to glucose, goes into the bloodstream faster than anything else. So if you have low blood sugar and you eat fruit, it will stop the symptoms of hypoglycemia very quickly. There's nothing better for low blood sugar than fruit. But people with hypoglycemia have to eat quite frequently to stem the symptoms. No problem. When mono-dieting, if you have hypoglycemic tendencies, eat as frequently as you feel you need to.

If you mono-diet for a week or longer on all uncooked foods—salads, in addition to juices, fruit, smoothies, and vegetables—you might crave something cooked but still want to continue your mono-diet. There is a way to do that that allows you to continue to cleanse but also to eat a little heavier. Add steamed vegetables to your salad. Choose whatever vegetables you like: broccoli, cauliflower, zucchini. Always try to use a wide variety of colorful vegetables. Steam one, two, or three, put them in your salad, add dressing and you will have an incredibly tasty and satisfying meal.

I suggest, however, that you don't add steamed vegetables on short mono-diets of only three or four days. But if you're going for a week, ten days, or two weeks, add steamed veggies for the last part of the mono-diet.

In other words, on a one-week mono-diet, add steamed vegetables the last two days. On a ten-day mono-diet, add them the last three or four days. Also, make sure there is more salad than steamed vegetables, not the other way around. Remember, it is the regular eating of uncooked food that is the goal.

A beautiful side effect of periodic mono-dieting is that your overall diet tends to improve. After eating clean, healthy food for a while, you're not so anxious to put just any ol' thing in your body. Sometimes the change is obvious, sometimes it's subtle, but as time goes by and you feel free of pain, you've lost weight, and you're feeling very good about yourself, you'll to want to keep it that way. You'll find yourself making healthier menu choices in restaurants and eating those death-burgers less frequently at the thousands of fast-food places that contribute so greatly to the level of ill health suffered by so many.

Be particularly careful what you eat the first one or two days after a mono-diet of five days or more. Eating a lot of very heavy foods too quickly can make you feel horrible. Your body becomes accustomed to a diet of light, clean, uncooked food and you can catch it off guard by eating too heavily too quickly. Let's say you do a one week mono-diet of juices, fruit, and salads. If on the eighth day you consume a big lunch of pizza or fried chicken or a burger and fries, and a dinner of steak and potatoes, bread, and apple pie, you're going to feel miserable the next day. It would be better to eat very lightly in the morning, only fruit and/or juice. Have a salad for lunch with a baked potato or a piece of toast if you need more than a salad for dinner. This way you gradually reintroduce the cooked food without jumping straight into consuming the heaviest foods possible. Wait until the second or third day after a mono-diet before having meat, chicken, or fish, and eat them sparingly.

You are sure to ask, "How often should I mono-diet and for what duration?" Generally speaking, if you have never mono-dieted or fasted, or taken any other measures to cleanse or detoxify your system, and you are fairly certain your inner body could use a good cleansing, the more frequent and the longer, the better. In other words, at first, diligently mono-diet at regular intervals, more frequently than later, when you know your body is pretty clean. Later, your mono-diets will be more for maintenance, especially if you upgrade your diet so as to minimize foods that would encumber your lymphatic system. Use a high-quality green drink daily when you mono-diet.

My Experience

When I was introduced to natural hygiene and mono-dieting, I was highly motivated. I was sick, fat, tired, in pain, and living in fear because of the death of my father from cancer. The person who taught me the fundamentals of mono-dieting assured me that a series of mono-diets and simultaneous improvement in my dietary habits would quickly bring me to a level of health I had not enjoyed for a very long time.

He sounded totally sure of himself and I sorely wanted to believe. But for as long as I had been dealing with excruciating stomachaches, for as many weight-loss diets as I had been on, for as frustrated as I was over my continually declining health, I have to admit that I was more than a little skeptical that it would all be wiped away by what seemed to be hardly any effort. But there was something else. I was willing!

My mentor told me that the first thing I needed to do, since I was eating anything I desired at any time, was to have only fruit and vegetable juices and fresh fruit for five days. At that particular stage of my life, the idea of eating only fruit and juices for five days was like suggesting that I wet my finger and stick it in a light socket. But I did it because I desperately needed something to turn things around for me. The first day was the hardest. The first day is *always* the hardest. But on the sixth day, when I was supposed to start eating other foods, the most amazing, most unexpected thing happened; I felt so darned good, so energetic, so positive, so light and clean, I decided to go for another five days! Me! The guy that would rather fall down a flight of concrete stairs than miss a meal.

I was riding my bicycle every day and reading books by Herbert M. Shelton, the acknowledged father of natural hygiene. At the end of ten days, my life was forever changed. I simply could not believe how good I felt. My stomach, which had hurt every day for more than 20 years, did not bother me at all. I had lost about twelve pounds. My energy level was through the roof, and I felt as if I owned the world.

My mentor, who had a rather quirky sense of humor, said to me, in a totally professional, serious tone, "Well, you have a decision to make now. You can either alter your dietetic lifestyle a bit and continue to cleanse your system, lose more weight, and feel euphoric, or you can go back to the way you were eating before your ten days and have your health go back to what it was. What's it going to be?" I didn't say anything. I just looked at him in a way that left no doubt what my decision was.

He told me that for the best and quickest results I should cut out all meat, at least at first. Then after I felt really good, I could reintroduce meat into my diet, but not the way I was eating it before, which was not only every day, but every *meal*!

Astonishingly, I lost 50 pounds in one month. Not only was my body ready to heal itself, I also helped it along by improving my diet, continuing to ride my bike every day, and flooding my consciousness with positive thoughts about how well I was doing and how successful I was going to be.

I made a commitment to do a ten-day mono-diet at least four times a year, one every three months. For the next two years, I did exactly that; every three months I did either ten days on juices and fruit or ten days on juices, fruit, and salads. In between, I ate very few animal products, exercised regularly, and did shorter mono-diets of one or two days in a row every week. After the first two years, with my weight loss maintained, no pain, and an exuberance for life that I thought I'd never achieve, I knew I had found a lifestyle that would serve me forever. Now I do ten-day mono-diets two or sometimes three times a year, and I mono-diet every other day.

I tried different kinds of mono-dieting routines. Once I ate only uncooked foods (fruit, vegetables, juice, and salads) every other day for three months. In between, I ate what I wanted. It was great! I felt absolutely incredible. When I was preparing for my first television tour to promote *Fit for Life*, I ate only fruit and juices for two weeks and only uncooked food for a month. Touring is unbelievably grueling, but I sailed through three weeks of nonstop work with interviews from morning until night and a plane ride every day, with an abundance of energy and positive feelings.

Where to Begin

Start with a three- or five-day mono-diet of fruit and vegetable juices and whole fruit just to see what it feels like. Mono-diet one or two days a week with longer ones (a week or ten days) every two to three months, depending on how much you feel you need to cleanse your body and how motivated you are to get your lymphatic system cleaned out so that no lymph nodes fill with detritus. As I have said above, the duration and frequency of your mono-diet is up to you.

Some people prefer to follow a more definitive program—something that removes the guesswork. Once again a quick analogy: If you were in a canoe or a rowboat that had a lot of water in it because of a leak, you would have to bail aggressively to lower the water level and prevent cap-sizing. Once you reduced the level of water, you could relax and bail only periodically to keep the level low. So it is with your body. To start, you should mono-diet more frequently and for longer durations to lower the level of toxins in your body. Then you can mono-diet more infrequently as a means to keep the level of toxins low.

For the first year, mono-diet for at least ten days every three months. That's four ten-day mono-diets for the year. Two should be only juices (both fruit and vegetable) and fruit, and two should comprise all raw foods (fruits, vegetables, their juices, and salads). In between the ten-day mono-diets, mono-diet at least two days a week, either two days in a row or twice within the week. It would, of course, be ideal to continue the same pattern every year for the rest of your life, to be absolutely certain that your body's toxic level never gets out of control and your lymph nodes never become swollen, but as a maintenance program you can cut it in half. That would be two ten-day mono-diets a year and at least one day a week.

Understand this: You cannot mono-diet too much! The more you do it, the healthier you'll be and the likelihood of your developing cancer will diminish. You can, however, mono-diet too little. Therefore, you have to find out what your personal comfort level is and determine how motivat-ed you are.

When you are mono-dieting, you are allowing your body to be cleansed. You are cleaning and rejuvenating your lymphatic system. Do not make the mistake of taking periodic mono-dieting lightly or minimiz-ing the extent to which it can achieve that much-desired goal of helping you live your life without the fear of becoming a cancer statistic. Considering the havoc that cancer has caused in so many people's lives and its apparent complicated and puzzling characteristics, I can under-stand an initial reaction being something like, "Yeah, right. Eating nothing but fruit and vegetables every so often is going to prevent something as pervasive and bewildering as cancer." Is there a problem with the solution being more simple and straightforward than you have been led to believe? If it was more complicated, expensive, and difficult to do, would you have more confidence in it?

If you have not experienced periodic mono-dieting, try it just to see what, if anything, you've missed. Having done so, you will certainly know your body better. If you own a fax machine or computer, you have probably marveled at the way such machines have revolutionized our lives. Imagine how you would feel if suddenly you had to give them up. It would be one thing if you had never experienced the benefits and were not aware of the ways in which they could dramatically improve your life, but to have them and use them and then lose them would likely be unbearable. And that is exactly what periodic mono-dieting is like. If you don't know what you're missing, then you don't know, and that's it. However, once you discover firsthand how periodic mono-dieting can transform your health and, therefore, your life, you will never want to give it up. You mustn't allow the fact that mono-dieting is simple, inexpensive, and totally in your control to discourage you from trying it. Mono-dieting is a gift, a blessing, and once experienced, you'll thank the day it became a part of your life. Let periodic mono-dieting be the "healing balm" that will encourage you to rejuvenate and maintain superior health and well-being.

6 POINT SUMMARY

- Periodic mono-dieting is a powerful way to cleanse and strengthen your cells, lymphatic system, and digestive tract.
- Periodic mono-dieting involves eating fresh, ripe fruits and/or colorful vegetables and their juices, uncooked, for a length of time that can range from one day to several weeks.
- Periodic mono-dieting can transform your health.
- Periodic mono-dieting will give you enormous energy.
- There is no "right" or "wrong" way to periodic mono-dieting.
- I have lost, and kept off, 50 pounds by mono-dieting. I now do a ten-day mono-diet two or three times a year, once every three months.

3 POINT ACTION PLAN

- For superior good health, find a way to incorporate periodic mono-dieting into your lifestyle, whether it is your one-day-a-week "detox day," or a longer period.
- Daily incorporate part of the mono-diet by drinking a glass of fresh vegetable juice in between meals. Try mixing a green drink in the juice.
- Have a large colorful, organic salad with fresh herbs at one meal a day.

Fuel, For Peak Performance

You can immediately change the course of your life
by making better choices.

*We stumble over the truth from time to time—but most of us pick ourselves up
and hurry off as if nothing happened.*
Winston Churchill

Life is such a very, very precious gift.
Dr. Albert Schweitzer, M.D.

Part 1: How Much Protein, Fiber, Fat, and Carbohydrates Do You Need Daily?

Given the faster-is-better lifestyle that most of us lead whether we want to or not, fueling our bodies for peak performance and optimum health is even more challenging. To keep pace and to improve our performance and stamina, we need to pay careful attention to what we eat and the amount we eat. It is also imperative that every day we maintain the right balance of proteins, fiber, fats, and carbohydrates.

Now that you have the facts about the power of Superfoods, you are ready to personalize a Superfood dietary strategy to suit your exact daily requirements. Let's examine these dietary building blocks and determine your optimal daily requirements for each.

Superfood Protein for Peak Performance

High-quality, low-fat protein is a Superfood. Your body needs this nutrient on a daily basis. One-fifth of a person's total body weight is protein. Protein is second only to water as the most plentiful substance in the body. Skin, hair, nails, eyes, muscles, hormones, enzymes, and nerve-transmission chemicals are mostly protein. Enzymes are made of proteins. Every body function is controlled by one or more of the body's 2,700 recognized enzymes. The blood's hemoglobin, which carries oxygen to cells, is a protein. The structure of genes and brain cells is protein. Antibodies that protect the body from disease and infection are proteins. Without protein, cells could not produce or store energy. The human body requires the nitrogen in proteins to build and repair body tissues like muscle—fats, fiber, water, and carbohydrates cannot do this job.

Protein derived from food is needed to replace the protein and amino acids that are constantly being broken down and lost in the daily wear and tear of living. The protein from food does not supply the body directly with protein; rather, it supplies the amino acids from which the body can build its own protein. The body makes protein from 22 recognizable amino acids. It can synthesize most amino acids, but eight must be obtained from foods: these amino acids are isoleucrine, leucine, lysine, methionine, phenylalanine, threonine, tryptophan, and valine. In addition, some people cannot manufacture the amino acid histidine.

To make protein, your body requires that all eight essential amino acids be available simultaneously. Proteins that supply them are termed complete protein and they contain all the essential amino acids in amounts and proportions adequate for human development. The Net Protein Utilization Index (NPUI) is a measure of a food's ability to deliver all the amino acids needed by the body. The ratings listed by the highest to lowest NPU Index are:

1. hydrolyzed, lactose-free whey protein, egg white protein powder (egg albumin), and low-fat soy protein isolate powders;
2. fish, free-range eggs, skinless poultry, lean meats and wild game;
3. low-fat, non-fat dairy products;
4. seeds, nuts, legumes (beans), sea vegetables (chlorella and Hawaiian spirulina), bee pollen, whole grains, and nutritional yeast.

Protein must be accompanied by both naturally occurring fiber and "healthy" fats. (Healthy fats are found in organic olive oil, organic flaxseed oil, hemp seed oil, or northern, cold-water fish such as salmon, bluefish, herring, mackerel, and sardines.) Protein helps slow the rate of entry of carbohydrates into the bloodstream, thereby maintaining a steady amount of insulin secreted by the pancreas and assuring a steady energy source.

BEAN ME UP

Until recently, most nutritionists believed that plant-based proteins had to be combined at each meal ("complementary protein") to assure an adequate supply to the body of all eight essential amino acids. Numerous studies now demonstrate that the body's protein pool can combine various plant proteins, eaten throughout the day, to achieve its full amino acid quota. So you can eat bulgur at breakfast (low in methionine) and garbanzo beans (high in methionine) in a colorful salad at lunch. A vegetarian diet provides plenty of protein if it is drawn from a wide variety of sources.

How Much Protein Do You Need Daily?

When you eat more protein in your diet than your body needs for repair and rebuilding, the extra is converted to fat and stored in adipose tissue (brown fat that, once stored in the body, is difficult to lose) rather than muscle. You can't store protein for later use, as you can carbohydrates and fats. Excessive protein generally draws calcium from bones. Calcium is an alkalizing mineral that buffers the corrosive acids of excessive protein; when protein intake increases from 42 to 142 grams daily, the excretion of calcium in the urine doubles. Excessive protein also dehydrates the body, since an enormous amount of water is required to help excrete protein wastes in urine. On the other hand, if you do not get enough protein, you will feel tired and weak, and be susceptible to colds, flus, and infections. Athletes crash and burn without enough protein.

Most North American adults do not need to increase their protein intake. The average adult eats from 80 to 120 grams a day, more than twice the U.S. RDA (Recommended Daily Allowance) of 0.75 grams of protein per kilogram of body weight. At the other extreme some people are carbohydrate-overdoer types who might be omitting enough protein from their diet.

Calculating Protein Needs

Exercise physiologists and nutritionists generally suggest you calculate your protein needs based on your weight and level of activity. Use the following classifications to determine how much protein you need daily. (Note: Exercise causes the body to use protein at a much faster rate and more protein is needed to maintain a positive nitrogen balance.):

Sedentary adult	0.4 of a gram per pound of body weight
Active adult	0.6 of a gram per pound of body weight (exercising at least three times a week)
Endurance athlete	0.75 of a gram per pound of body weight (long-distance runner)

| Strength athlete | 0.8 of a gram per pound of body weight (avid weight-resistance trainer) |
| Elite athlete | 1.0 gram per pound of body weight |

To calculate your daily protein requirements, multiply your weight by one of the above five classifications. For example, a 130-pound active adult would require 130 x 0.6 = 78 grams daily; a 150-pound endurance athlete would require 150 x 0.75 = 112.5 grams daily.

Most adults require between 45 to 90 grams of protein daily, depending on body weight. Use the same method as when you "visually measured" the amounts of alkalizing foods and acidifying foods (see Chapter 5). Imagine the protein portion on your palm. Never eat more than one palm-size piece of protein from meat, or one cup of beans or dairy at a meal. The palm-size piece of protein (firm or extra-firm tofu, turkey, white-meat poultry, fish, or meat) should be no larger than a deck of cards. Spread your protein intake over three meals and one of your two daily snacks. It is not necessary or advisable to try to meet all your protein needs at one sitting. Protein works as a stabilizer to offset a rise in blood sugar from carbohydrates; this stabilizing effect helps to moderate appetite, especially if the meal contained 5 to 10 grams of fiber.

PROTEIN FINDER

	Amount	Grams of Protein
Beans		
garbanzo beans	1 cup	15
lentils	1 cup	18
pinto beans	1 cup	14
soybeans	1 cup	28
tempeh	1 cup	32
tofu (firm or extra-firm)	1 cup	26
textured vegetable protein (TVP)	1 cup	20
Dairy		
cottage cheese, no fat	1 cup	28
milk, skim	1 cup	8
swiss cheese	1 oz.	7
yogurt, plain, non-fat	1 cup	13
Non-Dairy Beverages		
oat milk	1 cup	4
rice milk	1 cup	2.1
soy milk	1 cup	6.6

PROTEIN FINDER

	Amount	Grams of Protein
Eggs (free-range)		
large with yolk	1	6
egg whites only	2	9
Grains		
alfalfa, barley, or wheat grass	1 cup	8
bread, whole-grain	2 slices	6
millet	1 cup	8.4
oatmeal	1 cup	8
pasta, whole grain	1 cup	6
rice, brown	1 cup	3
Fish		
albacore tuna, water-packed	3 oz.	25
halibut, broiled	3 oz.	23
salmon, broiled	3 oz.	20
snapper, broiled	3 oz.	23
sole, broiled	3 oz.	15
trout, broiled	3 oz.	24
Fruit		
berries	1 cup	2
small avocado	1	4
small banana	1	1.2
cherries	1 cup	1.7
Meat		
ground beef, regular store-bought	3 oz.	17
beef steak	3 oz.	25
pork loin roast	3 oz.	23
bacon	3 oz.	5
(above meats are poor choices—all high-fat)		
chicken breast, skinless, broiled	3 oz.	26
rabbit	3 oz.	23
turkey breast, skinless, broiled	3 oz.	22
freshly ground lean beef	3 oz.	22
flank steak	3 oz.	27
wild game	3 oz.	28
Nuts and Seeds		
almonds	3 oz.	12
peanut butter	2 Tbs.	7.7
pumpkin seeds (or pumpkin butter)	3 oz.	21
sesame seeds	3 oz.	14.5
sunflower seeds	3 oz.	18.5
cashews	3 oz.	8
macadamia nuts	3 oz.	10

PROTEIN FINDER

	Amount	Grams of Protein
Yeast		
nutritional yeast	3 oz.	33
Protein Powders		
egg white (albumin)	3 oz.	33
soy protein isolates	3 oz.	32
lactose-free whey protein	3 oz.	35
Sea Vegetables		
chlorella	3 oz.	12
spirulina	3 oz.	13
Vegetables		
sweet potato, baked	1 medium	2
raw sprouts	1 cup	9
almost all vegetables	1 cup	4.4

Source: Adapted from J.A.T. Pennington, Bowes and Church, "Food Values of Portions Commonly Used," 15th ed. (Philadelphia: J. B. Lippincott, 1989).

Superfood Protein Notes

- Always choose lean cuts of meat and remove all visible fat before cooking.
- Broil chicken or turkey with the skin removed.
- Avoid high-fat meats. To get the lowest fat content in meats, consider both the cut and grade of the meat. The marbling (fat content) of the meat determines its meat grade and tenderness. Prime grade has the most fat, Choice grade somewhat less fat, and Select grade the least amount of fat. Choose your cuts from the parts of the animal that get the most exercise, which are the round (upper back leg), shank (lower leg), flank (belly), and chuck (neck and shoulder). These leaner regions generally contain one-half the fat of other cuts from the rib, loin, or sirloin.
- Chew meat well so that it is broken down sufficiently, which allows for proper digestion in the stomach.
- Avoid luncheon or processed meats such as bologna, turkey roll, and sausage, which generally comprise 90 percent fat calories. These meat products usually contain high amounts of salt, potentially carcinogenic nitrites, and other toxic additives.
- Your low-fat animal-protein choices should consist of wild game, white-meat poultry and eggs from free-range chickens.

- Whenever possible, buy meats and poultry from animals bred and raised free of antibiotics and growth hormones.
- Always choose low-fat, or better still, fat-free yogurts, cottage cheese, milk, soy milk, rice milk, and protein powders.
- If you are a vegetarian or vegan, pay special attention to your protein needs. Do not rely on tofu as your only protein source. Since firm or extra-firm tofu is fermented longer than regular tofu, most of the carbohydrates are removed in the longer fermentation process. I highly recommend this type of tofu, as it has less fat and is more protein-rich. Vary your protein sources. Do not rely too heavily on seeds and nuts that are also high in fat. Chew seeds and nuts well. Although incomplete in their protein profiles, used in moderation, nuts and seeds are a great addition in a vegetarian diet. Consider using a low-fat soy or whey protein powder in a "protein shake" two or three times a week, or add it to your oatmeal to balance the protein, carbohydrate, and fiber ratio.
- Many companies advertise that if you use their protein powder you will gain two or three pounds of muscle a week. This is a myth. Muscles grow only in response to the "trauma" of intense exercise. Muscles that are "traumatized" by weight-resistance training create a demand for more amino acids to repair and build. The protein powders do nothing to stimulate more muscle growth; they only supply the amino acids (building blocks), just as beans, poultry, dairy, meat, fish, nutritional yeast, grains, beans, seeds and nuts do.
- Avoid protein sources that contain oxidized cholesterol. Oxidized cholesterol is found in powdered eggs, powdered milk, mass-produced baked goods, and baking mixes.
- If you experience rheumatoid arthritis, for six full months try a vegan diet, consisting of no flesh, no eggs, and no dairy. A prostaglandin called PG-2 is formed by consuming animal protein and fat. It is an intracellular hormone that promotes inflammatory diseases. PG-2 is most abundant in the arachidonic acids found in saturated animal fat, peanuts, and egg yolks. If you have arthritis, it would be wise to avoid these protein sources.
- Free-range eggs are fine in moderation, unless you fry them. When yolks are exposed and eggs are scrambled or fried, the cholesterol is oxidized or partially oxidized to a number of toxic by-products. This is also true for frying meats, poultry, or fish. The safest way to maintain an egg's unoxidized integrity is to soft-boil, hard-boil, or poach it with the yolk intact and not exposed to air.

Superfood Fiber for Peak Performance

Fiber is a necessary Superfood. Fiber, as described in Chapter 3, is the part of plant foods that you cannot digest. Research on people that consume a high-fiber diet indicates that they rarely experience colon cancer, blood clots, or varicose veins. Plant-based diets of fruits, green drinks, vegetables, nuts and seeds, sprouts and legumes are all naturally high in fibers. Plant fibers detoxify, or clean out, the digestive tract by gently "sweeping" it clean. Fibers in the intestines remove the clogging "bad" LDL cholesterol, elevate "good" HDL cholesterol levels, and soak up excess hormones such as estrogen. This function is especially important to women, as fiber in the intestines encourages the conversion of estrogens to harmless by-products that are easily excreted, balancing hormonal ups and downs.

Fiber and water combine to help keep the body regular, thus preventing conditions like constipation, candida yeast infections, and irritable bowel syndrome. Fiber masterfully stabilizes blood sugar levels by slowly releasing sugars from digesting foods, vital if you want to reduce body fat. It is also efficient at removing many toxins and toxic heavy metals from the body. Fiber holds 30 times its weight in water, acting as a safe, natural appetite suppressant. Fiber also slows the rate of entry of carbohydrates into the bloodstream, thereby reducing insulin response and assuring the body of a steady energy source.

There are seven basic fiber types: bran, cellulose, gum, hemicellulose, lignin, mucilages, and pectin. Each fiber type has a unique function. If you eat from a wide variety of organic produce, whole grains, pumpkin seeds, hemp seeds, flaxseeds, beans, a few whole nuts, and sea vegetables, you will receive each fiber type daily for peak performance. Do not try to "mega-dose" on one type of fiber like oat-bran as you need each of the seven basic fibers for proper bowel cleansing.

Since most convenience foods are refined, the typical North American diet includes only 15 grams of fiber a day. Your goal should be 35 to 40 grams of fiber daily. Once you reach this goal, and drink the correct amount of water (8 to 12, 8-ounce glasses, depending on body size), you should have copious bowel movements (average 3 bowel movements every 24 hours) and your stool will have a proper consistency. Let me caution you, though, the body likes homeostasis—balance. Increase your water consumption *gradually;* also increase your fiber intake gradually to allow your intestines an adjustment period.

To increase your fiber intake, buy organically grown produce which does not need to be peeled. Eating the peel ensures that you get all the unique fibers and colorful phytochemicals from the rind or skin of produce.

Superfoods contain the entire range of necessary fibers to keep you regular and support your goal of achieving optimum health. It is vital that you spread your fiber intake over your three meals and two snacks daily, with roughly 10 grams at each meal and 5 grams at each snack. This will ensure peak performance, allow your body to accelerate healing, and slow down the entry of sugar from carbohydrates.

FIBER FINDER

	Amount	Grams of Fiber
Fruit		
apple	1 medium	4.5
apple pectin	1 cup	12
prunes	3	4.2
peach	1	3
banana	1 medium	4
raspberries	1 cup	3.7
elderberries	1 cup	10
Vegetables		
colorful, mixed salad	3 cups	12
carrots	3 large	9
broccoli	1 cup	4
any steamed vegetables	3 cups	10
Nova Scotia dulse	1 cup	9
Grains, Legumes, Nuts and Seeds		
oat-bran	1 cup	20
kidney beans	1 cup	4
oatmeal	1 cup	8
whole-grain bread	3 slices	9
grapenuts cereal	1 cup	9
lentils	1 cup	18
beans	1 cup	18
pumpkin seeds	1/4 cup	2
black walnuts	1/4 cup	1.8
almonds	1/4 cup	8
pine nuts	1/4 cup	6
baby lima beans	1 cup	6.5
refried beans	1 cup	8

Source: Adapted from G. J. Kirschmann and J. D. Kirschmann, *Nutrition Almanac*, 4th ed. (New York: McGraw-Hill, 1996).

Superfood Fats for Peak Performance

All nutritional experts agree that the human diet must contain a sufficient amount of fat, especially the omega-3 EFAs and omega-6 EFAs found in fresh fatty fish, fish oil capsules, olive oil, and flax oil. Eating too many of the wrong kinds of fats can seriously impair the body's healing ability, clog the arteries, and injure optimum performance.

On average, North Americans consume 40 percent of their daily calories from dietary fat. Government agencies dealing with health suggest that teenagers and adults reduce their total intake of fats to 30 percent of daily calories, with saturated fats less than 10 percent of calories. Health authorities agree that we should lower our fat consumption; what they disagree on is how low we should go. Some maintain no more than 10 percent of our daily calories from fat, others say 20 percent, and still others recommend 30 percent. My recommendation is to stay in the 20 to 25 percent range. Reducing the quantity of fat in your diet is not as critical as eliminating the wrong kinds of fats from your diet, and including the right kinds. However, it isn't easy to figure out which fats are good and which aren't. Consider the following:

- Some fats make you fat; other fats actually burn fat in your body.
- Some fats make "good" eicosanoids (powerful hormones); other fats make "bad" eicosanoids.
- Some fats slow you down; other fats give you energy.
- Some fats clog your arteries; other fats clean them out.
- Some fats slow the rate of carbohydrate entry into the bloodstream, preventing the overproduction of insulin; some fats accelerate the body's insulin response.

The Composition of Fats

Fats are digested more slowly than proteins or carbohydrates and are the last thing to leave the stomach; that's why they make you feel full. As for the enjoyment factor, many of the flavors in foods are actually dissolved in the fats. Fats also give food the substance nutritionists call "mouth feel" or creaminess.

Fats are a mixture of fatty acids consisting of fat and acid. They are made up of a lengthy chain of carbon atoms with hydrogen atoms attached at one end. Different fatty acids simply have different lengths of chains. Fatty acids can be classified by the lengths of the chains and by whether all the available chemical bonds of the carbon atoms are saturated (occupied) with hydrogen atoms. For example, the fatty acids in butter have short chains of four carbon atoms; the fatty acids in fish oils have long chains of 20 to 24 carbon atoms.

Types of Fats
Saturated Fatty Acids
Saturated fatty acids remain solid at room temperature. The greater the saturated-fat content of a product, the higher the melting temperature. Animal fats are highly saturated, as are two vegetable fats—the oils of palm kernels and coconut, which have all their carbon atoms occupied (saturated) with hydrogen atoms. Saturated fats are associated with raising "bad" LDL cholesterol. Some sources are butter, beef, chicken, and dairy products.

Polyunsaturated Fatty Acids
Polyunsaturated fatty acids remain liquid at room temperature and stay liquid in colder temperatures. The lower the temperature at which solidification occurs, the greater the degree of unsaturation. They have many (poly-) empty spaces where carbon atoms are missing hydrogen atoms. Polyunsaturated fats are associated with a higher incidence of cancer. Some examples of polyunsaturated fats are corn, safflower, sesame, soy, and sunflower oils.

Monounsaturated Fatty Acids
Monounsaturated fatty acids remain liquid at room temperature and get harder with cold temperatures. They fall halfway between saturated and polyunsaturated fatty acids and have one (mono-) empty space where a carbon atom is missing a hydrogen atom. Examples of these fats (oils) are avocado, canola, olive, and peanut oils. These monounsaturated oils are associated with raising "good" HDL cholesterol.

The Big Fat Lie

Saturated fats have no empty spaces (links) and are not biologically active in the human body except that they add calories to be burned as energy. Examples of saturated fats are beef, chicken (unskinned), lamb, pork, turkey, whole milk and its products (cheese, creams, and butter), and processed foods made with palm or coconut oils. Saturated fats are directly linked to atherosclerosis (damaged arterial walls or hardening of the arteries, which impedes circulation), restrictive blood flow, increased "bad" LDL cholesterol, and an impaired cardiovascular system.

Even more dangerous are the unnatural sources of "processed" saturated fats: margarine, solid vegetable shortening, and all mass-produced, processed bakery items or foods made with hydrogenated or partially hydrogenated oils. These foods are extremely hazardous to health as the oil has been artificially saturated with hydrogen to make it solid or semi-solid at room temperature and increase its resistance to spoilage.

You can easily reduce your consumption of saturated fat by cutting out or cutting back on the amount of meat, eggs, whole milk (and its products), artificially solidified oils and palm kernel oil you eat.

Mono- and polyunsaturated fatty acids have empty spaces (links) and are more biologically active in the human body. However, commercially processed monounsaturated and polyunsaturated fats are often rancid as a result of a change called peroxidation that starts as soon as the oil is extracted from its source and exposed to heat, light, atmospheric oxygen, and a trace amount of metallic elements (from machines that are used to process the oils). This process damages the oil's molecular structure. When you eat these oils, they attack your cell membranes and disrupt normal cell metabolism with a vengeance. The worst of these rancid oils is used in commercial salad dressing, where seasonings mask the odor of their rancidity. View prepared salad dressings as unattractive foods. Only oils that are expeller (cold) processed without heat, light, or oxygen are not rancid.

The U.S. Department of Agriculture reports that from 1909 to 1985 the consumption of refined vegetable oils increased a whopping 1,536 percent. The increase in vegetable fat consumption is the most significant change in fat consumption this century. While total fat intake increased 35 percent, vegetable fat consumption rose 270 percent. Contrary to popular opinion, animal fat consumption actually decreased. As processed, hydrogenated, bleached, chemically treated vegetable oil consumption has increased, so has the rise in cancer. During the hydrogenation process, harmful trans-fatty acids are formed. The unnatural shape a trans-fatty acid takes adversely affects cell membranes and other EFAs, and interferes with the production of the necessary prostaglandin hormone PG-1 and PG-3. PG-1 and PG-3 act as anti-inflammatory hormones and are made in the body when alpha-linolenic acid (flax, hemp or pumpkin–seed oils) are converted to EPA (eicosapentaenoic acid). Although refined and partially hydrogenated vegetable oils are unquestionably "bad" fats, the consumption of these oils has skyrocketed. Avoid them, and the salad dressings, commercial baked goods, prepackaged fried foods, and ice creams they are used in. Only use the ultra-healthy oils recommended in this chapter to maintain optimum health, healing, and peak performance.

The Great Debate—Butter versus Margarine

Heating any oil to fry, sauté, or stir-fry foods compounds the problem further. When any oil is heated, the rate of peroxidation increases quickly, doubling with every ten degrees Celsius rise in temperature. Do not fry with oils. (See the recipes in Chapter 18 for examples of preparing foods by sautéeing them in water and adding olive oil once they are cooked crunchy tender.)

You may well ask, "Is it better to substitute margarine for butter?" The answer: Margarine is not acceptable and should never be substituted for butter. Margarine is completely unnatural and is generally treated with petroleum-based solvents. Use unsalted butter in small portions. One step better is to use butter from organically fed cows with no salt or food coloring added to the product. Beta-carotene is sometimes added for color, an added benefit.

Superfood Oils and Fats

If you were to look inside my refrigerator you would find just two small bottles of oils and a little unsalted, organic butter. I use only one monounsaturated oil, olive oil, which makes "good" eicosanoids (powerful hormones) and is the safest oil to eat.

I use and recommend only cold-pressed extra-virgin "green" olive oil. Of all oils, olive oil has a great correlation to good health in the Mediterranean diet. Olive oil contains cis-oleic acid, which lowers "bad" serum cholesterol. Monounsaturated fat has no effect on insulin and it supplies the EFAs necessary to build "good" eicosanoids. Olive oil is hormonally neutral. Buy this oil in smaller opaque glass bottles with tight-closing lids so it remains less exposed to oxygen to preserve its freshness. You may add a capsule of vitamin E and/or a capsule of alpha-lipoic acid (both fat-soluble antioxidants) to the oil once it is open to prevent "auto-oxidation" (once the oil starts to spoil, the free radicals formed add to the rapid spoilage). Keep oil refrigerated once it is opened. It will harden in the refrigerator. This is a sign that it is real olive oil and has not been filled ("cut") with some cheap rancid oil or treated with chemical solvents and bleaches. To make the oil fluid again, hold the bottle under hot water for 30 seconds. Use one tablespoon of olive oil a day per person on your colorful salads, crunchy-tender vegetables, or raw vegetables.

The second bottle of oil in my fridge is organic, expeller-pressed flax oil. Your body can make all the saturated and unsaturated fats it needs by changing the lengths of the carbon atom chains. There are only two fats you cannot make, linoleic (omega-6 EFAs), and alpha-linolenic acid (omega-3 EFAs). These two fats must be provided in your diet for superior health, optimal performance, and healing ability. They are called essential fatty acids (EFAs). They are hard to find in most everyday foods and must be part of your health and healing diet. Flax oil and hemp oil do, however, provide them.

As with olive oil, use only certified, organic, expeller-pressed, unprocessed oils. Again, purchase them in smaller opaque glass bottles, which have been flushed with nitrogen and sealed with an inert gas like nitrogen or argon. Flax oil and hemp oil must be refrigerated and the date of extraction and pressing process must be clearly stated on the label. Use these oils within three months of the pressing date on the label. They are available in health food stores and some specialty markets and grocery stores. Use one or two tablespoons of either the flax or hemp oil daily on your vegetables. I like to include flaxseeds in my oatmeal or other whole-grain cereals. Simply grind one or two tablespoons of these wonderful seeds in a coffee grinder, for ten seconds. Sprinkle them on top of cooked cereal, soups, stews, salads, or vegetables. Keep flaxseeds refrigerated.

To obtain your essential fatty acids, you can also eat the high-fat, northern, cold-water fish that contain omega-3 EFAs (called EPA and DHA) such as bluefish, herring, mackerel, salmon, and sardines, and to a much lesser extent, albacore tuna. If you eat fish, eat two to three servings of these fish a week. Or you can take capsules of fish oils that are highly concentrated sources of EPA and DHA. If you take fish-oil capsules, use fish oil that has been molecularly distilled to remove impurities. Eating the fish suggested above, or taking these oils (or cod liver oil) saves your body the step of converting omega-3 EFAs to EPA. If you eat the suggested fish or their oils (or one teaspoon of cod liver oil a week), you do not need alpha-linolenic acid, which is the flax or hemp seed oil. The EPA (eicosapentaenoic acid) is vital to producing "good" eicosanoids and reducing the production of "bad" eicosanoids as described by Barry Sears in his book *The Zone*.

If you are sick or recovering from an illness, your body may not be able to convert alpha-linolenic acid (omega-3 EFAs) from flax or hemp seed oils to make the very necessary EPA. It is critical you use cod liver oil, broiled fresh fish, or fish-oil capsules during this period to ensure your EPA supply and "good" eicosanoids.

If you do not eat meat, or even if you do but do not eat bluefish, herring, mackerel, salmon, or sardines, or prefer not to use fish-oil capsules high in EPA and DHA, you can obtain alpha-linolenic acid, omega-3 EFAs, from flaxseeds (linseed) or hemp seeds. Alpha-linolenic acid will produce EPA and DHA in your body. Dr. Alexander Leaf, of Harvard University, an expert on EFAs, believes that our hunter-gatherer ancestors consumed a five- or six-to-one ratio of omega-6 EFAs to omega-3 EFAs. Wild game ate lots of green vegetables, especially purslane, rich in omega-3 EFAs. EFAs were abundant in the animals' flesh and body fats. In the technologically advanced feedlots of today, cattle, chickens, pigs, and turkeys are fed an almost exclusive diet of grains. Grains are almost void of omega-3 EFAs. The current ratio in most North Americans' diets is a dangerously imbalanced one of about 24 omega-6 EFAs to 1 omega-3 EFAs.

Superfood Suggestions for Fat

- Always select the leanest cuts of beef, lamb, pork, veal, or wild game. Remove all visible fat before cooking.
- Substitute red meat with fish, and the white meat of chicken or turkey, roasted or broiled, with the skin and subcutaneous fat removed, to limit your saturated fat intake.
- Use dairy products with the lowest fat content. Check that your dairy products contain no bovine growth hormones (rBGH). Dairies do not need to indicate rBGH on their labels. Ask your store to find out if their supply contains rBGH.
- Use herbs, apple cider vinegar, horseradish, sea vegetables, lemon juice, garlic, onions, or veggie purees to replace fatty sauces and gravies. Both dandelion and purslane, which many people consider to be weeds, are rich sources of omega-3 EFAs. Collect them from unsprayed areas and put them in your salad.
- Severely limit your intake of rancid oils or hydrogenated fats found in commercial, mass-produced desserts, cakes, pies, cookies, or muffins. Support your local whole-grain bakery. (Even Salt Spring Island, the little island where I live, has three great sources of whole-grain breads, Barb's Buns, The Crescent Moon Café, and Nature Works.)
- Include salmon, herring, mackerel, sardines, or bluefish in your meal plans at least two times a week, if you eat fish. This will provide your body with about 300 mg of EPA. You may use a fish-oil capsule of EPA-DHA. Both are sources of omega-3 EFAs. You can also use one teaspoon of cod liver oil a week, which supplies about 500 mg of EPA.

- Become acquainted with plant-based sources of omega-3 EFAs—flax oil, pumpkin seed oil and hemp oil. Use 1 to 2 tablespoons of one of these oils daily, depending on your body size. Grind hemp, pumpkin seeds, and/or flaxseeds and sprinkle them on your food. One tablespoon of flax, pumpkin seeds, or hemp seeds contain 14 grams of fat.
- Avoid consuming margarine and use small amounts of unsalted organic butter.
- Eliminate polyunsaturated oils such as safflower, corn, soy, peanut, cottonseed, and sunflower seed oils from your diet. You really do not need them as they add no nutritional value to your body, but add a lot of excess calories. If you do use them, only use the certified organic, cold-pressed oils in tinted glass or special plastic bottles.
- Use one tablespoon daily of cold-pressed, extra-virgin "green" olive oil as your source of monounsaturated linoleic acid. Purchase it in smaller color-tinted glass bottles. One tablespoon contains 14 grams of fat and makes "good" eicosanoids.

Calculating Fat Needs

Follow this simple method to figure out your fat needs in grams:

1. Calculate your calorie needs per day. (For active men, daily calorie requirements range from 2,200 to 3,500 depending on workload and length of exercise. For active women, daily calorie requirements range from 1,800 to 2,600 depending on workload and length of exercise.)
2. Calories per day x 0.25 = your number of fat calories.
3. Fat calories divided by 9 calories per gram of fat = number of grams of fat.

I eat 2,200 calories daily, so my personal calculation is 2,200 x 0.25 = 550 divided by 9 = 61.1 grams of fat daily. Check all food labels, which list

BLOOD FAT RISK FACTORS

Most health professionals use the following guidelines to evaluate the risk of heart disease when checking blood cholesterol and LDL levels (mg/100cc).

Blood Fat	Risk Factor		
	Desirable	Borderline high risk	High risk
cholesterol	less than 200	200-240	240+
HDL cholesterol	65 or more	50	35 or less
LDL cholesterol	130 or less	130-160	160 or more

Source: Adapted from the National Cholesterol Education Program (Ottawa; Washington, D.C.).

grams of fat per serving, so you can stay in your fat zone. Try to spread your fats among your three main meals to ensure that the protein, carbohydrates, and fats you consume each day are evenly distributed.

Fat or oil consumption must be accompanied by both low-fat protein and naturally occurring fiber. Fat helps to slow the rate of entry of carbohydrates into the bloodstream, thereby reducing insulin response and assuring the body of a steady energy source, without dietary fat being stored as body fat.

Fats—Not a Four-Letter Word

By now you realize that fats are both good and bad for you. Unfortunately, most North Americans are running scared of the four-letter word "fats." In sharp contrast to destructive fats, you absolutely need EFAs daily for your optimum health and healing.

High-quality dietary fats, eaten with low-fat protein and naturally occurring fiber, satisfy our sense of hunger and work as natural appetite suppressants. Fat is responsible for the release of the hormone cholecystokinin (CCK) from the stomach lining. This hormone signals the brain to stop eating. As funny as it may sound, it takes fat to burn stored body fat.

Superfood Carbohydrates for Peak Performance

The most important Superfood nutrient for achieving peak stamina is complex carbohydrates. There are two types of carbohydrates, affectionately called "carbs." The first group are the simple carbohydrates made from one or two ring-shaped molecules called sugar units. The second group are the complex carbohydrates, made up of a large chain of simple sugar units. Both simple and complex carbs occur in foods such as fruits, whole grains, and vegetables.

Simple carbs circulating in the blood are termed blood sugar. The basic blood sugar supplying the body and brain with energy is called glucose. You must get glucose from the foods you eat since your body's metabolic systems cannot produce enough. Simple carbohydrates are found in foods like white sugar and honey (which are virtually pure simple sugar) and in foods with added sugar such as muffins, cookies, doughnuts, milk, beer, pastries, ice cream, pies, cakes, and other sweet-tooth goodies. Fruit is also full of simple sugars, mainly fructose. Simple sugars taste sweet.

Complex carbohydrates do not have the sweet reputation of simple sugars, even though they are made up of long links of simple sugars. The most common complex carbohydrate is called starch, composed of hundreds of glucose units linked together. Starch is found in vegetables, grains, some fruits, legumes (beans), peas, sprouts, and grasses. It is easily broken down in the digestive tract into glucose. The body then takes the glucose to wherever it is needed for energy—the muscles, organs, brain—and stores the rest as a future reserve.

Reserves of Energy

Glycogen is a complex carbohydrate that occurs only in the body, never in food. Glycogen is the reservoir of glucose the body stores in the muscles and liver for future energy. Glycogen from the liver is taken through the bloodstream to supply your brain and organs with a steady amount of glucose, so they can function optimally. Glycogen in the muscles gives you quick glucose to sustain you during a hatha yoga class, a session on an exercise machine, or the spurt of energy you require to catch the elevator before the door closes.

A certain amount of glucose must be in your blood to keep you alert and spontaneous. Whenever you are sleeping or sitting down, only a small amount of carbohydrates is used by the body for energy; at rest, the body uses fat as its primary energy source. But the moment you rev up the 100 trillion cellular engines to walk briskly, run, swim, dance, or climb stairs, your muscles rely on the stored glycogen to energize those muscles for movement.

Your performance, both the quality and endurance of muscle function, is dictated by the amount of glycogen stored in those muscles. A low glycogen level means early fatigue. When blood sugar levels drop below normal, the pancreas responds by releasing the hormone glucagon, which stimulates the breakdown of fat and glycogen to provide energy for the body, especially the brain. Once glycogen reserves are exhausted, the body must break down muscle to provide the glucose needed by the brain.

To build up a good glycogen level you must consume 55 to 60 percent of all your calories from complex carbohydrates such as seasonal ripe fruit, colorful vegetables, and whole grains. Because carbohydrates are good for us, many people mistakenly think they can eat all the carbohydrates they want. When carbohydrates are eaten, blood sugar levels rise, and the pancreas responds by secreting a hormone called insulin. Insulin is designed to restore blood sugar equilibrium or balance. It removes excess glucose from the bloodstream and stores it first as glycogen in the liver and muscles and what is left over as fat. High insulin levels promote fat storage and block the release of fat-burning glucagon. This means that even though carbohydrates are fat-free, if you eat too many, you will store them as fat. Furthermore, they will prevent your body from burning fat.

Daily Carbohydrate Requirements for Peak Energy Performance

From 1977 to 1997, consumption of processed carbohydrates like crackers and pretzels increased 200 percent. In this same time span, processed breakfast cereals are up 60 percent and processed, carbohydrate-rich grains made into pizzas, pasta, corn chips, and nachos are up 115 percent. During the same time span that processed grain consumption increased, the percentage of overweight North Americans increased from 25 percent to 40 percent!

To calculate your carbohydrate calorie needs, multiply your total daily calorie needs by 55 percent (if you are active) or 60 percent (if you are extremely active). If I need 2,200 calories a day at 55 percent: 2,200 x .55 = I need 1,210 calories daily from Superfood carbs. To find the number of grams (since there are 4 calories per gram of carbohydrates), I divide 1,210 by 4 = 302.5 grams of carbohydrates daily.

Check carbohydrate information on food labels. Only use whole, unprocessed foods to get your carbs. The best choices are fruits, vegetables, and whole grains. Each of these Superfoods provide extremely high-octane fuels, which give you more miles per gallon of necessary energy for peak performance.

Guide to Eating Carbs

Just like fats, some carbohydrates are "good" for you and some carbohydrates are "bad" for you. It all comes down to the quality, source, and processing. That is, if a carbohydrate is processed (cooked or heated), it gives off its sugars too quickly. When choosing foods for your diet, always stay in the Superfood categories (high-octane fuels) and avoid processed (low-octane fuels) foods. Complex carbohydrates from veggies, fruits, and whole grains take longer to digest, are mixed with natural fiber, and slowly give their sugar to the bloodstream in a smooth, steady supply. This will assure you of a constant, steady energy supply to your muscles and brain.

What to Avoid: Low-Octane Fuels

- Avoid processed convenience foods full of refined white flour and hidden sugars. Reduce your consumption of refined grains such as white bread, white pasta, and white rice, which are void of nutrients.

- Avoid refined sugar, excess honey, maple syrup, and sweeteners. When eaten in excess, they encourage yeast overgrowth (candida) and tooth decay.
- Avoid too many carbohydrates or carbohydrates that are high-glycemic without sufficient protein, fiber, or fat, to slow down the release of sugar. Try to eat carbohydrates with proteins and fats to balance insulin interaction. Processed carbohydrates cause too much insulin to be secreted, to balance the sharp rise in blood sugar levels given off when these foods digest. Sharp insulin levels throw your hormone balance off and cause the excess sugars from these carbohydrates to be stored as fat.

What to Eat: High-Octane Fuels

- Eat whole-food carbohydrates like fruits, vegetables, whole grains, and legumes, which are full of fiber, vitamins, minerals, antioxidants, and phytochemicals.
- Choose water or herbal teas over high-carbohydrate (insulin-raising) sodas, juices, coffee, and alcohol.
- Choose the least processed carbohydrates, selecting brown rice over white rice, whole-grain hot cereals over boxed cereals, an apple over applesauce, and an orange over orange juice. Always choose whole Superfoods.

The Glycemic Index

The glycemic index is another system of classifying carbohydrates. This index refers to the rate that glucose enters the bloodstream after a carbohydrate is eaten. Glucose is rapidly absorbed and enters the bloodstream quickly because it is already in the form the body can use. Since complex carbohydrates are digested more slowly than simple carbohydrates, most nutritional researchers assumed that the release of glucose from complex carbs was slower than from simple carb sources. This is not always true. Some of the foods with the highest glycemic index rating (foods that give off glucose quickly, raising both blood sugar and insulin levels) are inferior food choices. Examples of these complex carbohydrates are raisins, white rice, parsnips, puffed rice cakes, honey, processed breakfast cereals, white potatoes, bananas, white bread, and white flour pastas, corn, or corn products like corn chips. These are universally dubbed "empty calories." Carbohydrates with low or moderate-glycemic ratings (foods releasing their glucose more slowly and requiring a more moderate insulin response) are superior food choices. Examples of these foods are apples, oranges, grapefruit, pears, plums, berries, cherries, peaches, sweet potatoes, lentils, soybeans, kidney beans, pinto beans, non-starchy vegetables like broccoli, sprouts, lettuce, sea vegetables, herbs, whole-grain breads, whole-grain pastas, and brown rice.

The higher the glycemic index of a carbohydrate, the faster it enters the bloodstream as glucose; and the faster glucose appears in the bloodstream, the more insulin the body is forced to make. This quick entry of glucose is not healthy. In 1992, the University of Toronto conducted the first experiments showing that glucose from table sugar actually entered the bloodstream slower than glucose from a dietetically correct puffed rice cake. Linked by chemical bonds, the pure glucose of the processed puffed rice cake is quickly broken down in the stomach, allowing the glucose to literally rush into the bloodstream at a faster rate than even table sugar. The puffed rice cake has become the cornerstone of many dieters' food strategy or of those with candida yeast infections. Research shows that any processed or cooked (heated) complex carbohydrate removes natural fiber and fats. Processing breaks down the cellular structure of the food, which allows for faster digestion and the lightning-fast entry of glucose into the bloodstream!

Superfood dietary strategies incorporate unprocessed, whole foods. These foods, with all their protein, carbohydrates, fats, and fiber, slow down digestion and the rate of glucose entry into the bloodstream. This slow entry gives you greater energy and allows just enough glucose to allow your brain to function effectively. This diet was exactly suited to the feast-or-famine lives of our hunter-gatherer ancestors. They found berries, fruits, or grains perhaps only every second day. Their bodies learned to store the extra glucose as a reserved energy storage system—fat—for future energy. Insulin performs the job of storing fat just fine.

Today, we have a lot of choice and can avoid our ancestors' genetic "fat bomb." We need some revolutionary thinking about reducing chronic hyperinsulinemia, the body's response to too many high-glycemic carbohydrates and the underlying cause of many disorders and diseases such as obesity, arthritis, heart disease, and a lack of energy.

Superfood dietary strategies are based on limiting your high-glycemic index rated foods and emphasizing the low- and moderate-glycemic rated fruits, vegetables, and grains for powerful mental agility and peak physical performance. Superfoods will always provide you with supercharged health! Always eat high-glycemic foods with low-glycemic foods, or with

GLYCEMIC FOOD INDEX

High-Glycemic Foods (glycemic index between 82 to 133 percent)	Moderate-Glycemic Foods (glycemic index between 50 to 82 percent)	Low-Glycemic Foods (glycemic index below 50 percent)
Rapid Insulin Secretion	*Moderate Insulin Secretion*	*Reduced Insulin Secretion:*
puffed rice or wheat cakes	whole-grain pastas	apples, oranges
puffed rice or grain cereals	whole-grain breads	cherries, peaches
corn	brown rice	all berries
corn chips	buckwheat pancakes	plums
glucose	rolled oats	watermelon
honey	pinto beans	pears
parsnips	black beans	pink grapefruit
white potatoes	navy beans	vegetables
instant, processed grain mixes	garbanzo beans	sea vegetables
cakes, pies, doughnuts, pastry	adzuki beans	sweet potatoes
processed breakfast cereals	raw carrots	yams
instant grain cereals		fat-free, plain yogurt
cooked carrots		all herbs
raisins		stevia (herbal sweetener)
white rice		lentils, barley
white bread or flour products		kidney and lima beans
		soybeans
		firm tofu, tempeh, etc.
		soy lecithin
		green drinks (GREENS+)

some protein and fat. This slows down the quick release of sucrose from the high-glycemic foods, and allows them to be digested as medium-glycemic foods.

Part 2: The 60/20/20 versus the 40/30/30 Meal Construction Plan

Most nutritional researchers recommend a high-carbohydrate dietary strategy: 60 percent of calories as carbohydrates, 20 percent protein, and 20 percent fat. However, six prominent authors recommend a lower carbohydrate dietary strategy of 40 percent of calories as carbohydrates, 30 percent protein, and 30 percent fat. These authors generally endorse the concept of reduced carbohydrates. In 1972, Dr. Robert Atkins published his first high-protein diet in *Dr. Atkins' New Diet Revolution*. In 1991, Rachael and Richard Heller published *The Carbohydrate Addict's Diet*. Then, in 1995, Barry Sears published *The Zone*. Each of these authors endorse the concept that people reduce their carbohydrate intake dramatically. In 1996, Michael Eades and Mary Dan Eades published *Protein Power*, which recommends that carbs be eliminated even more than the 40/30/30 but doesn't restrict fat. *Protein Power* and *Dr. Atkins' New Diet Revolution* eliminate almost all carbohydrates from the diet, except modest amounts of fruits and vegetables. These diets may be as low as 10/60/30. *The Zone* and *The Carbohydrate Addict's Diet* restrict carbohydrates and generally maintain a dietary ratio of about 40/30/30.

Which dietary strategy gives you a winning combination? The 60/20/20 or the 40/30/30? A dietary strategy must supply you with meals that meet five criteria: they should satisfy hunger; reduce carbohydrate cravings; provide mental focus; provide steady energy; and provide adequate amounts of colorful fruits and vegetables, with their natural protective and ultra-health-supportive antioxidants and phytochemicals.

On this basis, let's look at the two strategies in depth.

The 60/20/20 Diet Strategy
Thumbs Up
- It supplies lots of carbohydrates to keep you fueled with energy, if the

carbs are from complex, low- or moderate-glycemic, whole fruits, colorful vegetables, and a few whole grains.

- It is a great way to include a huge array of colorful Superfoods with a wide range of antioxidants and phytochemicals—this is an anti-free-radical diet.
- It includes a wide range of all seven fiber sources and a guarantee of 35 to 40 grams of fiber daily. This large fiber content ensures the release of glucose in a smooth steady supply, taking pressure off the pancreas and reducing insulin interaction.
- It supplies a minimum amount of fat for flavor, satiation, and EFAs that are metabolic boosters.
- It supplies sufficient protein requirements for most people.
- It increases both active thyroid hormone and noradrenaline.

Thumbs Down
- Carbohydrate content could be too high for insulin-resistant individuals, but this number is not as high as some researchers suggest.
- If carbohydrate content is derived mostly from grains (rice, corn, bread, rice cakes, pasta) or high-glycemic foods, excess sugar (glucose) in the bloodstream that is not needed for immediate energy can be stored as the fuel reserve—fat.
- It may limit adequate protein for elite athletes or strength athletes (avid weight-resistance trainers).

The 40/30/30 Diet Strategy
Thumbs Up
- It is good for short-term weight loss. A high-protein, low-calorie diet may supply a very meager 800 to 1,200 calories a day, guaranteed to cause some weight loss in everyone.
- It promotes the progressive idea of consuming a ratio of protein, fat, and low- or moderate-glycemic carbohydrates together, in a balanced proportion; it also promotes awareness of low or fat-free protein.

Thumbs Down
- It provides far too few calories for very active adults, those who exercise five days a week, and for athletes involved in endurance training.
- Reducing carbohydrates would reduce the workload on the pancreas, promoting weight loss in people who have to some degree lost their response to insulin or who lose weight on a low- or high-calorie diet.
- The lack of fiber may cause digestive problems.

- The body will detect carbohydrate reduction and long-term performance will suffer.
- Protein metabolism produces a nitrogen by-product that is toxic to the body and is flushed out with lots of water. In the absence of adequate carbohydrates, the body gets this extra water by breaking down muscle tissue.
- A high-protein diet favors a loss of muscle mass over body fat and causes water loss, as excess protein works as a diuretic.
- High-protein diets put an extra burden on the liver and kidneys that may result in excessive calcium loss.
- High-protein diets may supply only 12 grams of fiber, which can leave you constipated and prone to high blood pressure and a higher risk of colon cancer.
- This diet strategy is too low in all seven fiber sources. Sufficient fiber slows the absorption of the sugars contained in complex carbohydrates, preventing rapid spikes in blood sugar and surges of insulin, and allowing a constant source of energy.
- A high-protein diet potentially provides too much cholesterol and fat.
- It is not recommended for pregnant or lactating women.

My recommendation is a 55/25/20 ratio: 55 percent calories from complex carbohydrates (fresh vegetables, fruits, and some whole grains), 25 percent low-fat protein, and 20 percent fat that use organic olive oil and fish, or olive oil and flaxseed oil (as major sources of EFAs). If you are a serious endurance athlete, you need more calories from complex carbs and your dietary ratio should be 60/20/20.

Are You Better Off with More Carbs or More Fat?

The danger of eating the 40/30/30 diet is that you will consume less carbohydrate and more fat and cholesterol.

The danger of eating the 55/25/20 diet is that you will consume more carbohydrates and less fat. If you eat extra calories, you are better off consuming extra complex carbohydrate calories rather than extra fat calories. This is the simple reason: If you eat 200 extra fat calories, 194 end up as body fat and 6 calories are used converting it to body fat. If you eat 200 extra carbohydrate calories, 154 end up as body fat and 46 calories are used converting it to body fat.

The Winning Combination

Keep yourself in the "energy zone" for peak performance and accelerated self-healing. Each person has a unique, biochemical individuality and so must make slight adjustments to the amount of fat, fiber, and carbohydrates eaten daily, to meet their specific biochemical demands. Use Superfoods in a 55/25/20 or 60/20/20 meal construction plan to keep you fueled with high-octane Superfoods that will leave you supercharged with more powerful mental and physical performance.

2 POINT SUMMARY

- For peak performance and optimum health, assess the amounts of protein, fiber, fat, and carbohydrates you need daily to fuel your body properly.
- Spread your daily protein, fiber, fat, and carbohydrate needs evenly among your three meals and one of your two snacks each day.

2 POINT ACTION PLAN

- Calculate your daily protein, fiber, fat, and carbohydrate requirements and do not supersede them.
- Use Superfoods in a 55/25/20 or 60/20/20 meal construction plan to give you more miles per gallon of energy for peak performance.

Say Goodbye to Dieting

A health-sustaining diet is a matter of proportions.

Accept that you are a beautiful and unique individual,
then take responsibility for your own life.
Dr. Marcus Laux, Natural Woman, Natural Menopause

Take small but persistent steps; this will keep you on a positive path,
without overwhelming you.
Gaylene Lahue, fitness professional

Say goodbye to dieting once and for all! Tear up all those diets you may have tried in the past and file them in the garbage. Take your scale and donate it to a friend. The ultra-healthy strategies that I have been suggesting will help you reach your right weight *naturally*. As a matter of fact, research shows that you may not need to lose any weight to be healthy.

You don't need to be skinny to look good. Unfortunately, many people see excess weight as a character flaw, not a medical problem. Our national obsession, which equates acceptable appearance with thinness, has driven Princess Diana, Jane Fonda, Cathy Rigby, and countless others to bulimia, an eating disorder characterized by constant bingeing and purging. Since 1980, when bulimia nervosa was officially recognized as a disease, reported cases have more than doubled. Women comprise 90 percent of the sufferers. An article in *The American Journal of Psychiatry*, in 1991, concluded that one in 25 women are at risk for developing the full syndrome at some point in their lives. There are even more who suffer from some lesser version of bulimic-like behavior.

The fault lies in our obsession with thinness. We have to change our outlook on food, and see it as the way to health; we need to recognize each human being as a unique, beautiful part of the human race. In diversity there is unity.

The State of Affairs

Although our obsession with being thin may lead to ill health, too much weight can create other problems. A long-term study by the Centers for Disease Control and Prevention, in Atlanta, show that the number of Americans who are seriously overweight has jumped from 25 percent in the 1980s to 30 percent in the 1990s. *The Journal of the American Medical Association* estimates that 58 million people in the United States and 7 million in Canada weigh at least 20 percent more than their ideal body weight. Dr. F. Xavier Pi-Sunyer of New York City's St. Luke's-Roosevelt Hospital feels that the fattening of North Americans will put millions at an increased risk for diabetes, hypertension, heart disease, stroke, gout, arthritis, and some forms of cancer. There are some alarming signs that the next generation may be steamrolling along in the wrong direction. The percentage of overweight teens is now a minimum of 21 percent, up from 15 percent in the 1970s.

What accounts for this dismal state of affairs? Nutritionists are unanimous that it boils down to this: North Americans ate too much and exercised too little in the 1980s. In true thermodynamic terms, we took in more calories than we burned and stored the rest as excess fat. After all, we are encouraged to do this by advertising and the media. There are no advertisements for brussels sprouts, only for candy bars, soft drinks, fast foods, and sugar-coated cereals. In addition, foods that used to be dished out in modest proportions are now served in "king-size," "super-size," and "1/4 bigger size." The 8-ounce traditional soft drink has quadrupled in size. Even our emotional states encourage overeating. A study conducted by Duke University and Structure House, a facility for weight control based in Durham, North Carolina, concluded that women tend to binge on food when they are lonely or depressed. Men tend to binge when they are in social situations where they feel happy, excited, or are encouraged to eat.

Did All Those Diets Backfire?

The focus of most diets in the 1980s and 1990s was to reduce fat. In our low-fat zeal, we idolized reduced-fat foods. We began to eat carbohydrates such as chips, bagels, muffins, and prepackaged goodies that boasted low or no fat. These foods led us into self-delusion—eat all you want of huge, Godzilla-like portions, just keep them reduced fat. This diet came back and hit us with a whammy, right on the waistline and buttocks. Calories are calories, regardless of where they come from, and extra ones get stored as fat. Remember, "fat-free" does not mean "problem-free."

The way we have been eating and what we have been eating is a sure-fire prescription for lagging energy, poor work performance, deteriorating health, less mental acuity, and a low-level ability to self-heal. We have been led down the path of ill health by advertising executives who collectively spend 40 billion dollars a year to entice us to forgo Superfoods like colorful organic salads, fresh fruit, lean protein, and to eat their giant fries, triple cheeseburger, 32-ounce king cola, and huge garbage-can-size tubs of theater popcorn. Many of us tried to avoid fats, but began to eat nutritionless, high-density carbohydrate foods like fat-free cookies, desserts, and muffins that our bodies convert first into sugar, then into fat.

Overconsumption Malnutrition

The real problem is that the site in our brains that signals it has enough nutrients never gets the message! And the reason it doesn't get the message is that the foods we eat are deficient in vitamins, minerals, EFAs, fiber, protein, phytochemicals, and antioxidants. We eat and eat but the brain says, "Keep eating. I still haven't been able to locate those 150 micrograms of essential iodine or the micronutrient selenium, to make glutathione peroxidase to prevent cancer-cell development" or, "I am in a battle to save your eyesight from macular degeneration. Keep eating. I can't find enough beta-carotene yet." Remember, the body wants homeostasis and is fighting on our behalf 24 hours a day to self-diagnose and self-heal. We only need to support it in its efforts.

The minimum we should do is take a high-quality multi-vitamin-mineral-antioxidant capsule daily so the site of satiation can be signaled that some basic nutrients are available in a moderate, daily food supply. I define a high-quality multi-vitamin-mineral-antioxidant as one derived from natural sources that incorporate the full natural range of carotenoids and vitamin E tocopheryls such as alpha, beta, and gamma tocopheryl. (See the Appendix for sources.)

Don't Turn Down the Thermostat

As discussed in Chapter 1, our digestive and metabolic systems evolved in our hunter-gatherer ancestors. They didn't have a "ready-made" food supply. When food was not available, their metabolisms just slowed down to preserve their energy reserves. Today, when you go on a low-calorie diet, your body assumes there is no food available and that it is "starving." Your metabolism automatically slows way down to burn less calories, and hunts for any dietary fat it can find in your diet, which it stores directly as body fat.

Dr. George Roth, molecular physiologist with the National Institute on Aging, in Bethesda, Maryland, demonstrated that animals placed on a calorie-restricted diet automatically reduce their body temperature by about one degree Celsius. Lower temperature means a less vigorous metabolism, which means less food is metabolized. "In order to compensate for the reduction in diet," Roth says, "the animals switch from a growth mode into what can be thought of as a survival mode." They get fewer calories, so they burn fewer.

Since the body is always fighting to maintain homeostasis, in its infinite wisdom it simply turns down the thermostat to avoid "starvation." Your body will actually slow your respiration, heart rate, and the metabolic activity in your muscles to a "famine mode." Trying to lose weight by dramatically lowering your calorie intake will never work—it can't! It is irrefutable that it will not work, regardless of commercial weight-loss claims. Your whole resting metabolic rate adjusts downward to defend itself against the calorie shortage, even when you are active. Regular meal skipping and starve-and-binge eating patterns cause your calorie-burning furnace to slow down.

It gets worse! Surveys and studies show that dietary success tends to be temporary. Each year, 85 million North Americans go on a diet, but no matter how much weight they lose, 95 percent gain it all back within five years. As soon as the diet is over, we go right back to our old habits and not only put on the weight we lost but gain more weight. Do you want to know why we put the weight back on? Read on.

The Yo-Yo Effect

When you eat too few calories for function, you start to burn vital muscle tissue. You also lose your necessary water supply. This loss of water is responsible for the initial euphoria you feel, when it appears that you've shed ten pounds. Your body, however, senses a "starvation" or a "famine" and immediately increases the amount and activity of lipoprotein lipase, an enzyme that governs how efficiently digested fat in your bloodstream is stored in cells. The body thinks it needs to store fat to survive the "famine" period, and it locates every molecule of fat it can find, even to the point of not letting your body use any of it as an energy source. Without fat to burn as energy, the fat-burning furnace slows down to compensate for the absence of fuel. The body is now greedily looking for fat to store. This is why a dieter gains more weight eating a strawberry sundae than a nondieter. A low-calorie diet actually makes your body more efficient at hanging on to and storing fat.

On a low-calorie diet, your body also burns muscle tissue as an energy supply. When the diet ends, your body wants to replace its lost "reserve" of fat stores, and you gain back the weight as fat, not as the muscle you lost. This difference is significant because a pound of muscle burns 50 calories of fat a day. If you had not dieted but had gained ten pounds of muscle instead, through proper exercise, you would look great, feel great, and enjoy the bonus of burning 500 more calories a day.

Eat, Be Happy, and Lose Weight

To stop storing fat and start burning fat, take the following 15 steps in the Superfood diet.

15 Steps To Sensible Superfood Weight Reduction

1. Start to drink 6, 8-ounce glasses of water every day through a straw. This will prehydrate you and help you cleanse your body of toxic debris. Depending on your body size, slowly build up to 10 to 12, 8-ounce glasses of water a day.
2. Make sure you eat ten servings of colorful vegetables and three servings of fruit daily. The combination of the water and fiber will work as a natural appetite suppressant and promote a feeling of satiety.
3. Use a green drink mixed in pure water, twice a day, to alkalize your body fluids. Also take a high-quality multi-vitamin-mineral-antioxidant capsule to ensure your micronutrient supply is sufficient.
4. Measure your body fat once a month at a fitness center. Use this approach, and how your clothes fit, as your only guide.
5. Eat a low-fat diet and be vigilant, watching for hidden fats in chips, cookies, skim milk, meats, and salad dressings. Remember, "low-fat" does not mean "problem-free."
6. Eat three meals and two snacks every day. Spread out your daily protein so you get a little at each of your three meals and one of your two

snacks. Make sure you consume Superfoods full of natural fiber and some of your grams of fat calories at each of your three meals. Do not skip a meal. Do not overeat: control the size of your portions.

7. Never go more than four hours without food, as a steady supply of food keeps your blood sugar, and therefore your energy levels, constant.

8. Do not eat processed sugars that add excess calories that must be stored, eventually, as fat. Eat seasonal fruit and colorful vegetables and organic whole grains in moderation.

9. Research stresses that you should lose no more than a half a pound of fat per week. We saw earlier that dieting slows metabolism, increases fat storage, and increases appetite. If you lose more than the half pound of fat a week, you will defeat your efforts since your body will restore its "fat set point" to replenish its fat reserve.

10. Since fat is burned only in muscle, exercise is the key to build muscle and burn fat. You may use your own body weight and do push-ups, squats, and resistance training by pushing your hands against the sides of a doorjamb. Or you can simply tighten a muscle and hold the contraction. You may also want to join a fitness center and receive professional weight-resistance training.

11. (a) Consider supplementing your diet with 200 to 400 mcg of chromium picolinate daily to maintain insulin metabolism and help reduce body fat.

   (b) Your fat is stored in adipose cells, but burned in the mitochondria (metabolic "furnaces") of each cell. Acetyl-L-carnitine or L-carnitine moves body fat from adipose tissue to the mitochondria. This is especially true if you exercise and use L-carnitine. L-carnitine is related to the vitamin B family but is usually considered similar to an amino acid and classified as a biocatalyst. Most researchers suggest a dosage of 500 to 1,000 mg daily.

   (c) Coenzyme Q_{10} enhances energy production in the mitochondria. This may cause fat stores to be burned in your mitochondria. Most researchers suggest a dosage of 30 to 100 mg daily.

   (d) Another safe herb to use as part of a weight-loss program is Gymnema sylvestre. This plant, native to the forests of India, maintains blood sugar levels and reduces food cravings.

   (e) Garcinia combodia, also known in India as Indian berry, is a fruit. The extract of this fruit, hydroxy citric acid (HCA), has been used for centuries in India and South Asia as a spice in curry. It promotes the burning of body fat as fuel. It reduces appetite and fat storage from a high-fat meal by up to 30 percent. Researchers suggest a dosage of 250 to 300 mg with each of your three meals.

12. Eat low-glycemic foods. The higher the glycemic index, the quicker that food gives off its sugar into the bloodstream. The lower the glycemic level, the more even and slower the sugar is given off. (See page 137 for a list of high-, low-, and moderate-glycemic foods.)

13. Reduce stress. According to Dr. Per Björntorp, of the Sahlgrenska University Hospital, Göteborg, Sweden, stresses that range from anxiety to depression prompt the adrenal glands to secrete the hormone cortisol. Cortisol prepares the body for an emergency, including telling it to store more fat, especially in the belly where cells have more receptors for cortisol than do superficial fat cells under the skin. Cortisol is like a key in a lock, opening fat cells, allowing fat to be stored. Cortisol also eats away lean muscle mass, which the body needs to burn fat. In addition, high cortisol levels significantly reduce growth hormone output. L-carnitine or acetyl-L-carnitine supplementation, as suggested above, can reduce cortisol, as can being happy and reducing stress. Stress causes cortisol levels to skyrocket. Be happy, reduce stress, keep a smile on your face, and keep cortisol out of your lean muscle mass.

14. You may want to experiment and raise your metabolic rate so that your body burns more calories all day. This process, called thermogenises, encourages the body to burn a type of fat called brown adipose tissue (BAT), which is difficult to lose under normal circumstances. Initiate thermogenises by using a herbal fat-loss supplement. These supplements generally contain the substance Ma Huang (ephedra); caffeine or kola nut, theophylline (from tea); white willow bark or aspirin; naringenin (from grapefruit). Use this formula *only* when monitored by a knowledgeable health-care professional, since this combination can elevate blood pressure, may cause heart palpitations, and initiate nerve injury.

15. Human growth hormone (HGH) is the most abundant hormone made by the pituitary gland. Production peaks during adolescence then steadily declines as we age. HGH replacement, administered only under the care of a qualified health professional, restores many bodily systems to a much more youthful level. Some speculate that cutting caloric intake one day a week, as on a "detox day" (see pages Chapter 5), or "periodic-mono diet" (see Chapter 8) may cause small amounts of HGH to be secreted into the body by the pituitary gland.

The Superfood approach to sensible food consumption will keep your body's metabolic pathways operating at an optimum level and keep your weight, measurably and predictably, in your ideal range. You do not need drastic self-restraint. You need only to follow natural, healthy dietary principles!

Do Diet Pills Work?

If you desperately want to shed pounds, you may look for a quick fix. A number of obesity drugs curb appetite by regulating serotonin levels and promoting feelings of satiety. Dexfenfluramine, sold under the name Redux, became available to North Americans in 1996. It is an improved version of the obesity drugs fenfluramine and phentermine, known as fen-phen, available since 1973. Redux prescriptions are approved for one year only and are intended for the clinically obese, those who are 20 to 30 percent overweight. Some neuroscientists are concerned about the negative long-term effects of obesity pills on brain functions and general health. Studies show that once patients stop taking the drug they put the weight right back on. Use the dietary strategies set out in this book for sensible, healthy approaches to weight loss. If you use an obesity drug, use it only under the care of a health-care professional, and follow the recommendations contained here. My goal is simple: to keep you ultra-healthy and to help you balance your weight naturally but quickly.

Energize Your Thyroid for Peak Performance

The thyroid gland is a small endocrine gland at the base of the throat. It functions as a central command post, sending hormonal messages to every cell in the body, directing the maintenance of body temperature, heart rate, muscle contraction, and the rate at which food is turned into energy. Many people suffer from a condition termed hypothyroidism (underactive thyroid), which manifests itself as fatigue, subnormal body temperature, and unexplained weight gain. Health-care professionals usually prescribe a synthetic thyroid hormone or a natural thyroid extract from an animal source.

The Superfood approach will *naturally* support better thyroid functioning. Colorful salads, sea vegetables, sprouted seeds and grains, seasonal fruit, raw vegetables, and freshly extracted organic vegetable juices all bolster and strengthen the thyroid function. The thyroid requires iodine to function optimally. Sources of iodine-rich Superfoods are sea vegetables (Nova Scotia dulse, spirulina, chlorella, kelp, nori, agar, kombu, and wakame), cod liver oil, herring, halibut, salmon, garlic, watercress, egg yolks, and nutritional yeast.

The Science of Fat

Researchers Angelo Tremblay, Jean-Pierre Despres, and Claude Bouchard, of Laval University, Quebec City, have been studying the science of fat. They have determined that visceral fat deep in the abdomen—under the muscles and between the organs—puts us at a greater risk for heart disease, high blood pressure, and diabetes, than the fat that sits just under the skin, called subcutaneous fat. Men generally store the dangerous visceral fat and women generally store subcutaneous fat, in the hips, thighs, and under the skin.

Visceral fat is much deadlier since it is in the abdomen, in direct contact with organs, and its small cells actively pick up and release fatty acids. Subcutaneous fat cells are larger, more sluggish, and not as active or problematic.

Researchers at the Garvan Institute of Medical Research, Sydney, Australia, found that the more intra-abdominal fat, the higher the body's insulin levels. This can lead to insulin resistance, weight gain and, in the long term, type II diabetes. Excess insulin may lead to increased fat storage.

The best low-tech method for calculating how much visceral fat your body is storing is to measure your waist at the narrowest point above your navel but below your armpit. If it's more than 34 inches, you're probably carrying too much abdominal fat, and running a significant health risk.

For years, doctors used the Metropolitan Life Insurance Company's height-weight tables to determine if a patient was overweight. The more sophisticated calculation is the BMI, or body mass index. You can compute your BMI by dividing your weight in kilograms by the square of your

HOW TO DETERMINE YOUR BODY MASS INDEX (BMI)

1. Multiply your weight in pounds by 0.45 to get your weight in kilograms (Example: 150 pounds x 0.45 = 67.5 kilograms).
2. Multiply your height in inches by 0.025 to get your height in meters (Example: if you are 5'10" tall that is 70" x 0.025 = 1.75 meters).
3. Square the number you calculated in step 2. (Example: 1.75 x 1.75 = 3.063)
4. Divide your weight in kilograms (the number you calculated in step 1), by the square of your height in meters (the number you calculated in step 3). (Example: 67.5 divided by 3.063 = 22.04). This is your BMI.

height in meters. You can also click into http://www2.shapeup.org/sua on your computer and it will do it for you.

A BMI from 19 to 25 is in the healthy range, 26 and above puts you at risk for hypertension, cardiovascular disease, and diabetes.

Even more important than your BMI is where you carry your fat. If you look like an apple, round in the middle section, you are storing the more dangerous intra-abdominal fat (visceral fat). If your shape is more like a pear, storing fat from the waistline down, you are storing the less dangerous subcutaneous fat. Many researchers believe that the body's propensity to build up either of these types of fat is pure genetics.

A healthy weight is not defined by numbers on a scale but by where fat is stored in the body and how different types of fat cells behave. A Vanderbilt University (Nashville) study found that women who kept down their fat intake to 25 grams a day and their calories at 1,200 daily lost 18 pounds on average over a five-month period. The other good news is that it is easier to lose the problematic intra-abdominal fat by exercise. Exercise is now being recognized for its ability to stave off some of the worst of the health effects of being overweight. It mobilizes and burns both types of stored body fat to give you back your health and self-healing capabilities. Exercise slows the physiological aging process. Even modest weight reduction may result in improvement in many metabolic coronary heart disease risk factors. (For more on exercise, see Chapter 11.)

No-Diet Weight-Loss Success: Case Study

At North End Fitness, the Ganges exercise facility where Leslie Simpson works out, regulars often offer her support with comments like, "Way to go," "Looking good," and "Good work, Leslie," as she goes from the stair-climber to the weight-resistance machines. Leslie is still trying to get used to all the attention. "Who would have ever imagined that I would be a fitness role model?" she asks. Certainly no one who knew Leslie 18 months ago when at age 30 she weighed 162 pounds and stood exactly 5 feet tall.

Like many people who struggle with obesity, Leslie slowly started to gain weight in high school and college, where hamburgers and french fries were the norm, and she was described as "chunky." Leslie had her first child, a daughter, while teaching English in Japan. During this time her older brother died in a diving accident. Within one year her other brother was diagnosed with AIDS; six months later, he died. Leslie fell into a deep depression and ended up on medication. When she got pregnant with her second child, she and her husband decided to return to North America. "After giving birth I suddenly was shocked to discover I weighed 162 pounds. I tried to put on an old tent dress that now was too small, and cringed when I looked in the mirror—I looked 45, not 30. I had the shape of an apple."

Leslie visited a friend who had one child and had just lost 30 pounds. She explained the Superfood dietary strategy to Leslie, with exercise incorporated as a full regimen. Leslie altered her diet to include fat-free protein, olive oil, lots of colorful vegetables, fresh ripe fruit, moderate amounts of whole grains and herbs, and a green drink. She stayed at 1,200 calories a day and began to drink 10, 8-ounce glasses of water daily. She stopped eating excess table salt, fat, ice cream, chocolate, sweets, and high-glycemic foods.

She also joined the fitness club and walked on the treadmill or stair-climber for 45 minutes, five days a week. As she got in better shape she started aerobics classes, and stretching and weight-resistance training. On her thirty-first birthday she weighed 50 pounds less than she had 12 months earlier. She made a vow to lose 17 pounds in the next six months. Leslie was successful, and after one and a half years, she has returned to her normal weight of 95 pounds. All the weight loss was pure excess body fat.

Leslie says she now enjoys the little things many people take for granted. She can bend over and tie her shoes or walk up a flight of stairs without being winded. Shopping is no longer a nightmare and social outings aren't opportunities for embarrassment. She is more confident now, and friendlier, which prompts other people to be friendlier to her.

Leslie has a couple of tips for others who want to follow the Superfood dietary strategy:

- "Never go more than four hours without eating one of the three Superfood meals or two snacks each day. At each of the three meals, I combine some of my protein, fat, fiber, and low-glycemic carbohydrates, for good hormone response. This keeps my insulin output even all day.
- "Always eat some protein first, at each meal, not the carbohydrate. This then slows down the body's response to the carbohydrate and ensures that insulin will be released in moderate amounts.
- "Daily, I consume 10, 8-ounce glasses of pure water through a straw, 10 servings of colorful vegetables, and 2 to 3 servings of fresh fruit. All my protein sources are low-fat. This is manageable.
- "I forgive myself if I miss an exercise session or am faced with an inevitable setback. I am not dieting, I am on a permanent dietary

strategy, to keep me healthy and happy, and it is designed to have some flexibility in it. I do deep breathing to reduce stress. Relief from stress is critical.

- "Whenever I want a piece of candy or a dessert, I eat some protein and fiber like celery or fat-free cottage cheese first so I have an effective protein-to-carbohydrate ratio for balanced insulin response. The protein and fiber slow down the rate of digestion and absorption of the sugars. Just keep the dessert to a moderate portion and enjoy it. It is an anti-nutrient, so make it a rare occasion. Getting older no longer has to mean gaining weight."

Leslie's story is an example of the power of Superfoods to balance the body's nutritional needs and help remove excess and unwanted body fat.

6 POINT SUMMARY

- Portion sizes in North America dramatically increased in the 1980s and 1990s.
- In the 1980s and 1990s, North Americans consumed more calories than they used up, storing those extra calories as fat.
- In their fat-avoidance zeal many people overconsume low-fat or no-fat foods, forgetting that these foods are still loaded with calories.
- Severe calorie-restricted diets turn down the body's "thermostat," causing the fat-burning furnace to slow down, to compensate for the absence of fuel; these diets do not work.
- Diet pills are not the answer to permanent fat loss.
- The Superfood dietary strategy for weight reduction is sensible, natural, allows you to find your own natural weight, and leaves you ultra healthy.

4 POINT ACTION PLAN

- Say goodbye to dieting once and for all. It does not achieve permanent fat loss.
- Control the size of your food portions throughout your three meals and two snacks a day. Do not consume excess calories.
- Establish your Superfoods dietary strategies one meal at a time; never skip a meal or a snack.
- For maximum fat loss and balanced hormonal responses, consume some of your daily allotted protein, fiber, low-glycemic complex carbohydrates, and fat at each of your three meals and one of your two snacks.

Exercise Your Way to
Optimum Health

HEALTH REFLECTION

Exercise is your only fat-free, indoor-outdoor stress reliever.

*If you do not have enough time for exercise, you better reserve
a lot of time for illness.*
Michael Colgan, Ph.D., *Optimum Sports Nutrition*

Physical exercise benefits the healing system.
Dr. Andrew Weil, M.D., *8 Weeks to Optimum Health*

The almanac may predict a heavy rainfall for spring, but no matter how much you squeeze it, you will not get one drop of water out of it. A menu may read beautifully and match our particular food needs, but to get the flavor, taste, nourishment, and benefit, we have to eat the food it describes. Exercise books, videos, gyms, fitness centers, and magazine articles can encourage us to exercise, and researchers can prove its great benefits to optimum health, but unless we make it a consistent part of our lifestyle, we enjoy no benefit from it.

If Not Now—When?

You may have neglected exercising regularly and feel you have lost your suppleness, but there is nothing to prevent you from beginning now. My father, Papa Joe, began to walk and exercise at age 86. My sister-in-law, Lani, began an exercise program after 35 years in a wheelchair. She must be lifted from the wheelchair and put on the floor. She lies on her back and with assistance enthusiastically completes her weight-resistance and flexibility-building routine. These two examples encourage us all to get exercising.

The most important aid to longevity is exercise. Without it, the body's composition gradually alters in favor of fat at the expense of muscle. This progressive deterioration is a primary, but unnecessary, component of aging. In *Biomarkers: The Ten Determinants of Aging You Can Control*, co-authors William Evans and Irwin H. Rosenberg show that people who engage in mild exercise are healthier and enjoy longer life expectancy than people who are sedentary. In one of their studies, a group of adults aged 87 to 96 almost tripled their thigh-muscle strength and increased their muscle mass by 10 percent in only eight weeks. Evans also compared young endurance-trained men with 45-to-60-year-old endurance-trained men. He found that aerobic capacity and percentage of body fat are related to time spent exercising, not to age. Age alone was not a factor in predicting anything, only exercise was. A lack of exercise parallels every aspect of aging.

Wear Out Your Sneakers, Not Your Body

You do not need a complicated fitness program or expensive exercise equipment. As a matter of fact, the exercise I recommend needs no equipment other than a good pair of shoes. That exercise is walking. Unfortunately, we live in a society full of energy-saving devices and not many people are vigorous walkers anymore. Walking tones and stimulates the entire body. Walking exercises all body systems simultaneously, both our brains and our musculoskeletal systems.

Walking is a contralateral movement; that is, alternating simultaneous movement of the right arm and left leg with the left arm and right leg. This is the way the body was intended to move, and it has a harmonizing influence on the whole central nervous system. As a toddler, it was probably difficult for you to learn the coordination of precise contralateral movements. So once you have it, don't give it up! As we age we tend to move from contralateral movements to a shuffle. Keep your contralateral movements swinging in rhythm by brisk walking.

Once you begin walking, you will feel refreshed and energetic. You will also sleep better. Walking will only wear out your sneakers. Unlike your body, they can be replaced. (If you prefer, other activities also provide benefits: swimming, golf if you walk from tee to tee, aerobic dance, aerobics classes, bicycle riding, and weight-resistance training.)

To get the best effects from this exercise, walk briskly for at least a half-hour every day or one hour every other day. While walking, keep your head straight and your chin up and look forward, not down. Walk tall. Keep your shoulders up and level, not rolled forward or hunched. Relax your neck, back, and shoulders. Swing your arms but never let them go above your shoulders. Trace an arc with your hands from your waistband to your chest height. Keep your stomach muscles gently contracted and your back flat. This will keep your posture perfect and give you free-flowing contralateral movements. The wonderful surprise of a good walking technique is how free and fluid it feels.

15 Reasons to Walk Each Day

Walking has to be regular and last for at least 30 minutes to give you the following 15 benefits:
1. builds self-esteem and sense of well-being
2. reduces the risk of heart disease and cancer
3. helps you lose weight, especially fat weight
4. helps to preserve lean muscle mass
5. increases maximum oxygen uptake
6. increases both heart and lung capacity and strength
7. reduces anxiety, stress, and worry
8. slows the rate of joint deterioration
9. elevates mood and alleviates depression
10. helps to keep the bowels regular
11. improves blood circulation to the brain and organs
12. increases "good" HDL cholesterol and reduces "bad" LDL cholesterol
13. increases bone density and helps to prevent osteoporosis
14. strengthens muscles
15. maintains coordination and balance

HOW MANY CALORIES

To determine how many calories you burn while walking, follow this formula:
1. Divide your weight in pounds by 132.
2. Multiply the result by the number of miles you walked.
3. Multiply that result by 75, for the calories burned.

Therefore, a 160-pound person who walked four miles has burned:
1. 160 divided by 132 = 1.22
2. 1.22 x 4 = 4.88
3. 4.88 x 75 = 366 calories burned

Turn Up the Flame

If you commit yourself to a brisk, half-hour walk every other day or, better still, five days a week, you will cover 10 miles each week. That is 40 miles a month or close to 500 miles a year. Not only will your physical health improve, but you will burn fat calories and turn up the flame of your resting metabolism rate (RMR).

Exercising in the morning raises your resting metabolism rate, not only while you are exercising (walking), but for up to 16 to 18 hours after you exercise. This means that you not only burn 150 calories in your 30-minute morning walk, but your body will burn more calories throughout the day. Keep a daily log of the distance you walked.

Set Goals

To make walking a habit, set weekly walking goals such as: (a) walk for 30 minutes, three days a week; and (b) walk briskly for 60 minutes, two days a week. Aim for a total walking time of about 210 minutes. Include shorter half-hour walks, and on two days a week walk for 60 minutes. Use these walks to explore parks, river pathways, college campuses, conservation areas, or wilderness paths. Walk slowly for five minutes to warm up, then walk briskly for 50 minutes. Walk slowly for the last five minutes to warm down. Every 15 minutes, try a "challenge minute" where you walk as fast as you can.

To add some extra walking time to your day, take the stairs rather than the elevator. Park at the end of any parking lot so you walk farther to your destination. Invite a neighbor or friend to walk with you daily, or get a four-legged friend to walk daily. Join a hiking club that walks at your pace. Walk briskly to work.

Superior Combinations

Do not accept quick weight-loss witches' brews or a gimmick-of-the-week diet. The only way to burn fat permanently is to exercise and cut back on the calories you consume each day. As mentioned in Chapter 10, fat is burned only in your mitochondria, the "furnaces" in each cell that burn glucose to give you energy. The more lean muscle you have, the more capacity you have to burn fat. Build lean muscle mass and use low fat protein choices in your diet.

Dr. Neil McCartney and others at McMaster University in Hamilton, Ontario, ran a 10-week study comparing the effects of aerobic exercise alone to aerobics plus weight training in patients with coronary heart disease. The aerobics group showed a 2 percent increase in cardiovascular capacity and an 11 percent increase in endurance, measured as the time to exhaustion on a stationary bike. The aerobics–weight training group showed a 15 percent increase in cardiovascular capacity and a sizzling 109 percent increase in endurance. The aerobics group showed no real increases in strength in leg pressure, leg extensions, or arm curl tests. The aerobics–weight training group showed a 21 percent gain in leg presses, 24 percent gain in leg extensions, and 43 percent gain in arm curls. Which group would you want to be in? The law of optimum health is that all good things reinforce each other.

Walk each day but also do some weight-resistance training (anaerobic exercise) or isometric exercises. Weight-resistance training builds strength, more durable bones, and flexibility. It is the most reliable and measurable form of exercise, and is the only exercise able to develop both bone density and lean body mass. It also increases balance and tensile strength to reduce the likelihood of your falling.

Moreover, it is fun and does not have to be a challenge. If you need help, join a fitness club and receive professional weight-resistance training and monitoring. Strength training has evolved to a science and is extremely sophisticated. Receive training from a qualified staff member before you begin any weight-resistance training, as the correct form is necessary to build lean muscle and avoid injury. Always properly warm up muscles before this exercise.

Your Training Heart Rate

Fitness charts generally advise you to subtract your age from 220 then calculate 70 percent of your answer as your training heart rate. This is supposed to represent 70 percent of your maximum heart rate and the perfect training level for fat loss. (My calculations at 51 years of age would be 220−51 = 169 multiplied by .70 = a training heart rate of 118.) Follow this format for your calculations: 220−your age x .70 = your training heart rate. This is supposed to be the highest level of exercise at which your body mostly burns fat, called the anaerobic threshold. I believe this rate is incorrect.

If you are breathing hard, you are running short on oxygen and have gone beyond the aerobic (using oxygen) threshold. At this stage you do not burn fat, only sugar and some protein. Recent research demonstrates that a walking pace of 40 to 55 percent of your maximum heart rate is the optimal intensity of exercise for fat loss. At this rate you can walk and still carry on a conversation. You do not need to be an athletic star to achieve this goal, just patient and persistent.

Take Some Class Action

In addition to strength training at a fitness center, the YMCA, YWCA, or a community center, consider joining organized classes in some form of aerobic exercise that challenges the heart rate and causes increased oxygen consumption. Some fitness centers, clubs, community swimming pools or Y's offer water exercise classes. Also consider taking yoga, Tai Chi or Feldenkrais classes, which are wonderful centering exercises that will also increase your flexibility, sensitivity, and awareness.

Introduction to Yoga, Tai Chi, Feldenkrais

For some people, these names conjure up images of exotic, esoteric, and foreign practices. However, those who have made yoga, Tai Chi, and Feldenkrais part of their exercise routine know that these great health-giving traditions of movement and posture improve circulation and flexibility, and reduce stress. Yoga, Tai Chi, and Feldenkrais should be performed with a deep sense of appreciation and confidence. Conscientious breathing and movement combine to foster the correct mental setting and attitude. Awareness is brought into every aspect of breath, movement, and pause. Join a class or take private lessons with a qualified instructor in your area.

Yoga

Yoga means union or joining, a controlled effort toward self-integration. There are different expressions of yoga. Hatha yoga (there is also Raja, Karma, and Jnana yoga) gives first attention to the physical body. It is a means of exercise to bring about health and integration in body, mind, and spirit.

Each posture (asana) in hatha yoga is preceded by slow, deliberate, conscientious movements propelled by the breath. The posture is "held," allowing the breath to work as an instrument to release and relax the muscles holding the posture. Coming out of each posture is also attended to with the awareness of movement and breath. In between each posture or pose there is a brief period of relaxation and breathing.

Hatha yoga is based on the belief that when the energy flow of the body is blocked by tension, health is diminished, resulting in sickness. By holding the yoga postures and practicing deep breathing and relaxation, tensions are released, allowing the now-unimpeded energy to flow throughout the system. This is life-giving, life-healing energy.

Tai Chi

Tai Chi was developed by the Taoist monk Chang San-feng in 12th-century China. Tai Chi is often described as a moving meditation. These movements demand a clear concentration of mind so that no disturbance enters the process of breath and movement. Tai Chi is a sequence of generally slow natural movements specifically designed to improve one's health by reducing bodily tension, improving circulation and breathing, and calming the heart and mind. Each movement allows the entire body to be exercised in a balanced, harmonious fashion. The movements increase the circulation of blood and oxygen to all parts of the body; they help to achieve proper alignment of the spine; they use all the major skeletal muscle groups; and they develop balance, coordination, and fine motor control. Moreover, like hatha yoga and Feldenkrais, there are subtle aspects of energy work in Tai Chi that play a vital role in the health and balance of the practitioner.

Feldenkrais

The Feldenkrais method was developed by Moshe Feldenkrais, a physicist, engineer, and judo master. It was designed as a system of education to draw the attention to the entire range of movement. Each movement is made with the utmost care and attention. The movements are slow, fluid, and mainly repetitive, with some variations. This system of movement draws attention to very fine detail and neither stresses, strains, nor forces any muscles or joints. Feldenkrais aims to improve the subtle and the larger movements of the body. It is suitable for all ages, ability or disability, for athletes as well as those with neurological impairments.

In essence, Feldenkrais movements are "relearned" movements. They are designed to change the "set" pathways or patterns in the brain associated with movement. This may sound simplistic and perhaps not very impressive, but let me tell you, the results can be impressive! These "relearned" movements replace the inefficient habitual movements we have become "set" with that may be causing us structural and muscular problems, compounding chronic pain and stress. Through changing our patterns of movement, we also change our patterns of thinking and behavior. The habitual patterns are replaced by new dimensions in thinking, understanding, and behavior, which opens up the opportunity for personal growth.

Walking, plus weight-resistance training, and either hatha yoga, Tai Chi, or Feldenkrais are a perfect combination of aerobics, strength, and flexibility for the human body. Together, they slow down the physiological aging process.

Add spice to your life—try a variety of group activities and begin your class action process now.

Some Other Exercises

Here are other exercises to integrate into your creative day.

Eye Exercises
The eyes take on a heavy workload. Their muscles need to be exercised so tension held in eye muscles will be reduced. Eye exercises bring healing, nutrient-rich blood to eye tissues. Whole-food stores carry booklets dedicated to eye exercises. They are beneficial, easy to do, and remarkably rewarding. One exercise involves first pressing on your temples and rotating your eyes. Next, gently massage the bony ridges of the eyes, pressing firmly on sensitive acupuncture points. Now press eyes shut firmly for ten seconds. Then open them wide and hold for ten seconds. Repeat this cycle of alternate pressing and wide-opening ten times. Another exercise is to move eyes in small circular movements, then trace a large square box and finally trace an imaginary X inside that box.

Face Lift
Raise your eyebrows and open your eyes as wide as possible. At the same time, open your mouth to stretch the muscles around the nose, chin, and mouth. Do this ten times, holding the stretch for 10 seconds each time.

Massage is particularly beneficial. Place your fingers on your chin, move them with upward sweeping movements, making large circular motions around the eyes. This releases stress and fatigue and brings tone to facial skin around the eyes. Focus on your cheekbones and temples. These exercises stimulate the flow of qi (chi)—universal life energy you can feel in your body—over meridian channels in the face, to help tone sagging skin, maintain skin elasticity and flexibility, and revitalize skin tissue.

Scalp
Place your fingertips on your scalp. Do not rub. Rather, massage vigorously so the scalp moves. Try this at many different sites on your scalp. This helps to stimulate hair follicles that causes the shaft to thicken. The massage causes better blood flow to hair roots, and the hair grows quicker; it affects, positively, both its thickness and sheen.

Skin

Before you bathe or shower, rub your entire body vigorously and quickly with either a dry, white cotton washcloth or a natural, soft bristle brush. Begin at your feet and work up towards your head. Do this for three minutes. This causes a greater flow of blood to skin cells that invigorates them with nutrients and also allows the skin to release toxins.

5 POINT SUMMARY

- To derive supercharged health, you must make exercise a consistent part of your lifestyle.
- Walking is a neurologically coordinated body movement termed contralateral movement.
- As we get older, we do not walk, we tend to shuffle if we do not walk regularly in our mid and older years.
- Walking and moderate weight-resistance training are a superior combination of human exercises.
- To develop flexibility and maximize sensitivity, consider joining classes of hatha yoga, Tai Chi, or Feldenkrais.

3 POINT ACTION PLAN

- Make aerobic walking a daily event; keep a daily log.
- Join a fitness center and receive weight-resistance training regardless of your gender or age.
- Join hatha yoga, Tai Chi, or Feldenkrais classes to increase flexibility, sensitivity, and awareness.

Breathing for Relaxation and Stress Management

HEALTH REFLECTION

Breath channels energy and vitality.

The enjoyment of life's gifts constitutes living,
not the number of days we are given to live.
Buddhist saying

If you haven't found a better way, it is only because
you haven't looked hard enough.
Ann Louise Gittleman, M.S., *Supernutrition for Women; Supernutrition for Men*

It is Sunday evening and you are in heavy traffic trying to get home after a relaxing weekend. Out of nowhere an inconsiderate driver cuts in front of you. An adrenaline rush causes your neck, shoulders, and abdominal muscles to tighten up, and your breathing to become rapid, shallow, and high in your chest. These are your body's responses to fear, anger, stress, sadness, and physical pain.

Examine a few more situations in your life. Recall a day when you felt carefree. You probably breathed in deeply, and felt calm and revitalized. At times like this we feel a sense of "being centered." Life is not out of control. Now think of a situation when you had to finish an important task, take a final examination, or complete a work assignment, and felt out of control. As panic, fear, or anxiety gripped you, you probably breathed shallowly.

Unfortunately, shallow breathing has become a way of life for most people, causing a limited amount of oxygen to reach the bloodstream. Shallow breathing also results in fatigue, gas, insomnia, muscle cramps, and feelings of anxiety and panic.

The physical body is an electromagnetic field of energy that operates at its own level of frequency or vibrational vitality. Breath channels energy, or vitality. In yoga philosophy this energy is called *prana*. In Chinese philosophy it is called *qi* (chi), and in Latin, *spiritus*. Deep-breathing patterns strengthen vitality, whereas shallow breathing depletes it.

Knowing how to relax and neutralize stress is the key to being happy. When you breathe deeply, fully, and completely, the fresh oxygen causes your electromagnetic field to vibrate at a higher, balanced rate, which allows you to counteract the stresses of modern life and helps to calm your mind and spirit.

Superfoods and Superbreathing are the inheritance Mother Nature gives equally to each of us. Breathing not only oxygenates the body's 100 trillion cells, it also releases carbon dioxide waste material from each cell. Smooth deep diaphragmatic breathing improves blood circulation, gently massages internal organs, promotes efficient elimination of carbon dioxide, strengthens the heart and lungs, and promotes deeper sleep patterns. Oxygenation also stimulates brain cells and enhances memory capacity. Deep breathing helps us to feel calmer and more centered or focused, both physically and emotionally.

We can survive without food for 40 to 50 days, without water for three to five days, and without oxygen for only three minutes. Oxygen is vital energy.

Breathing with Energy

For centuries Eastern philosophies have stressed the importance of calm, controlled, deep breathing. The Eastern Orthodox Church emphasizes the Jesus Prayer, or one of its variations such as, "My Lord Jesus Christ I Love You," which is conscientiously and mentally chanted in perfect rhythm with each inhalation and exhalation. Practitioners of yoga, martial arts, Tai Chi, stress reduction, aikido, therapeutic touch, full relaxation, and meditation use breathing to draw energy and focus it for use in physical or mental movement. This rhythmic chanting and breathing, accompanied by Divine inspiration, liberates us from the grip of fear, anxiety, attachment, and panic, and brings us to the center of our Being. Calm breathing also has an alkalizing effect upon the body!

Most of us think of the nose as a single passageway and don't pay attention to the fact that the nose is divided into a right and a left nostril. Yogis have regarded the nostrils not as passive entranceways for air, but as connecting points leading inward to a vast system of energy. Put your open palm two inches from your nostrils. Breath in and out forcefully three times. Your exhaled breath should be of equal force from both nostrils, but after years of shallow, unconscious breathing, most of us breathe predominantly through one nostril. We need to unblock and balance the flow of vital energy coming into the body.

Ancient yoga studies conclude that the two nostrils have different energy potentials. The left nostril gives the incoming air a negative charge, while the right nostril gives it a positive charge. This is the same "ionic dance" that creates electrical power at the cellular level when positively charged sodium and potassium shuttle in and out of a negatively charged cell. Opposites attract, so the unified stream of energetically charged air energizes the body and nerves.

Anxiety-Reduction Breathing

Calm breathing exercises, accompanied by visualization techniques, are important for the prevention or release of anxiety. Most anxiety manifests as emotional distress, but it can also trigger strong physical symptoms such as rapid heartbeat, shortness of breath, muscle tension, and tension in the abdominal region.

To practice anxiety-reduction breathing, lie on your back with your knees bent and feet slightly apart. Breathe in and out through your nose. Keep your mouth gently closed. Inhale deeply, visualizing the healing air entering your lungs. As you breathe in, allow your stomach and muscles to relax. Feel the air moving from your lungs to every cell in your body. Now fully exhale through your mouth. As you breathe out, let all your muscles relax and visualize the cells releasing toxins, waste, exhaustion, and tension into the lungs and out with the exhalation. Use the full motion of your lungs with each deep inhalation and exhalation. Repeat this sequence ten times. At the end of the exercise, your entire body will feel tension-free and relaxed.

Purification Breathing

Purification breathing involves breathing through one nostril at a time to force the blocked nostril open and to open energy pathways. When your diaphragmatic breathing (deep breathing) is a steady stream, alternated from one nostril to the other, it deeply calms and strengthens the nervous system, leaving you relaxed and stress-free. In this breathing style there is a modest expansion of the chest wall, but diaphragmatic contraction and expansion predominates.

This pattern takes only two to three minutes and should be practiced as soon as you wake up in the morning and prior to going to sleep at night.

1. Sit comfortably in a chair with your head, neck, and body in a straight line. Or lie on your back, with your arms at a 45-degree angle to your body, palms up. Let yourself relax.
2. Let your breathing continue in a deep, smooth manner. Feel your abdomen, sides, lower back, and chest expand with each inhalation and contract with every exhalation.
3. Bring your right hand slowly to your nose. Use your thumb to gently close the right nostril. Shut your eyes. Exhale through the left nostril, then begin a series of three breaths, in and out, all through the left nostril. Keep the breaths deep, full, smooth, silent, and equal in length.
4. Now close your left nostril with the fourth finger of your right hand while you release the thumb from your right nostril. Exhale deeply, then begin the same series of three deep, full, smooth, silent, equal-in-length inhalations and exhalations. Do this alternating nostril-breathing for nine rounds from each nostril. When complete, sense your breathing, like a deep refreshing stream, coming in and out of both nostrils.

Deep, complete, full breathing is a harmonizer of the body and mind. At least once a day try to do this purification breathing exercise outside in fresh air.

Mind, Breath, and Energy One

Your breath will now be effortless, relaxed, and calm. Your mind can now be easily focused. Focus on your breathing until your mind is not distracted by thoughts. Your attention will now stay wherever you place it. Let yourself "be breathed" at this point. The gracious universe that gave you life now gives you the breath of life. Let the universe breathe in and out of you. Be calm, be passive. This practice will accelerate physical or emotional healing. Feel that you are pure energy, not confined by the limits of a body. You are grounded now. When you are grounded in reality, you can begin to accept life as it is. To struggle against each present moment is like struggling against the physical universe. Keep your attention on what is, and see and appreciate the fullness of every moment.

By going beyond the incessant dialogue of inner turbulence, you change your previous programming. Try to remain nonjudgmental, to become quiet and still, to become free of your mind. Let go of your beliefs, assumptions, opinions, fears, expectations, and self-image of who you think you are. Spend time with yourself and get to know who you really are.

It is here that the miracle of existence is renewed each day. Try it, just for today. Do not hesitate!

Look to this day,
For it is life,
The very life of life.
In its brief course lie all
The realities and verities of existence,
The bliss of growth,
the splendor of action,
The glory of power —
For yesterday is but a dream,
and tomorrow is only a vision.
But today, well lived,
Makes every yesterday a dream of happiness
And every tomorrow a vision of hope.
Look well, therefore, to this day.

—Sanskrit proverb

6 Point Summary

- Shallow breathing is your body's response to fear, anger, stress, sadness, and physical pain.
- Breath channels energy, which is synonymous with vitality.
- Proper breathing oxygenates your 100 trillion cells and removes the waste residue of respiration – carbon dioxide.
- Most of the time you only breathe through one nostril as the other one is blocked.
- Proper breathing will accelerate your physical or emotional healing and reduce emotional or physical anxiety.
- Deep, conscientious breathing harmonizes body and mind.

4 Point Action Plan

- Whenever you feel anxiety, spend two minutes doing anxiety-reduction breathing techniques.

- Use an alternate-nostril breathing technique to unblock both nostrils and oxygenate your body. Do this type of breathing before you go to sleep and when you wake up in the morning.

- Once you have completed the purification breathing exercise, quietly spend time getting to know who you are.

- At least once a day, try to inhale and exhale outside, to get fresh air into your system to accelerate oxygenation and healing.

13

Superfoods and Supernutrition for Women

HEALTH REFLECTION

The law of optimum health is that all good things reinforce each other.

You have to start somewhere. Don't obsess about where you are now;
anticipate where you are going.
Dr. Jesse Lynn Hanley, M.D., director of the Malibu Health and Rehabilitation Center,
and author, *The Definitive Guide for Women*

Women have to empower themselves with superior dietary strategies.
Aim to integrate all the different aspects of health —physical,
mental, emotional and spiritual.
Dr. Gayle Black, director of the Breast Cancer Survival Clinic, New York City;
author, *The Sun Sign Diet*

Of fundamental importance to your energy level is the amount and quality of
food you put in your body. Too many women are eating inadequately. Some
women do not allow themselves adequate time for rest and recreation.
Dr. Carolyn DeMarco, M.D.; author, *Take Charge of Your Body*

In my 25 years of nutritional research I have noted that it is women who are most informed about nutrition and more eager than men to eat their 10 servings of fresh vegetables a day and 2 servings of fruit. Women explore alternative therapies and have taken the lead in the consumers' movement to purchase organic produce, nonprocessed foods, and healthy protein alternatives. Women have demanded that the traditional medical establishment explore and change their practices with the wave of growing natural alternatives. And it has generally been up to women to persuade, inspire, coax, encourage, and push their male friends into beneficial lifestyle changes.

Women's health is a multifaceted challenge: only women experience childbirth, breast-feeding, and menopause. Along with those challenges many women experience premenstrual syndrome (PMS), infertility, endometriosis, fibroid cysts, and perimenopause, none of which men have to deal with. Women must address the whole picture of their health—physical, mental, emotional, and spiritual.

Considerable progress has been made in women's health, and respect for the awesome burden a woman carries has increased tremendously.

Love Your Body the Way It Is

Many women are unhappy with aspects of their body image such as their height, weight, thighs, nose, or hair. If you feel this way, you are not alone. Almost every woman thinks that her body could look a little better.

Moreover, women have been subject to prejudices, patronizing attitudes, and unrealistic expectations. Many women who experience inexplicable feelings of depression, malaise, or anger are told, "Oh, it's probably just your hormones," or "Don't be hysterical." Just last century, pelvic surgery was a common treatment for "emotional instability." (The term "hysteria" is derived from the Greek word *hystera*, which means womb.)

Many women themselves also have unreal expectations of themselves, and become obsessed with achieving youthful skin or trim thighs. These desires make them targets for slick advertising wizards, who play on their fear of aging.

More than ever, women need dietary strategies that give them the self-assurance and ability to accept themselves the way they are. The details of this plan, based on the Superfoods approach to optimum health and well-being, must be put together by each woman individually and followed with a good degree of discipline. Every woman's very best friend, and greatest ally in her quest for optimum health, is her body.

Physical–Mental–Emotional–Spiritual

Change is hard. It is far easier to follow safe old patterns than to burst into new territory. As we age, spontaneous choice and personal growth becomes harder. But new awareness can lead to new ideas, new hopes, new strengths, and new habits. And conscious repetition of new patterns can reinforce the newly awakened woman and cause her unconscious, repetitive, destructive actions to evaporate. The new learning experience creates its own fuel. The awakened woman creates a new model of awareness.

A woman comes into her own when her awareness shows that outside events, images, ideals, and appearances can never hurt her. Once she is free from self-destructive emotions, interpretations, unresolved hurts, negative self-images, and self-judgment, the doors will open to true Reality, which is always here and now. Once she is open to her inner life, and motivated by the truth within, her latent potential will pour out, and she will break free of social expectations. She will allow herself to be guided by her flawless intuition rather than by externally imposed interpretations.

In her silent moments of nonattachment she will experience her intimate stillness. In her active moments she will become love, the profound nurturing balm. She will share her reality unstintingly, for she is inexhaustible—not that she is physically inexhaustible but that she has touched the inexhaustible part of herself that eclipses the physical. She is now ready to nurture and to sustain that part of her. She is both physician and patient.

It is important to realize the imbalance factors early. Symptoms are signs of imbalance; a symptom is not the imbalance itself. Correcting underlying imbalances automatically relieves the symptom.

Breast Cancer

Breast cancer is a devastating disease that takes a terrible toll on women, but there is some good news. After decades of continuously rising cancer rates, statistics indicate a decline in breast cancer mortality. As reported in 1997 in the "University of California at Berkeley Wellness Letter," between 1990 and 1995 there was a 3 percent average decline among breast cancers, and experts predict that within 20 years the rates may drop another 25 percent, as people use better diets to protect themselves from the disease. The bad news is that rates of both lung and lymphatic cancers are up among women. Women can guard themselves against these cancers by not smoking and by eating Superfoods, which cleanse the lymphatic system.

A study led by Inger Thune at the Institute of Community Medicine of the University of Tromso in Norway suggests that regular exercise gives women some protection against breast cancer. The study's 25,624

CANCER RATES AND WOMEN

Cancer Type	Women	Cancer Type	Women
All cancers	-1.1%	Lymphatic	+3.2%
Lung	+6.4%	Breast	-6.3%
Colorectal	-4.8%	Ovarian	-4.8%
Oral	-10.5%	Cervical	-9.7%

female participants, aged 20 to 54, who exercised four hours a week, reduced their risk of developing breast cancer by 37 percent. The more these women exercised, the less susceptible they were to the disease, investigators found. One leading hypothesis is that the less estrogen women are exposed to, the less their risk of contracting breast cancer. That may be the reason, for example, that women who begin menstruating late are at a lower risk, as are those who enter menopause early. Research shows that exercise reduces the amount of estrogen pumped out by a woman's ovaries. In 1996, *The Journal of the National Cancer Institute* reported that dietary modification can reduce estrogen levels in a woman's body. A diet that contains 20 percent calories from fat and that provides 40 grams of fiber each day for 7 to 10 weeks resulted in a decrease in estrogen. This program is essentially the same as the Superfood dietary strategies and the 55/25/20 Superfood meal construction plan recommended in Chapter 9. If a woman combines exercise, the Superfood meal construction plan, which includes protective phytochemicals with 3 to 5 servings of a soy-food source weekly, and the breathing-meditation exercises suggested in Chapter 12, she will be taking action *before* she develops the symptoms of cancer.

A Woman's Superfood Strategy

For the best preventive approach a woman should:
- Eat a minimum of 10 servings of organic vegetables daily and two ripe, whole fruits.
- Include miso, soy milk, tofu, tempeh, textured vegetable protein (TVP), soy isolate protein powder, a green drink, sea vegetables, sourdough whole-grain breads (no wheat products), 1 to 2 tablespoons of omega-3 EFAs such as flaxseed oil daily and one tablespoon of extra-virgin organic olive oil on your salads.
- Take a high-quality multi-vitamin-mineral-antioxidant supplement daily that contains 200 mcg of selenium, 200 mcg of chromium picolinate, the full range of carotenoids, and the full range of at least 400 IU vitamin E tocopheryls as dietary antioxidants and nutrients to help the cells defend themselves from cancer processes. (See Appendix for sources.)
- Daily, consume sea vegetables and Celtic sea salt, essential for their easily absorbable iodine and sodium, which support the health of the thyroid gland.

- Include a quality green drink such as GREENS+ to support peak performance and accelerated healing.
- Take special care to eat organic produce and drink pure water. There appears to be a direct link between toxic chemicals and breast cancer rates. In areas of substantial pesticide use, where highly contaminated groundwater is the sole source of drinking water, the breast cancer rates are unusually high. Carcinogenic chemicals in unfiltered water should be avoided.
- Avoid alcohol consumption. There is a correlation between alcohol intake and breast cancer. The Harvard School of Public Health tracked the nutritional habits of a group of nearly 90,000 nurses for four years. Women in this study who consumed between three and nine alcoholic drinks a week experienced nearly a 150 percent increased risk of breast cancer.
- Drink your 6 to 12, 8-ounce glasses of water with 6 tablespoons of fresh lemon or lime juice daily to properly prehydrate.
- Exercise 3 to 5 times per week incorporating both aerobics and weight-resistance exercises.
- Practice daily visualization techniques; close your eyes and feel a healthy, revitalizing energy cleansing and healing your breasts, ovaries, and uterus. Visualize the flow of more supportive nutrients to the breasts and feel the heat as concentrated energy bathes the breasts.
- Daily, both when you wake up and before you go to sleep, practice the breathing and meditation exercises outlined in Chapter 12.
- Hatha yoga, Tai Chi, or Feldenkrais movements are particularly influential in supporting women's optimum mental and physical performance. These activities realign the energy patterns in the body.
 (Note: If you do have breast cancer you may have to eliminate all dairy foods except plain white organic yogurt (which is necessary for superior intestinal ecology and is very alkalizing). Eliminate red meat (a source of saturated fat), refined sugar, and hydrogenated oils. Eat moderate amounts of whole grains, and more beans and vegetables that decrease estrogen levels.)

Hormones

Superfoods can be hormone helpers. They contain genistein, protease inhibitors, and daidzein that are phytoestrogens that help to regulate estrogen levels. Specifically, soybeans, soy-based foods, green peas, dried beans, split peas, lentils, garbanzo and green beans are most beneficial.

The best source of unheated phytoestrogens occurs in organically sprouted soy sprouts, also contained in high-quality green drinks. (See Appendix for sources.) Superfoods are low-fat but include the necessary EFAs and fiber to support hormonal production.

Asian women on their traditional low-fat, high-fiber diets have anywhere from a 400 to 600 percent lower incidence of breast cancer than North American women. Asian women's diets are generally 20 percent fat calories with 35 grams of fiber. North American women typically consume a diet that is a staggering 40 percent fat with only 15 grams of fiber. Fiber reduces estrogen by binding with it in the small intestine and eliminating it from the body. If there is not enough fiber in the diet, the estrogen is reabsorbed and causes an estrogen overload that may be responsible for the initiation of breast cancer.

Flaxseeds contain phytochemicals called lignins. Like soy phytoestrogens (isoflavones), lignins bind to estrogen receptors and help to inhibit the growth of estrogen-dependent cancers, in the same fashion that the phytochemicals (phytoestrogens) daidzein and genistein, from soy, do. Add two tablespoons of flaxseeds, which you have ground to a powder in a coffee grinder, to your cereal or soup or salads. Superfood cruciferous vegetables such as broccoli, cauliflower, and brussels sprouts contain protective chemicals called indoles and isothiocyanates, which, respectively, help to inactivate estrogen and increase the activity of enzymes that help to detoxify carcinogens.

Personal Hygiene Products

Tampons and pads that are whiter-than-white contain rayon. Rayon is a wood-pulp derivative that undergoes chlorine bleaching to give it that gleaming sanitary look. Dioxin, a by-product of chlorine bleaching, is a known carcinogen. It accumulates in fatty tissue and has been linked to cancer, endometriosis, and immune system suppression.

Rayon may also be implicated in the amplification of TSS-T1 (staphylococcus aureus bacteria), the cause of toxic shock syndrome (TSS). A study published in 1994 in the journal *Infectious Disease in Obstetrics and Gynecology* suggests that all-cotton pads and tampons may reduce the risk of TSS when compared with rayon or rayon-blend pads and tampons. Health food stores, pharmacies, and quality grocery stores now carry 100 percent unbleached cotton personal hygiene products.

Premenstrual Syndrome

Premenstrual syndrome, or PMS, is a range of 150 symptoms that can occur one to two weeks prior to menstruation. Bloating, weight gain, acne, migraines, moodiness, irritability, and breast tenderness are some of the most common symptoms. Here are some strategies that might help:

- Reduce or remove coffee, alcohol, sugar, and table salt from your diet since these substances tend to aggravate PMS.
- Eat high-fiber foods, since they bind with estrogen and help carry it out of the body, and PMS symptoms are the result of too much estrogen circulating in the body.
- Eat a large colorful salad daily, 10 servings of vegetables, herbal garnishes, and 2 to 3 pieces of ripe, seasonal fruit or berries.
- Use flaxseed, hemp seed, borage, black currant and evening of primrose oils or fatty fish (or their oils) such as salmon, which seem to help a wide variety of symptoms because of anti-inflammatory properties contained in their essential fatty acids (EFAs).
- Drink 6 to 12, 8-ounce glasses of water daily and try a herbal tea combination of dandelion leaf, skullcap, and parsley. St.-John's-wort and kava kava are two herbs that are also helpful for stress reduction.
- Use a natural progesterone cream during the two weeks prior to menstruation. PMS symptoms are caused by a progesterone deficiency which somehow causes an estrogen imbalance. Consult you healthcare professional to fine-tune your exact progesterone needs. (See Appendix for source from Transitions for Health, or check your local health food store.)

Pregnancy

Pregnancy is another area of a woman's life where preventive health can be especially rewarding. A Superfood dietary strategy offers a pregnant woman the opportunity to give a new human being the best possible start to a healthy life, both mentally and physically.

If you are able to plan your pregnancy, begin to use Superfood dietary strategies *before* you become pregnant. A growing fetus can drain your nutritional stores; therefore, the higher your nutrient levels to begin with, the better off both you and your baby will be. It is, however, never too late to start.

In addition to diligently following the Superfood dietary strategy, supplement your diet to ensure that the developing child has sufficient vitamins and minerals that are being drawn from your supply and rapidly incorporated into the brain and developing organs of the fetus.

A multi-vitamin-mineral-antioxidant supplement that contains at least 50 mg each of the B vitamins, 400 IU of vitamin E as a full range of tocopherols and also carotenoids such as alpha- and beta-carotene are necessary daily. In addition, consider taking 800 mcg of folic acid and 30 mg of zinc as an amino acid chelate. Most multi-vitamin-mineral-antioxidant supplements contain 400 mcg of folic acid, so you may need to take an additional 400 mcg of folic acid. You may require between 2,000 and 4,000 mg daily of vitamin C in divided doses. Take an iron supplement only under the care of a health-care professional. If you are directed to take iron, generally you will take 30 mg daily, and it should be ingested with one of your doses of vitamin C for better absorption. Take the iron and vitamin C between meals and all other supplements with your morning meal, or better still, half your supplements with breakfast and half with supper. (Check with your health-care professional and midwife for sources of good supplements. Also, see Appendix for sources.)

Exercise regularly and maintain your normal weight while pregnant. Researchers at Boston University School of Public Health found that the incidence of neural tube defects in infants escalated with increasing pregnancy weight.

Breast-feeding

A healthy woman should breast-feed her child if possible. Breast-fed babies suffer less infections, allergies, colic, and diarrhea. The most convincing argument for breast-feeding is that human milk is the perfect food for infants. If the mother eats well on a Superfood dietary strategy, her milk will be far superior to any store-bought formula. Breast milk is also customized to the needs of the baby. The nutritional content of breast milk is different for premature and full-term infants, and it's different still for older babies. Infant formulas can never reproduce this made-to-order quality of mother's milk.

Breast-fed babies have a health advantage over those given formula: the immunity factors in human milk. Nature guards newborns with an infection-fighting elixir designed to carry them safely through the first few years of life. In an article in *Pediatric Infectious Diseases Journal* in 1993, researchers noted that people who were breast-fed as infants are less likely to get diabetes and some types of cancer.

Infants' brains and nervous systems grow rapidly. It is vital they receive adequate nutrients for proper neurological development and that the mother receive them first.

Menopause

Long before menopause occurs and menstrual cycles cease, some women in their thirties and forties are subject to distressing symptoms. The transition from fertility to infertility, called perimenopause, is a time of wild hormone swings as a woman's body produces less and less estrogen. This change can trigger a long list of problems, among them hot flashes, dry skin, facial blemishes, insomnia, depression, and lapses in memory.

For years women thought they had only two choices for dealing with menopause: avoid taking synthetic hormones altogether and suffer the occasional debilitating effects of menopause or accept a prescription for Premarin (an estrogen derived from pregnant mares' urine) and Provera (synthetic progesterone) and with it perhaps an increased risk of some cancers. Women in their thirties were also given birth control pills. Many women have been unhappy with the options given to them by mainstream medicine.

There are, however, other choices than the ones mainstream medicine has to offer. Superfoods such as flaxseeds and soy-derived products like tofu, tempeh, soy milk, and miso contain phytochemicals known as phytoestrogens, which are estrogens made from plants. These plant-sourced estrogens mimic regular estrogen and help balance the diminishing estrogen levels a woman experiences beginning approximately at age 30. In her book *Dr. Susan Love's Hormone Book*, Dr. Love questions the efficiency of regular hormone-replacement therapies. At 49 she has entered perimenopause. To cope, she exercises daily, adds phytoestrogen-rich Superfoods like soybeans (or their products) and flaxseed to her diet, and drinks black cohosh herbal teas to natural-balance her hormones. In their book *Natural Woman, Natural Menopause*, Dr. Marcus Laux and Christine Conrad also highly recommend plant-derived hormones from the Superfoods soy and flaxseed.

You can use these suggestions to increase and balance your estrogen levels. To balance your progesterone levels use a topical cream (see Appendix for sources). You may want to talk to your health-care professional about using other hormones such as DHEA and testosterone.

More than anything else, nothing matches paying attention to diet. Each day, consume 2 tablespoons of organic flaxseeds, ground in a coffee grinder, and sprinkled on cereals, soups, or salads. Drink low-fat soy milk daily, and consume either firm tofu, miso, or tempeh as a plant-sourced protein and phytoestrogen.

High-quality green drinks contain soy sprouts high in the two most active phytoestrogens—genistein and daidzein. Soy sprouts are the only unheated sources of phytoestrogens. And because they are not heated, they also contain the full natural range of vitamins, minerals, fiber, and enzymes. Use a green drink mixed in a liquid of choice twice a day, once before breakfast and again midafternoon, about 4:00 p.m.

Superfood herbs also ease the changes of menopause. Whole-food stores carry combinations of skullcap, licorice root, angelica root, red raspberry leaves, Siberian ginseng, dong quai, black cohosh, red clover, blessed thistle, wild yam, vitiate, and chaste tree berry that appear to contain plant hormones that increase estrogen and progesterone levels in the body and help to balance hot flashes and mood swings.

Osteoporosis

In 1993, an estimated 1.8 million women in Canada were afflicted with osteoporosis, a deterioration of bone mass that can eventually lead to fractures and curvature of the spine. In addition to the suffering caused, the disease cost at least $465 million in acute health care, and more than $800 million in long-term care, according to Dr. Carolyn DeMarco. A bone scan is the most accurate way to assess whether you are losing bone.

A Superfood dietary strategy can protect against the ravages of osteoporosis. The single biggest factor in preventing osteoporosis is to remain with a diet of 75 percent alkalizing and 25 percent acidifying foods. In central Africa and Japan, where women naturally eat this way and their diet averages only 300 mg of calcium a day, osteoporosis is uncommon. Monitor your urine pH to determine if your urine is slightly alkaline. An acidifying diet encourages calcium to be stripped from the bone to help neutralize or buffer strong corrosive acids in the diet (see Chapter 5). In addition, eat calcium-rich foods such as dulse, sunflower seeds, sesame seeds, deep green vegetables, fat-free organic yogurt, fat-free cottage cheese, whole grains, broiled chicken, or fish.

In *Preventing and Preserving Osteoporosis*, Dr. Alan Gaby stresses a comprehensive holistic program that includes diet, walking, weight-resistance training, avoidance of environmental toxins such as pesticides and herbicides on produce, and natural hormone therapy. He also recommends a broad range of nutritional supplements such as 1,200 to 1,500 mg of calcium daily combined with 600 to 800 mg of magnesium for women who eat meat, and for vegetarians (no meat or dairy) 1,000 mg of calcium daily and 500 mg of magnesium.

Exercise causes calcium to stay in the bones. Walk briskly for 30 minutes five days a week. Walk briskly for at least a half-hour every day, and one hour every other day. One day a week go for a two hour walk. Ideally, arms and legs should be exercised to maintain strong bones. Research suggests that women who exercise, even if they begin after the start of perimenopause or menopause, can improve their bone mass. In her book *Strong Women Stay Young*, Miriam Nelson, of the Tufts Centre for Aging, Boston, writes that women who do weight-resistance training at least twice a week for 40 minutes a session had greater gains in bone mass than women who did no weight-resistance training, even if they walked daily.

From her twenties to her early forties a woman is at the height of her reproductive capacity. This is a prime time for taking preventive-health measures to strengthen bones and establish a Superfood dietary strategy that will ensure strong healthy bones.

Breast Cysts

Breast cysts are fluid-filled lumps that cause pain, tenderness, swelling, and sometimes nipple discharge. They usually occur prior to or during menstruation. Cysts are caused by either estrogen excess or an increase in sensitivity of breast tissue to localized estrogen. Symptoms occur with the body's monthly changes in estrogen levels. These lumps are actually normal changes in breast anatomy, and are not associated with an increase in breast cancer. Lumps that do not go away after menstruation should be examined by a health-care practitioner.

Breast Cyst Therapy

Natural therapies can greatly mitigate the symptoms of breast cysts. Try some of the following:

- Since the liver is the organ that alters estrogen and allows the body to excrete it, follow a diet that supports liver function. An alkalizing dietary strategy will help (see Chapter 5). Soy lecithin granules, choline, and inositol have antioxidant actions that detoxify the liver. Licorice root helps to protect and regenerate liver cells. Three other herbs that stimulate liver function are dandelions, burdock, and chicory root. Eat them in salads or drink them as unsweetened herbal teas.

- Consume nutritional yeast (such as Red Star) that contains the whole vitamin B family.
- Evening primrose oil or, my preference, omega-3 EFAs from organic flaxseed oil, helps balance all hormones, including estrogen.
- Sea vegetables or Celtic sea salt are good sources of potassium iodide, effective in reducing breast tenderness.
- Women with breast cysts should avoid caffeine and even decaffeinated beverages, which many women are sensitive to. The culprit in the coffee, tea, cola, or chocolate (caffeine sources) is a compound called methylxanthines that causes breast cyst overstimulation in some women.
- If you consume meat, try to purchase organically fed animals not raised with hormones and antibiotics. Over half the antibiotic used is with animals. These substances may interfere with women's natural hormones, as may the rBGH hormone (bovine growth hormone) used in dairy cows. If you drink milk, ask your store to check that it is free of rBGH as it does not need to be shown on the label.
- For both breast cancer protection and breast cyst lumps, avoid alcohol consumption.
- Make sure you get enough sleep and reduce your stress levels with exercise and breathing-meditation sessions.
- Try therapeutic touch, massage therapy, reflexology, or acupuncture to stimulate blood and healing energy flow to the breasts. Aerobic exercises promote lymph flow to the area of the breast, helping to remove metabolic waste and increase the flow of nutrients.
- Have a qualified health professional teach you how to do your own breast self-examinations (BSE) so you know exactly how a healthy breast feels.
- Apply natural progesterone cream (such as Pro-Gest, which contains more than 400 mgs of progesterone per ounce of cream—see Appendix for sources) on the tender lumps themselves or rub it in soft areas of skin such as the inside of the forearms, to help relieve breast tenderness. At first this increases breast tenderness by increasing estrogen receptors in the breasts, then it decreases them and the tenderness goes away.

Thyroid Deficiencies—Running on Empty

If you can't seem to connect with your friends, your children, your mate, or please your boss, and you can't concentrate, your thyroid may be malfunctioning. If you're too exhausted to get out of your favorite easy chair, are constipated, and can't remember what you had for lunch yesterday, if you are constantly feeling cold, if you spend the weekend sleeping, feel depressed or just plain stupid, your thyroid may be malfunctioning.

Thyroid disorders, to which women are particularly vulnerable, are generally very easy to treat, but are also easy to miss or misdiagnose. They can be detected with a blood test called a thyroid-stimulating hormone (TSH) assay. Many women like to piggyback the TSH assay with a cholesterol test. If you do this every five years after the age of 30 or 35, you can identify and treat thyroid problems before symptoms appear. If you have been suffering from a "laundry list" of symptoms, if you feel sluggish, tire easily, or are depressed, it is prudent to have your TSH tested.

The most common thyroid problem is an underactive thyroid; this condition is called hypothyroidism. Some experts estimate that one in five women will suffer from hypothyroidism. To test yourself for an underactive thyroid, keep a thermometer by your bed. When you awaken in the morning, place the thermometer under your armpit and hold it there for 15 minutes. Keep still and quiet. Any motion will upset your temperature reading. This is an ideal time to do your breathing exercises and meditation. A temperature reading of 97.6 degrees Fahrenheit or lower may indicate an underactive thyroid. Take your morning temperatures for five continuous days. If they are consistently low, have the TSH assay.

Thyroid-Supporting Strategies

- If you feel tired, cold, or continually rundown, consume a herbal tea containing bayberry and black cohosh to support thyroid function. A diet rich in iodine such as seafood, sea vegetables, and green drinks are a good addition to a dietary strategy to support the thyroid.
- Use nutritional yeast as a source of naturally occurring B vitamins.
- Consider using one amino acid—L-tyrosine. Most health professionals suggest 500 mg twice daily with 50 mg of vitamin B_6 and 100 mg of vitamin C to aid absorption.

Yeast Infections

Yeast lives in the body as a normal part of the flora. Its main home is in the 29 feet of the intestines where the moist, dark, warm temperature is an ideal breeding ground. It also lives in the mouth, vagina, skin, and intestinal tract of healthy people and is kept in check by "good" bacteria. When the yeast overpowers other bacteria and becomes dominant, irritation, itching, and burning occur. Generally, the origin of the infection is the use of antibiotics, which kill off the normal bacteria in the vagina and bowel and allow yeast to grow uncontrolled. When this happens, you feel as if you are being dragged through hell. Symptoms include fatigue, headache, muscle ache, depression, and disruption of the endocrine, immune, and nervous systems.

Any woman on antibiotics should take a "friendly" bacterial culture like acidophilus regularly (my personal favorite is a life-culture product called Bio-K+) or a homeopathic remedy toward the end of her antibiotic regimen and for a few days afterward. Just before menstruation, women are more apt to have yeast infections because progesterone is increased in the body and this hormone is more friendly to yeast development. Birth control pills dramatically increase the incidence of yeast infection in some women. It is estimated that 65 percent of all women deal knowingly or unknowingly with chronic yeast infections.

To tame the yeast, or candida albicans, your dietary strategy must include a vigilant anti-candida treatment program. I suggest you work closely with a knowledgeable health professional and consider the recommendations below.

An Anti-Candida Plan

It is impossible to eliminate candida completely. Your goal should be to control the overgrowth, and bring yourself back to health where a strong immune system prevails.

- Cut out all sugar—period! The average North American consumes 52 teaspoons of sugar daily, most of it hidden in processed foods or bakery items. You must avoid sugar, soft drinks, soybean products and tofu, wine, beer, alcohol, vinegar, all fruit except lemon and lime juice, flour products, nuts and nut butters, as they "feed" the fungus.
- Follow the Superfood dietary strategies carefully. If you eat meat, choose antibiotic-free turkey and chicken.
- Herbs that contain potent essential oils that are powerful candida-killing substances are garlic, ginger, echinacea, pau d'arco, cinnamon, thyme, and rosemary. You may use them raw in salads, as a tea, in a supplemental capsule, or in cooking.
- Use a probiotic supplement such as Lactobacillus acidophilus daily (try Bio-K+). This substance has been shown to inhibit the growth of candida. High-quality green drinks contain 2.5 billion "friendly bacteria" per

teaspoon, from seven various types of "good bacteria" that help to repopulate the intestinal tract with the proper healthy bacteria. Once these bacteria, whose natural home is the intestines, reinoculate the intestinal walls, candida overgrowth diminishes rapidly.

- Other oral anti-candida substances are grapefruit-seed extract, caprylic acid products, Bentonite clay, which absorbs bacteria, and diluting tea tree oil (a couple of drops) in a half-cup of water used as a douche. Tea tree oil mixed with water and drunk is an effective anti-fungal agent.

- An ingredient in spirulina called calcium spirulan is effective against a series of fungus, bacteria, and viruses. Twice daily, use a green drink containing spirulina mixed in water.

- Consume 40 grams of fiber daily to keep the inner ecology of your intestines healthy and cleansed. Reread the information on fiber and carbohydrates contained in Chapter 9. Innocent-looking puffed rice cakes feed candida albicans because their processed cell walls are broken down and they release their glucose like a lightning bolt. This allows rapid growth of candida.

- Avoid monosodium glutamate (MSG), a substance which is added to many prepackaged foods or which is used in Asian cooking.

- Try acupuncture, which has shown dramatic results with candida albicans balancing.

- Visualization techniques (sit quietly and visualize the candida albicans becoming less plentiful and less active) have been extremely helpful to some women. Remember, for visualization to work, you must believe in it.

- Homeopathic remedies (aquaflora, candex, and others) are beneficial for some individuals, if the treatment is supervised by a qualified homeopathic doctor.

- Locate a nutritionally oriented dentist to remove mercury amalgam tooth fillings. They leak mercury, which is an antibiotic that kills many bacteria, but encourages those that escape its power to develop into superstrains, which then flourish and grow unopposed. One of the beneficiaries of this process is candida albicans.

Be patient with candida albicans infection as it may take three to six months to balance your intestinal tract and reduce both the symptoms and the actual candida overgrowth itself.

Final Thoughts for Women

A Superfoods dietary strategy will rejuvenate every part of your body. You will be amazed at the energy, clarity, and mental acuity you will enjoy each and every day. You will have the ability to control the most fundamental aspects of your body chemistry: the antioxidant coursing through your bloodstream to maintain your vision; the fiber soaking up extra estrogen in your intestines; the phytochemical triterpenoids blasting a cancer cell; the micronutrients responsible for eliminating invading carcinogenic chemicals; the sulphoraphane or indoles helping to vigorously dismantle bacteria, viruses, and parasites; the acidophilus "friendly bacteria" giving your intestines and immune system the added advantage to defend itself against yeast infections; the vigorous chlorophyll protecting you from the ravages of early aging. You will be delightfully surprised with your progress, and you will be able to live a more robust life. It is all a gift of Nature, you only have to use it.

How you feel, how you look, and the quality of your life depend to a great degree on how you fuel your body and mind. Will the awakening woman, free of the psychologically manipulative, crafty, subtle images of advertising and past destructive behaviors, fuel herself with nicotine, alcohol, sugar, MSG, sodium aluminum sulfate (baking powders), mercury or methylxanthines, which lead to possible malignancies and cellular aberrations? Defy the advertising wizards who have no regard for your intricate and beautifully crafted body. Their genetically engineered and processed foods may look good, smell good, and taste good, but they carry a deadly price tag. Don't pay that painful price.

Simply put, you trigger your own physiological responses by your response right now. Don't speculate. Instead, accelerate your health and healing. You will never feel sorry you did!

What you hold, may you always hold! What you do, may you always do and never abandon. But with swift pace, light step, unswerving feet, so that even your steps stir up no dust, may you go forward securely, joyfully, and swiftly, on the path of prudent awakening.
—Saint Clare of Assisi (1195-1253),
friend and disciple of Saint Francis of Assisi

There once was an old wise woman dining on lentils and crusty bread. She was approached by a young maiden who lived comfortably dancing for the king. The maiden said, "Old woman, learn the wizardry of pleasing the king and you will not have to live on old bread and a few lentils."

The old woman smiled, "Learn to live on crusty bread and lentils—and you will not have to please the king."

—Old Sufi story

3 POINT SUMMARY

- More than ever, women need to become empowered with dietary strategies that give them the self-assurance and ability to formulate a comprehensive plan for self-preservation.
- Women must free themselves from self-destructive emotions, interpretations, unresolved hurts, negative self-images, and self-judgment and awaken to their own latent potentials.
- There are progressive Superfood dietary strategies that will protect a woman from breast cancer, breast cysts, thyroid deficiencies, and yeast infections.

6 POINT ACTION PLAN

- Employ the simple breathing and meditation exercise suggestions in Chapter 12 to help you develop your own intuition and to begin the inward journey to full awakening.
- Take time each day to consider what you will eat, why you will eat it, and exactly what effect the food will have on your physical and mental performance.
- Use a high-quality multi-vitamin-mineral-antioxidant supplement daily, to ensure your body obtains all its micronutrients.
- Avoid consuming processed foods.
- Eat 10 servings of organic vegetables and 2 to 3 pieces of ripe, whole fruit daily.
- Eat a large, fresh, colorful salad daily.

Superfoods and Supernutrition Mostly for Men

Forgiveness and thankfulness open your door
to unconditional love and dynamic health.

A Superfood diet allows your body's inherent healing system to work at peak
performance as you encounter the challenges of day-to-day life.
Dr. Zoltan Rona, M.D., *Return to the Joy of Health*

All I have seen teaches me to trust the Creator, for all I have not seen.
Ralph Waldo Emerson

It is one of the cruelest surprises of middle age that life holds challenges for
which no amount of time on the stairmaster can prepare one.
Jerry Adler, writer, contributor to *Newsweek*

Men have shorter life spans than women and are generally more reluctant to seek medical care when they are ill. Men also lead in eight of the top ten causes of death in North America (heart disease; hypertension; cancer; prostate cancer; breast cancer; stroke; severe liver malfunction; kidney disease; lung disease; circulatory diseases). Men's weight is concentrated in the middle of the body, and they are more prone to cardiovascular disease, heart attack, and emotional stress, which leave them more susceptible to fatalities in their forties, fifties, and sixties.

Reluctant to seek counseling or emotional support groups to share their anxieties and frustrations, men constitute only about 25 percent of the patients of psychologists, weight-loss centers, and stress-reduction clinics. At a superficial level, men feel confident if they can converse about the local baseball team, their job, or a recent fishing trip. At a deeper level, men feel estranged.

Men suffer because they feel limited, because they don't see how limitless they really are. They limit what is limitless, they try to control the uncontrollable, condition the unconditioned, and it makes them feel helpless or miserable. Becoming aware that every man knows but a little or understands but a little will give men inspiration to move forward. Instead of exploiting, awakened men explore new possibilities. By realizing that they are imperfect, men can become both accountable and responsible.

Write Your Own Future

Men desperately need a lifestyle change! To improve their health and their connections to the world, men must make a special effort to practice Superfoods dietary strategies, especially to limit their consumption of protein and fat—which means staying away from 12-ounce steaks, slabs of cheese, and salads smothered in salad dressing. Most men do not get their hormone-balancing omega-3 EFAs, their 8 to 12, 8-ounce glasses of pure water, colon-protecting fiber, or cancer and heart attack–preventing Superfoods. Inadequate nutrition puts most men in a subtle but profoundly altered state of consciousness that prevents their peak mental and physical performance. The awakened man must keep saturated fat, which is so unhealthy to the heart and arteries, to a minimum. As men age they have to make an effort to consume more stress-reducing fruits, anti-free-radical whole grains, cancer-preventing vegetables, and some vegetarian main dishes. Men must eat more slowly to enjoy eating life-sustaining healthy food.

Men need to reflect before consuming a meal, to thank the sustaining earth, the food itself, the food preparers, God, the limitless moment, and to think about all humanity without sufficient food at that moment.

Men need to be actively involved in writing the stories of their well-being. The good news for men is that increasingly, they are actively seeking to improve their health through nutrition. Write your own future! Don't wait to be another early-mortality statistic.

Success Strategies

How can I keep up? Do you fall into the trap of thinking that doing your best is enough? Have you found, though, that your best does not satisfy you, your friends, your spouse, or your co-workers? This unhealthy cycle, caused by a need to excel at all costs, is propelled by your ego. The harder you work, the more frustrated you feel and the more your job feels empty. You, unfortunately, are looking for approval and control. Begin to do the breathing exercises described in Chapter 12. Anxiety is built up structurally and can be relieved effectively with breathing exercises.

Study and apply the following ways you can remove stress and improve your health:

- Stop for two minutes twice a day and breathe deeply to ensure both nostrils are open and you are oxygenating your system fully.
- Keep a water container with a secure lid and straw in it near you at work and sip this pure water regularly throughout the day.
- Eat fewer processed foods like candy bars or chips. Instead, eat apples, oranges, berries, celery or carrot sticks for snacks at work.
- For lunch, eat a colorful salad with an organic olive oil dressing and a small portion of protein such as fat-free cottage cheese, water-packed albacore tuna, firm tofu, or a skinless chicken breast.
- Get exercising. Only 4 percent of the workforce in North America walks to work. Our hunter-gatherer ancestors used 2,900 calories a day. The average person burns up only 1,800 calories daily. Exercising in the morning or walking to work to raise your resting metabolic rate (RMR) gives your cellular motors that extra rev.
- Avoid taking antidepressants (prescriptions for these drugs are up 102 percent since 1992).
- Begin a session of meditation or prayer with your morning or evening breathing exercises, just before sleep, and when you wake up in the morning. Get to know your spiritual side, become familiar with it, trust it, feel the peace from your own spiritual unfolding.
- Get support with special problems. Seek out 12-step support groups such as Alcoholics Anonymous or positive people who support you and cheer on your daily successes.
- Get a walking partner!

Alcohol Gives Me Relief

Alcohol takes a terrible toll in our lives. It is involved in almost 50 percent of all traffic fatalities, and is often a factor in violent crimes. Alcohol can damage the entire body but it primarily affects the brain, by destroying neurotransmitters, the messengers of brain-body communication. It also depletes amino acids such as tryptophan, causing depression, sleeplessness, and confusion. But wait—it gets worse. Levels of serotonin, a brain chemical involved in neural mechanism, become imbalanced, replacing a natural inner sense of calm with anxiety.

The good news—change is possible. Many men have abandoned lifelong substance abuse and, as a result, watched their physical, emotional, and mental functions improve dramatically.

If you want to cut down your alcohol intake or give it up altogether, apply some of the following strategies:

- Avoid addictive or physiologically stressful caffeine-laden drinks.
- Practice portion control and reduce your sugar consumption.
- Drink from 8 to 12, 8-ounce glasses of pure water daily. This will help you to detoxify your liver and cells, and eliminate those toxins.
- Follow my suggestions for a detox day, one day a week, or Harvey Diamond's periodic mono-dieting program as outlined in Chapter 8. Both approaches are restorative.
- Use a high-quality multi-vitamin-mineral-antioxidant supplement. (See Appendix for sources.) Consider using homeopathic remedies. Inquire about them at a health food store.
- Consume more fresh, organic produce to help you detoxify.
- Use milk thistle daily or imbibe a high-quality green drink daily containing this herb. Conventional medicine has nothing to match the liver support that milk thistle gives.
- Engage in regular exercise; it will make you feel good and relieve stress from your liver.
- Locate a sauna, steambath, or a "sweat lodge" near you and use them twice a week. This will sweat toxins out of your system. Be sure to drink extra water when you take a sauna. Take your saunas in the evening, just before your meditation session, then sleep.

Your body is your ally. Support it one day at a time.

Prostate Problems

The prostate is a walnut-sized gland in men that surrounds the urethra, located at the neck of the bladder. Almost all men over the age of 50 develop benign enlargement of the prostate, which causes frequent urination, annoying night-time urination, and a decreased force of the urinary stream known as prostatic hyperplasia or BPH. This condition threatens millions of men's fertility and plays havoc with their sexual identity.

The encouraging news is that there is more support from natural sources than from drugs or surgery. Here are some suggestions:

- Adopt an alkalizing dietary strategy as defined in Chapter 5.
- Eat 7 servings of soy products weekly. This includes tofu, soy milk beverage, tempeh, miso soup, soy sprouts, soy isolate protein powder, and soybeans. Soy contains natural isoflavones called genistein and diadzein that help to detoxify harmful DHT (dihydrotestosterone), the male hormone metabolite linked with excessive prostate tissue growth.
- Cut back on saturated fat.
- Eat one heaping tablespoon both of organically grown pumpkin and sunflower seeds daily. They have a positive effect on symptoms of BPH.
- Eat 10 servings weekly of tomatoes (full of lycopene) and 10 servings of red-orange produce (full of alpha- and beta-carotene).
- Supplement with 150 mg twice a day (300 mg total) with each of these two herbs—pygeum africanum (the bark of an African evergreen) and saw palmetto berries (berries from a common tree grown in the southeastern United States). Saw palmetto extract actively inhibits the formation of DHT from testosterone by shutting down the enzyme 5-alpha-reductase that is necessary for its conversion. This herb also reduces inflammation of the prostate. Research indicates that it works effectively for 90 percent of users in two months. Pygeum africanum also works by limiting the formation of DHT and is a mild antibiotic. You must take both herbs. (See Appendix for sources.)
- Improve blood flow to the prostate with daily walking or exercise. Consider massage therapy, acupuncture to reduce swelling and bring healing energy to the area, and chiropractic stimulation to the entire pelvic region.
- Constipation aggravates prostate enlargement, so drink 10 to 12, 8-ounce glasses of pure water daily and eat lots of Superfood produce to ensure adequate fiber consumption.
- Use a green drink daily.
- Supplement with nutrients that aid healthy prostate function. Zinc regulates the hormone that converts testosterone to the troublesome DHT. Use 75 mg of chelated zinc daily or check that it is in your multi-vitamin-mineral-antioxidant supplement.
- Be vigilant and have either one of these: 2 tablespoons of flaxseed oil daily; EPA fish-oil capsules daily; or a teaspoon of cod liver oil daily for your EFAs.

- The micronutrient selenium is vital for the functioning of the prostate; use 200 mcg a day of Selenomax, a natural, high-selenium yeast, or check that it is in your multi-vitamin-mineral-antioxidant supplement. High-quality supplements will contain Selenomax and Chrommax, organic chromium, which you also need.
- If you are really prepared to go to war to prevent possible prostate cancer, take 250 mg of the following three amino acids, twice a day, between meals: alanine, glutamine, and lysine.
- Practice holding your urine for 5 to 10 seconds in midstream voiding to build up the muscle groups around the bladder.

Anger, Violent Temper

Many men find anger and violence to be a problem in their lives. If you are one of them, try these strategies:
- Exercise at a fitness center 5 to 6 days a week, preferably in the morning. Do aerobic training on a treadmill, stationary bike, StairMaster, or rowing machine. Do brief, intense, anaerobic weight-resistive workouts, paying strict attention to your form. Complete your sessions with tension-reducing stretching.
- Include an extract of the herb St.-John's-wort or SAMe, as a supplement, as they calm both the mind and the central nervous system. (See Appendix under Superfood Tips)
- Extend your breathing-meditation sessions in the morning and prior to sleeping for up to 15 minutes a session, gradually extending them both to a half-hour. On weekends extend these sessions to 45 minutes.
- Eat an alkalizing diet (see Chapter 5). You will notice that you feel more satisfied, are calmer, less irritated. Avoid violent movies, videos, daily news, and newspapers.

Hair Loss

When they lose their hair, some men feel they are losing their manhood. To halt premature hair loss, reduce stress in your life. Stress creates the hormone cortisol that eats away at lean muscle mass and may be associated with premature hair loss. Consider the following strategies to waylay hair loss:
- Increase circulation to the head with Tai Chi, hatha yoga, reflexology, acupuncture, and a vigorous scalp massage twice a day using the essential oils of rosemary and ginger, available at whole-food stores. These oils stimulate circulation on or under the scalp at the hair-root level.

- Eat more soy foods.
- Drink more pure water.
- Get sufficient sleep.
- Use white cotton pillowcases (since dyed pillowcases slowly give off their synthetic dye and the scalp and hair roots absorb it) and avoid synthetic, petroleum shampoos that irritate the scalp.
- Make sure your shampoo contains no sodium lauryl sulphate (a foaming agent from coconut oil that is nasty stuff).

A Healthy Heart

Each year cardiovascular disease kills about 500,400 North American women and 557,200 North American men. Twenty years ago women were rarely heart attack victims, now they constitute a major part of the statistics. Each year 20,000 women under the age of 65 die of heart attacks; 30 percent of those women are less than 55 years old.

The Haukeland University Hospital in Bergen, Norway, completed a Norwegian study showing an extremely high correlation between high homocysteine levels and coronary-disease mortality. Homocysteine is not the lone culprit in heart disease, but it is a co-conspirator—and one you can do something about. Homocysteine, an amino acid, is used by the body to help manufacture proteins and carry out cellular metabolism. Too much of it appears to cause blood platelets to clump together and vascular walls to begin to break down. Protein-rich foods contain an amino acid, methionine, that converts to homocysteine. By the age of 45, arteries begin to be scarred by elevated homocysteine levels and provides excess circulating cholesterol with a place to stick and grow. Three B vitamins, vitamin B_6, vitamin B_{12}, and folic acid, work to convert the amino acid into a molecular form the body can use. I highly recommend you increase your consumption of a range of Superfoods including leafy green vegetables, fruit, beans, peas, whole grains, fat-free, organic yogurt, and fresh cold-water fish that each contain an abundance of these vitamins, that keep homocysteine in check.

The message is finally beginning to permeate society: prevention is the answer. We know now that the heart is immediately influenced by lifestyle choices. The causes of cardiovascular disease—obesity, high levels of LDL cholesterol, high blood pressure, and cholesterol plaque buildup in the arteries—can be reversed through exercise, relaxation, and superior nutrition. All this is within our control.

Heart Strategies

To reduce your chances of contracting cardiovascular disease, follow these suggestions:

- Eat a colorful Superfood diet of organic, seasonal, local fruits and vegetables full of heart-protective antioxidants and phytochemicals like sulforaphane, lignins, cabinols, indoles, polyphenols, proanthocyanidins, and terpenoids.
- Eat the "good" olive oil (organic, extra-virgin) and organic flaxseed oil daily but avoid all hydrogenated, processed margarines, oils, fats, commercial baked goods, and prepackaged snacking goodies.
- Take coenzyme Q_{10} (CoQ_{10}) at 100 mg a day minimum, ingested with your olive oil or omega-3 EFAs (flax oil) to aid in absorption, to stabilize heart cell membranes, and to protect the cell's "furnace," the mitochondria, where your body produces energy both as adenosine triphosphate (ATP) and adenosine diphosphate (ADP). In 1994, *The Journal of the American Medical Association* reported that those with higher alpha- and beta-carotene levels had a decreased risk for coronary heart disease. In 1969, *The Lancet* reported a 77 percent decrease in non-fatal heart attacks with the daily supplementation of 200 IU of vitamin E daily. Use a high-quality multi-vitamin-mineral-antioxidant formula daily, with the full range of naturally occurring vitamin E tocopheryls and natural full range of carotenoids.
- Eat magnesium and potassium-rich foods.
- Drink 6 to 12, 8-ounce glasses of pure water daily.
- Use the heart-strengthening herbs hawthorn, motherwort, and garlic daily.
- Take a live-culture acidophilus that has been shown to lower cholesterol and to help normalize HDL/LDL ratios. An example of this is a product called Bio-K+.

Final Thoughts for Men

Take advantage of your body's full capacity for self-diagnosis and accelerated healing. Be an awakened man, a creative man, and create yourself anew. It is not beyond your power to rejuvenate your cells, muscles, organs, tissues, and hormonal balances. Men are on the verge of creating a new type of man—perhaps a better type of fully awakened man, fully accountable and responsible.

Adopt a lifestyle that will protect you from premature aging, degenerative disease, and disability. Fine-tune your dietary strategies for powerful mental and physical performance. A Superfood dietary strategy allows your body's inherent healing system to work at peak performance. It can supercharge your mental, physical, and spiritual health. You will look better, feel better, and slow down the physiological aging process. Most important, you will be up to life's daily challenges and become a powerful influence in the development of peace, joy, acceptance, compassion, nonjudgment, and harmony in your family, friends, and co-workers, in your community, in your country, and within yourself.

Use Superfood dietary strategies wisely. It is as simple as becoming aware of your next meal, then the next. You will never look back!

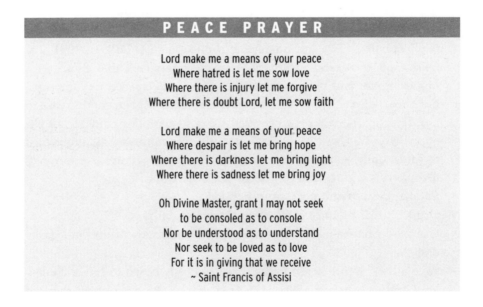

PEACE PRAYER

Lord make me a means of your peace
Where hatred is let me sow love
Where there is injury let me forgive
Where there is doubt Lord, let me sow faith

Lord make me a means of your peace
Where despair is let me bring hope
Where there is darkness let me bring light
Where there is sadness let me bring joy

Oh Divine Master, grant I may not seek
to be consoled as to console
Nor be understood as to understand
Nor seek to be loved as to love
For it is in giving that we receive
~ Saint Francis of Assisi

FINDING HAPPINESS

A wealthy merchant came across a fisherman in a small tranquil seaside village, eating a simple lunch of raw red peppers, some tender garden greens, a piece of unleavened dark bread and some roasted fish. The wealthy merchant said, "If you would remove your sails, put a motor in your boat, replace those old nets with modern nylon nets and use artificial bait, you would not be so idle, you would make a lot more money, eat much better and be a lot happier."

The simple fisherman looked up calmly at the wealthy merchant and said, "Ah, sir, but I am already as happy as I could possibly be."

–tale from the Canary Islands

3 POINT SUMMARY

- Many men might appear to be confident, but might ultimately feel estranged.
- Rather than feeling limited, men must feel their limitlessness. They must not try to control the uncontrollable.
- Men must consider a lifestyle change in which they eliminate some of the high-saturated-fat sources of protein, consume more natural fiber, and eat more fresh organic produce daily.

5 POINT ACTION PLAN

- Seek positive reinforcement to make a lifestyle change. This reinforcement might come from a fitness center, a professional weight-loss center, a church group, a 12-step program, or professional counseling.
- Take time to do the 10-minute morning and evening breathing-meditation exercises; on weekends extend these sessions to 45 minutes.
- Incorporate the exercise suggestions in Chapter 11 to increase your peak performance and meet the stresses of day-to-day challenges.
- Use a comprehensive multi-vitamin-mineral-antioxidant supplement daily. (See Appendix for sources.)
- Be conscientiously aware of eating your 10 Superfood servings of vegetables daily and 2 to 3 pieces of ripe, fresh organic fruit. Enjoy eating and take time to chew your Superfoods well.

15

Spiritual Fitness

HEALTH REFLECTION

A genuine sense of inquiry allows us to be a lamp
unto our own enlightenment.
Physical peak fitness and accelerated healing
of our physical health happens from the outside in;
spiritual peak fitness and accelerated freedom
from our confining perceptions happens from the inside out.

You shall know the truth and the truth shall make thee free.
Jesus Christ

It is our very search for perfection outside ourselves that causes our suffering.
Buddha

The temple bell stops, but the sound keeps coming out of the flowers.
Basho, a Zen poet

*I did not go to my master to learn his words of wisdom, but to see how he tied
and untied his shoes.*
Hasidic rabbi

Where is there anyone that is not you? You are the soul of the universe.
Swami Vivekananda

Ultimate balanced health must include spiritual fitness. Just as Superfoods dietary strategies and proper exercise are important to keep the body in shape, personal exploration that opens to deeper wisdom is necessary to keep the soul in shape. A sense of inner balance and deep spiritual awakening further accelerates mental and physical fitness. Research shows that if people with mild to moderate hypertension learn to unwind and become calmly balanced within, they may be able to take less medication or none at all. Researchers at the University of California in Los Angeles taught 22 patients to use techniques such as deep breathing, biofeedback, and calming imagery to manage stress. One year later, 12 had discontinued their blood pressure medications; four others had graduated to smaller doses. *Remember: Optimum physical health happens from the outside in; optimum spiritual health happens from the inside out.*

Spiritual fitness is the ability to realize our connectedness with God, Nature, Being, or the Eternal Moment. God is found in the immortal, eternal, and infinite. Our physical body, being finite, has limitations and cannot travel the terrain of the infinite. Only that part of us beyond the physical—the loving, vibrant, witnessing—can travel the roadless way. People from diverse cultures and religious backgrounds create spiritual fitness in a number of ways: reading sacred texts, praying earnestly, chanting, self-reflection, meditation, selfless charitable work, music, dancing, and community singing. Each of these spiritual fitness "practices" are really conversations or communions with God. They may be of different intensities and practiced at various levels, but they are the same fundamental type of activity—communing or talking with God.

Other methods of spiritual practice may take a humanitarian form: assisting flood victims, donating time to a senior citizens' home, caring for the welfare of animals, protecting the devastation of our watersheds and forests, vigilantly maintaining a healthy emotional atmosphere for children to grow in, giving time to hospice patients, inmates in a prison, a hospital or a center for the mentally challenged. Others may devote quality time to finding solutions to environmental issues and global problems or to resolving communication conflicts in the workplace. It could also be as simple as reaching out to a friend in need or calmly creating time to commune with Nature. If each of these activities is entered into with selfless nonattachment to personal praise or gain, they allow us to come to rest in our spiritual core. To be genuine, each activity must be motivated by unconditional love.

Every action, big or small, can be a spiritual fitness exercise, or learning opportunity, to integrate ourselves and be in clear communion with the Divine. Brother Lawrence, a 14th-century Christian monk, said, "It is not necessary to have great things to do. I turn my little omelet in the pan for the love of God." Spiritual exercises focus our attention from the outside finite world to the internal, infinite world. Marcus Aurelius, the Roman emperor and philosopher, put this in perspective when he said, "If you are distressed by anything external, the pain is not due to the thing itself, but to your own estimate of it; this you have the power to revoke at any moment."

Spiritual Fitness and Physical Health

Can these spiritual practices or conversations with God have an impact on our physical well-being? There is scientific evidence on the power of prayer and one of its most persuasive proponents is Dr. Larry Dossey, of Santa Fe, New Mexico. His *Healing Words* and *Prayer Is Good Medicine* contains a treasure chest of scientific proof of the healing benefits of prayer and meditation. Dossey cites many studies that show that prayer does have a favorable influence on physical and mental health.

In 1990, F. C. Craige and his colleagues reviewed ten years of publications of the *Journal of Family Practice* and found that, when participation in religious ceremony, social support, prayer, and relationship with God was measured, 83 percent of the studies showed benefit to physical health. In another review of mental health, 92 percent of the studies showed benefit from participation in some kind of spiritual practice.

Peak physical fitness requires that we place some of our attention on our lifestyle and Superfood selections. Likewise, peak spiritual fitness requires that we place some of our attention on the infinite and spiritual aspect of ourselves. Our goal is to connect with our spiritual core. Spiritual fitness, as it develops, has a positive effect on our own physical and mental well-being. Spiritual fitness can also serve as a conduit to channel our protective thoughts, love, strength, goodwill, hope, and clarity, sent in the form of prayers, to others.

Are You Spiritually Fit?

Spiritual fitness is as important, if not more vital, to peak "total fitness," as good nutrition and adequate exercise. To evaluate your spiritual fitness, answer the following eight questions.

	Yes	No
1. Do you read inspirational or spiritual literature daily?	❏	❏
2. Each evening, do you objectively review your day?	❏	❏

	Yes	No

3. In your evening self-reflection, do you learn from your day's experiences and determine always to be open to new ones? ❏ ❏

4. Do you regularly, each day, send loving thoughts, or offer your time as assistance to individuals, communities, Nature, or the global community? ❏ ❏

5. Do you feel like an integral part of all humanity? ❏ ❏

6. Do you react with genuine joy to the financial, employment, physical, or relationship successes of others? ❏ ❏

7. Are you encouraging and positive in your choice of words? ❏ ❏

8. Is prayer or meditation part of your daily schedule? ❏ ❏

To find your score, add up the "yes" answers. A score of 7 to 8 is optimal and suggests that your spiritual life is vital to you and that you are nurturing it properly. A score of 6 or less may still mean that your spiritual life is equally important to you, but indicates a need to work on certain portions of your life, to foster greater spiritual unfolding.

Spiritual fitness has no limits. Regardless of your score, commit to a deeper exploration of your spiritual fitness. Value it as a priceless treasure. Just as you supplement your physical health, consider ways to supplement your spiritual health.

Attitude and Spiritual Fitness

There is an old story told by the great sage Vivekananda, that emphasizes the attitude we must have to accelerate optimum spiritual fitness. Here it is:

A gem merchant had fallen upon hard times. Totally exhausted, weary and without food for the entire day, he checked into an inn for some food and rest. He could hardly stay awake and his body was shaking with exhaustion. As he was about to enter his room, he happened to overhear a conversation indicating that a man in the room next to him had millions of dollars' worth of rare jewels. Suddenly, the merchant shed his hunger and weariness and focused his full concentration on the wealth in the room next door. He became charged with adrenaline and both his body and mind felt revived just thinking of those jewels. He could not sleep all night as his mind joyfully thought of all the ways to spend that enormous wealth. The moral of the story is what Jesus Christ exemplified when he said, "Where your treasure lies, there will your heart be also."

We cannot allow our external life to take 100 percent of our energy, enthusiasm, and "heart." We must take time to develop a great treasure chest of experiences, unfolding as our spiritual enlightenment. We must give it such value that the time spent in spiritual fitness activities will revive us, reorient, remake, re-form, and balance us so we have a connectedness with God; and our body-mind-soul makeup is in perfect equilibrium. This attitude will also release us from any "spiritual heart disease" as we open to our true nature—love.

Spiritual Fitness Supplements

The seven main supplements to foster optimal spiritual fitness are:
1. Inspirational reading
2. Mindfulness (including humanitarian efforts)
3. Writing spiritual poems, stories, or letters
4. Reflecting at day's end
5. Prayer (including music and/or singing)
6. Meditation
7. Seeking spiritual guidance (or support groups)

Inspirational Reading

Spiritual or inspirational reading offers the soul needed nourishment. Your reading material can be scriptures, the lives of saints, or stories that communicate directly to your heart. Each person has different needs at different stages of his or her life. The right book, cassette tape, or video communicates to your soul profound wisdom that allows you greater insight and a sense of enlightenment. It opens you to your infinite intelligence and explains, inspires, interprets, and defines the spiritual way of life. For added stimulation, enjoy inspirational reading by the sea, a lake, a mountain meadow, or in the shade of a tree. Or share time with your spouse or a friend at a scheduled time each evening. Carry a small pocket-size book of inspirational sayings in your jacket, purse, bag, or knapsack.

Mindfulness

Our unconscious mind (subconscious) is full of the seeds of everything we have ever thought, said, or done. If we go through life unaware of our unconscious motivations, we will them to rule us. If, however, we are mindful of our past and its influence on our words, thoughts, and deeds, we can become more multi-dimensional, and not limited. We have to make a special effort to see the blue sky, the flowering bushes, the majestic trees, and the potential in all human beings. Wherever we are, at any time, we have the capacity to enjoy the moment and to bring a sense of peace into that moment. Correct behavior is focusing our full mindfulness into moment after moment of awareness.

If you catch yourself not being mindful, just rushing through life on automatic pilot, stop, and realize that to enjoy this moment is your most important task. Breathe in deeply and say, "This is the present moment," breathe out and say, "This is a unique and wonderful moment." Your mindfulness may take on a humanitarian form or be in the form of a financial donation to support a necessary service or cause. A potent, mindful practice is to smile, be kind, and be peaceful. Mindfulness allows us to develop the capacity to smile, to be at inner peace, and to make peace in each moment, to moment, to moment.

Writing Spiritual Poems, Stories, or Letters

We must understand the whole of Life, not just one little part of it. That is why we must read, look at the skies, sing, dance, laugh, reach out with compassion to others, and fully understand—for all that is life! Keep a blank book nearby in which to write down your new thoughts, sayings, or poems. They will be like signposts on the road map of your new journey into enlightenment. Do not rebuke or challenge others with your letters, but write letters to cherished friends describing your newfound awareness. They will celebrate with you. The goal of writing poetry is to dissolve our complexities into simplicity by arousing the memory of our true nature—the changeless soul.

Reflecting at Day's End

The quiet, calm minutes before falling asleep are a very precious time to review and reflect upon your performance throughout the day.

Discovering regret and dissatisfaction in your thoughts, actions, and responses is very constructive if it is a prelude to spiritual improvement. Do not feel desperate to change everything in one reflective evening. Resolve to reflect each evening with unflinching patience and perseverance. Examine where there may be any deep-rooted despair, selfishness, repression, bigotry, or anxiety in your life. They will each be cured as you bring them to full awareness. You will clearly see that they benefit neither yourself nor others. Remove them as obstacles to your growth. This silent, noiseless work will "bring peace that passeth understanding."

Finally, examine how you talk, think, act, and respond to those whom you cherish and love unconditionally. Picture them in your mind's eye, transferring one or two of those feelings, thoughts, actions, or responses toward others to whom you do not feel that way. This process develops a healthy self-love and sense of security, and then transfers it to an insecure, shallow relationship. Every human being has a few relationships that need work. Be determined to practice, to manifest a full loving nature, wherever or with whomever you need to work with!

Have you found places to work on? There, now perform random acts of kindness!

Prayer

The object of prayer is to have an intimate conversation with God. The faith that God is an equal participant in our conversations is important. We take for granted that our perceptions and senses are meant for outer exploration. Imagine the infinite vast regions of light and blessedness as a waiting discovery in the interior terrains of our soul.

Praying reprograms our subconscious and helps us discover our full potential. It gives us a feeling of fulfillment and prevents us from indulging in self-destructive behavior to fulfill our emptiness. There are various types of prayer: prayers of gratitude, prayers of praise, or just staying in Divine communion. Prayers may also be directed to a specific need that you or someone else requires help with.

Include songs or music in your prayer session. Singing or listening to calming music can elevate your mind, relieve stress, and deepen your mood.

Prayer allows you a daily personal connection with your spiritual core. As a daily practice, prayer will change your life at the deepest levels where you will find Peace and Love.

Meditation

Meditation is quietly and calmly forming a relationship with the Creator, a relationship we sadly neglect, abuse, or worst of all, to which we are indifferent. Just as our bodies require Superfoods, our souls require nourishment of cosmic proportions. Nothing short of God will appease the hunger of the soul. When we feel dissatisfied, uncertain, or ill at ease within, we generally turn outward in search of peace, security, comfort, love—anything to take away the nagging inner tension or disturbance. There is nothing in all of Creation that we can conquer that will appease the soul. The only satisfaction the soul seeks is to be found traveling inward. Meditation is the ticket to our interior quest.

The main point of meditation is to halt and put into reverse the outgoing tendencies of the mind. Think of the heart area as your center. It is the area of focus, or the residence of the soul. Sit quietly in a chair, in a calm place. Close your eyes and breathe calmly. Let go of the disturbances and turbulence in the mind. Do not try to achieve or gain anything. A room may be dark for one thousand years. How do you get light into it? You cannot force light from darkness. You get rid of darkness by opening a door or window and bringing in the light. Meditation is opening the door and window. Sit in meditation with no expectations or preconceived formulations—just enjoy the light shining in. True spiritual fitness requires an ambitionless quiet time, devoid of ego satisfaction. By offering this time simply to God, all your outer actions will slowly become spiritual fitness exercises.

Seeking Spiritual Guidance

Seeking help, advice, or suggestions from someone who has crossed this terrain before you is exceedingly beneficial.

Spiritual mentors come dressed in many disguises and from every walk of life. You may talk to your minister, priest, rabbi, an elder, a wise grandparent, or a recognized spiritual mentor.

Keep mindful, open, and alert. The worst pitfall is to think you are committed to a spiritual life, convinced that wonderful growth and spiritual awakening will only come in a preconceived way. Instead, feel a divine obligation to stay open to your mentors. Never be smug. Always keep an eager beginner's mind-set. This will guarantee you of mentors when you need them.

Mentors can take the form of a book (the Bible, for instance), a lecturer, a holy person, a new thought, a glance from a stranger, the swaying branch of a tree, or the colorful sky at a brilliant sunset. Mentors are those people, events, or places that encourage us to greater wisdom; enthusiasm to be accountable and responsible; faith in the Divine; and greater depth in our spiritual conversations with God.

5 POINT SUMMARY

- Spiritual fitness is the most important aspect of the body-mind-soul makeup.
- A deep spiritual awakening further accelerates mental and physical fitness.
- A thread of harmony connects each spiritual fitness exercise to our spiritual core.
- Spiritual fitness exercises have a positive influence on mental and physical health.
- Spiritual fitness exercises include inspirational reading, praying, meditating, chanting, self-reflectedness, practicing mindfulness, writing spiritual poems, stories, or letters, dancing, singing, playing or listening to calming music, or selfless charitable work, seeking spiritual guidance.

2 POINT ACTION PLAN

- Make some form of spiritual exercise part of your "total fitness" program.
- Supplement your daily spiritual exercises with one or more of the seven powerful spiritual fitness supplements described above. These are genuine spiritual practices, not merely methods to improve your physical health.

16

Clinical Applications of the Power of Superfoods

by David Schweitzer, Ph.D., M.D., president of the
International Albert Schweitzer Society

HEALTH REFLECTION

Remember, daily your health is won or lost at the cellular level.

*The real revolution in medicine is the important
transition from treatment to prevention.*
Dr. Kenneth M. Kroll, M.D., Fellow, International College of Surgeons

*Aging, debility and illness are not inevitable—learn to listen
to your body—significantly, predictably and measurably
invigorate your health and healing with Nature's Superfoods.*
Dr. Bernd Friedlander, nutritional researcher

Accelerated physical healing requires in-depth dietary strategies.
Dr. Morton Walker, *Toxic Metal Syndrome*

Dr. David Schweitzer, a medical doctor practicing in London, England, is an outspoken proponent of natural, organically grown Superfoods and Superwater. I asked him to share two clinical case histories of patients who responded favorably to the addition of Superfoods to their diets. First, let me explain Dr. Schweitzer's clinical style and his conclusions about diet and nutrition.

Dr. Schweitzer is a humoral pathologist monitoring body fluids. His life's work has led him to the conclusion that a doctor or health professional does not have to follow one healing strategy only. He believes that all appropriate alternatives need to be utilized, they need to reinforce each other in the diagnosis and natural healing of disease. His clinic, therefore, is staffed by health professionals from a number of disciplines: dietary and nutritional therapies, herbal medicine, naturopathy, chiropractic, osteopathy, cranial osteopathy, massage therapy, reflexology, acupuncture, acupressure, shiatsu, relaxation and breathing therapy, psychotherapy and counseling, clinical environmental ecology, iridology, and orthodox allopathic medicine. Dr. Schweitzer trusts nothing in isolation, stressing instead the importance of the holistic approach. He feels that the mind and body are inseparable and capable of self-repair if the individual is ready to take an active part in his or her own accelerated healing and optimal health.

Dr. Schweitzer's Superfood Observations

- Water comprises nearly 70 percent of the body and is the most important nutrient for the body.
- Proper breathing techniques are vital for optimum health and healing.
- Breathing brings in oxygen and vitalizing energy.
- Foods must be chewed well in the mouth, to allow for proper digestion.
- The body's genetic health maintenance and healing mechanisms are designed to function at peak performance with natural, nondeformed, organically grown foods.
- Excess cooking destroys vitamins and enzymes.
- The human diet should be composed of 75 percent alkalizing foods and 25 percent acidifying foods by volume.
- Cultures that eat simple, organic food do not know cancer or poliomyelitis.
- Chemically treated and processed foods ferment in the intestines, and by reabsorption in the intestinal canal, toxins enter the bloodstream and weaken the immune system.
- White refined sugar is a toxin. Follow it through the processing stages: in the first extraction, calcium and protein are removed and all vitamins are destroyed; the sugar is mixed with acid chalk, carbonic gas, and sulfur dioxide and natrium bicarbonate; sugar then is cooled so it crystallizes; it is then treated with strontium hydroxide; finally, it is colored with Indathren blue or Ultramarine. The final sugar has a composition as $C_{12} H_{22} O_{11}$, with an atomic density of 98.4 to 99.5 percent, which puts it in the category of a poison.

- White refined, bleached flour fits into the same category as sugar.
- Mass-produced bakery items contain hydrogenated fats and trans-fatty acids that are a health hazard; they also contain white refined sugar and white flour.
- Never use margarine or regular refined salad oils that line grocery-store shelves.
- Food additives create unknown chemical reactions that impede the body's ability to function or heal.

Case Study #1

A male, 56 years of age, was diagnosed with fungi-infested blood and eczema on various parts of his body. He suffered from severe itching, lack of memory, excessive weight, irritability, anger, poor sleep patterns, bloated abdomen, and lower back pain. He tired easily and had great difficulty getting out of bed in the morning. His morning urine average pH was 4.5.

In observing the oxidation of the man's blood, there was marked oxidation of the origin type fungi with its elimination by-product aflatoxin, which is a carcinogen.

Prior to commencing the new dietary strategy, the patient was put on a 10-day detoxification cleanse, concentrating on the adrenal glands, kidneys, liver, and colon. This cleanse also eliminated parasites, fungus, and compacted colon debris.

He was then put on a completely plant-based diet, received colonic irrigation, had intravenous chelation therapy. The diagnosis pointed to the need for an anti-fungal diet based on Superfoods, with the addition of a grapeseed extract, which retards fungal growth. He was not allowed sugar or starch, vinegar, alcohol, mushrooms, dairy products, meat, rice cakes, grains, fried foods, soft drinks, or processed foods. A large array of colorful vegetables except for parsnips, especially garlic and onions, were included. The diet had to be 70 percent raw and the remainder steamed. His Superfood diet contained many servings of cruciferous vegetables like mustard greens, cauliflower, brussels sprouts, bok choy, broccoli, kale, and rapini, all rich in the anti-fungal phytochemicals sulforaphane, indole-3-carbinols, and isothiocyanates. Legumes (beans) were the preferred protein source. GREENS+ was used to provide a full profile of micronutrients and for its immune system–boosting properties. All fruits except lemon or lime juice were to be avoided. Iodine is anti-fungal, so sea vegetables were included at two meals a day. He was given a number of herbal teas and digestive enzymes. An advanced acidophilus called Bio-K+, was utilized. (Bio-K+ is registered at France's Pasteur Institute and at Laval's Armand-Frappier Institute. The Food Research and Development Centre of Agriculture Canada, and labs at Laval University in Quebec were the sites for Bio-K+ research.) He was slowly encouraged to increase his water intake to 12, 8-ounce glasses a day with three of those being pau d'arco tea, two being from the GREENS+ mixed in water, and one being aloe vera juice.

Organic flaxseed oil and cold-pressed extra-virgin organic olive oil were used as they are both anti-fungal. Cloves, garlic, ginger, and cayenne were used liberally on salads and vegetables, as they are beneficial Superfoods in anti-fungal diets.

This was an aggressive anti-fungal diet. I guided him carefully through the first 10-day adjustment period. His entire diet was the Superfoods dietary strategy.

He also received Neuro Linguistic Programming (the science of associating words and images in a positive manner) so he could detach from old concepts and replace them with new progressive thoughts and a positive self-image. Visualization exercises, hatha yoga classes, daily walking, and correct, anxiety-reducing breathing techniques, were also included.

Slowly, his discomforts began to minimize, his anxiety was alleviated, and each symptom was reduced. After two months his dietary selection was expanded, and after three months he was stable with no symptoms. He continued on a maintenance Superfood diet and I continued to monitor his wonderful progress every three months.

Superfoods are a powerful anti-free-radical advantage that stop or slow down the oxidation process within the body. They are both preventive and curative.

Case Study #2

A female, 61 years of age, was initially treated for uterine and breast cancer. She underwent chemotherapy without success and was sent home for her final days. Her other symptoms were hypothyroid, hypofunction of thymus and adrenal glands. The GGT value (liver factor) was over 400 IU (it should be 20), indicating toxicity. She also had a urinary infection with haematuria (blood in the urine). Her muscles felt fatigued. She was far too acidic both emotionally and physically. I tested the pH of her first morning venous blood, urine, and saliva.

For one week I put her on a liquid detoxification fast during the waning moon cycle, since this is the best time to clean the body emotionally, physically, and intellectually. In the period of the waxing moon (an ideal time to rebuild physical health) I started the therapy of restoring her health with organic Superfoods, EFAs, high-quality protein, and clean water.

I followed the same sugar-free, high-fiber Superfood diet of the first patient (Case Study #1) except I incorporated more fruits, colorful vegetables, more fiber, plant-based protein, nutritional yeast, fresh vegetable juices, grated raw foods, and Essiac tea. She ate a wide variety of seasonal fruit except bananas. Salmon was included in her diet. I restricted her low-glycemic intake of pasta, rice cakes, and potatoes. She discontinued dairy but used high-quality, unsweetened soy milk and soy yogurt. Soy-derived foods were used daily for their phytochemicals, genistein, and daidzein. She also began growing sunflower and soy sprouts at home.

She received natural vitamin and mineral supplements, antioxidants, and my favorite green drink GREENS+ three times a day. Supplements were taken with this green drink, which protects the body from excessive free radical assault by providing cells with a greater oxidation-reduction potential. Her water intake was increased gradually and carefully monitored.

Improvement was immediate after these dietary changes. We also incorporated both electronic and manual lymphatic drainage techniques to clean her lymphatic system of accumulated debris. She began to walk daily and include relaxation-breathing techniques in her regimen. Digestive enzymes necessary to facilitate her digestion, as well as appropriate homeopathic remedies, were included. Cautiously, quadrant by quadrant, a knowledgeable, biological dentist, working closely with me, replaced her mercury amalgam dental fillings with dental ceramics. I used an antioxidant defense of Superfoods and supplements. This was necessary to prevent delayed reactions generally associated with mercury amalgam dental-filling removals, probably due to mobilization of tissue mercury and bacteria in the gingiva. It took two weeks to raise her from chronic acidemia.

She installed an air purifier in her home. She became very active in Tai Chi classes and our meditation groups. We had her eliminate all her cosmetics and personal-hygiene products and replace them with natural, chemical-free shampoos, deodorants, etc. Also, we had her replace all her household cleaners, dish detergents, and clothes-washing soaps with safer alternatives. She received extensive chiropractic and acupuncture treatments to allow her *qi* (chi), or energy, or "life force energy" to flow freely. She used unbleached, white cotton undergarments, sheets, and pillowcases.

She received intravenous ozone therapy. Once strong enough, she received colonic irrigations to cleanse her bowels.

Her attitude was outstanding, and that helped heal her. There are incurable diseases with a curable patient because they have a positive attitude. Nineteen months later she has allowed her body to heal itself and she now has a balanced biochemical equilibrium.

Summary

Superfoods are critical to a successful dietary strategy aimed at allowing the body to revitalize itself and accelerate complete healing. Superfoods offer several advantages: they are easy to digest and nutrient rich, and it is easy for the body to absorb their health-giving compounds. They boost activity of the immune system, gradually strengthening the body's innate system of defense and healing. The healing system, fortified with Superfoods, can restore the balance of health. Most illnesses are then self-limited.

20 Steps to Living Longer and Healthier...Now!

HEALTH REFLECTION

The foods you fuel your body with today, dictate your peak performance level and optimum self-healing capability.

Health can only be achieved through a healthful lifestyle.
Dr. Daniel Crisafi, Ph.D., author and lecturer

Superfoods sensibly and measurably give you dynamic health.
Susan Stockton, M.A., author, *Book of Life*

As powerful as they are, Superfoods will not avert or reverse every health problem. They can, however, readily transform your mental and physical health, change your future for the better, and redesign the effects of your past.

This final chapter examines 20 steps that have an extraordinary effect on the body's total health and healing ability. Most of these steps utilize the powers of Superfoods, but several of them are additional strategies that will take your health to a new level for greater mental and physical performance.

20 Steps to Living Longer and Healthier

1. *Begin All Meals with a Reflective "Grace" or "Thanksgiving"* A grace or thanksgiving before the sharing of food generates a feeling of healthy cohesiveness that generally encompasses the rest of the day. Food and nourishment, as a real art, combine science and spirituality, merging technology and philosophy.

2. *Eat as if Your Life Depended Upon It!* Eating is a very intimate process. Consider each food before you eat it. Analyze quickly but carefully. Ask yourself, "Do I want to incorporate this particular food into my 100 trillion cells?"

3. *Chew Foods Well to Begin the Process of Digestion* Chewing is critical to the formation of potent anticancer agents in foods that are *only* released with chewing. Your stomach has no teeth. Enjoy eating, take a few minutes longer to chew your foods well and enjoy the texture, color, smell, and flavor of each mouthful. Do not deny yourself this wonderful experience. Superfoods revitalize you in two ways: first, when you enjoy them; second, when their vital nutrients enter your body to support cellular metabolism. The potent cancer-inhibitor phytochemicals indole-3-carbinol (I_3C) and sulforaphane are only released from cruciferous vegetables such as cabbage, brussels sprouts, radishes, turnips, mustard, kale, kohlrabi, and collards, when these vegetables are well chewed and an enzyme called myrosinase is released from the vegetable cell walls that only then forms indole-3-carbinol and sulforaphane.

4. *Leave Your Stomach 20 Percent Empty for Complete Digestion* Practice portion control at each of your meals. Never "top up" your stomach. Digestive enzymes in the stomach need to "mix and tumble" to accelerate digestion. Leave a little room, or complete digestion cannot happen.

5. *Combine Foods Properly for Assured Assimilation* There are two rules I strongly suggest you consider. The first rule is, eat fruit only by itself, never with protein, fat, or carbohydrates. The only exception is that you can mix celery juice with other fruit juices such as organic apple juice. Better still, eat the whole fruit. The second rule is, make sure you have sufficient protein, fiber, fat, and carbohydrates in a good ratio and proportion at each of your three meals a day. Try to follow the 55/25/20 meal construction plan which includes 55 percent complex carbohydrates (colorful vegetables), 25 percent low-fat protein, and 20 percent fat. Use whole-grain products as condiments or a side dish, and not as the primary source of your low- or moderate-glycemic complex carbohydrate daily food intake. (See Chapter 10 for a full explanation.) Eating right foods in the wrong proportions is as bad as eating the wrong foods. Remember, total calories are not as important as where they come from. Never go more than four hours without eating one of your three meals or two snacks a day.

6. *Drink 6 to 12, 8-ounce Glasses of Pure Water a Day* The most important nutrient you can utilize daily is clean water. Depending upon your body size and level of activity, drink 6 to 12, 8-ounce glasses of pure water through a straw daily. Never allow yourself to become dehydrated. Rehydrate by drinking your water quota throughout the day. Each day use a total of 6 tablespoons of freshly squeezed lime or lemon juice in your water, two tablespoons upon rising, two midafternoon, and two in the evening. Avoid carbonated soft drinks, artificial fruit-flavored drinks, coffee, and alcohol—they are foreign to your body. Water is your powerful energizing Superdrink.

7. *Eat a Diet of 75 Percent Alkalizing and 25 Percent Acidifying Foods* Ensure that your diet includes 75 percent alkalizing foods and 25 percent acidifying foods, based on volume. This will guarantee robust energy and optimum potential for beneficial self-healing. Your body chemistry will be in balance ("homeostasis") and operate at peak performance. Monitor the pH level of your morning urine or saliva and adjust your dietary strategy to determine when you have the right balance of alkaline/acid foods.

8. *Eat Organically Grown Fruit, Vegetables, and Whole Grains* Include Sea Vegetables and Supplements. Try, as much as possible, to purchase foods that have not been exposed to pesticides, herbicides, fungicides, and ripening-retardant chemicals. Also, avoid milk or dairy products containing bovine growth hormone (rBGH). Be alert to the new wave of bioengineered foods, and foods that have been irradiated. Avoid chemical-laden and overly processed foods containing MSG, excess sugar, and hydrogenated oils. Incorporate sea vegetables into your menu selection 2 to 3 times a week. Add soy lecithin granules to your cereals, soups, or salads. Use a high-quality, natural, multi-vitamin-mineral-antioxidant supplement daily that includes 400 IU of mixed, naturally occurring tocopherols (vitamin E) and mixed naturally occurring carotenoids such as alpha- and beta-carotene. Consider using a capsule of 500 mg of vitamin C as ascorbates and take 6 to 8 capsules throughout the day for a total of 3 to 4 grams.

9. *Eat 10 Servings of Vegetables and 3 Servings of Fruit Daily* Be creative and utilize a wide selection of colorful, organically grown vegetables and ripe, fresh seasonal fruit, grown in your area. A serving is considered one-half a cup. Use raw foods daily in salads, and with entrées, as carrot sticks, celery sticks, zucchini sticks, red pepper slices, yam rounds, turnip sticks, or tomato slices. Grate beets, radishes, horseradish, sweet

potatoes, red cabbage, or daikon as garnishes with entrées. Sprinkle seeds and nuts, or ground pumpkin seeds, or flaxseeds on hot whole-grain cereals. Use fresh herbs and sprouts liberally to jazz up and electrify the appearance of your food. Be creative with raw foods. These Superfoods give your cells layer upon layer of protective phytochemicals and antioxidants, skillfully designed in the Divine Blueprint for optimal cellular protection.

10. *Take Care of Your Inner Ecology* Daily, eat one cup of plain fat-free white, organic yogurt that contains a "live" bacterial culture, or a non-dairy soy yogurt. Eat it without fruit or sweeteners. It will replace the beneficial "healthy" bacteria in your intestinal tract to maintain intestinal hygiene. "Friendly" bacteria aid in the digestion of foods and the manufacture of the vitamin B family. They skillfully dismantle viruses, bacteria, and parasites that enter our food chain or water supply. High-quality green drinks contain 2.5 billion "friendly" bacteria per tablespoon serving, from seven various types of "friendly" bacteria that each take up residence in specific sites on the gastrointestinal wall. These bacteria come from dairy-free sources grown on brown rice. Green drinks also contain fructo-oligosacharides (FOS) that feed these necessary bacteria and allow them to thrive for superior inner ecology.

11. *Keep the Colon Clean* The body requires motion to allow the bowels to cleanse properly. Walking is a contralateral movement that massages all the body's systems. Walk for at least a half-hour five days a week and consider joining a fitness club to begin some well-supervised weight-resistance exercises. Hatha yoga, Tai Chi, and Feldenkrais are all exquisite body movements that harmonize your internal organs, bowels, and musculoskeletal system. Daily, eat 2 to 3 pieces of organically grown, ripe seasonal fruit, whole grains, and colorful vegetables. Eating these foods provides the added fiber that will bulk up in your intestines, gently sweeping the colon clean of extra estrogen, hormones, toxins, waste debris of cellular metabolism and soaks up excess cholesterol. These foods will keep you regular. Maintain intestinal hygiene by consuming 35 to 40 grams of all seven fiber sources (bran, cellulose, gum, hemicellulose, lignin, mucilages, and pectin) daily to thoroughly cleanse the intestines and restore normal bowel transit.

12. *Eat Low-Fat Proteins, Quality Fats, and Low-Glycemic, Complex Carbohydrates at Each Meal* Your Superfoods dietary strategy includes combining vegetables, fats, and proteins at each of your three meals, in portions and ratios that help keep your glucose (blood sugar levels)

stabilized and reduce the body's insulin response. Effective protein-to-carbohydrate ratios are necessary to balance your hormonal response. (Review Chapter 10). Eat lean cuts of meats and remove all visible fat before cooking. Remove all chicken skin and subcutaneous fat before broiling. Try to eat salmon, mackerel, sardines, and trout two to three times a week. Only consume fat-free dairy products and eat free-range eggs soft-boiled, hard-boiled, or poached only.

If you are a vegan or vegetarian, try to mix your plant-based protein sources so you utilize a wide range of sources. Nutritional yeast, spirulina, chlorella, and either lactose-free whey protein powder or soy isolate protein powder add biologically complete protein to any diet. If you eat meat, substitute plant-based protein sources 3 to 7 times each week, to avoid the excess saturated fat in meats.

Avoid sugar and use honey in extreme moderation. A sweet no-calorie low-glycemic alternative to honey or sugar is the sweet-tasting herb stevia rebaudiana, available in whole-food stores. Substitute 2 tablespoons of stevia powder for every cup of sugar, or one-quarter teaspoon of powdered stevia extract for every cup of sugar in any recipe.

13. *Breathe Deeply—Reduce Stress Naturally* Clean your nostrils several times a day to ensure you are breathing through both nostrils. Conscientious breathing revitalizes the body with both oxygen and energy. Shallow breathing is our response to tension, fear, worry, anxiety, depression, or pain. Deep, full breathing is our response to joy and happiness. Each morning and each evening take five minutes to breathe calmly and perform breathing exercises. Relief from stress is critical to optimal health. How you respond to the stressor determines whether you are stressed or not.

14. *Exercise Daily* Exercise is life-supporting. Our bodies were meant to move in a natural, neurologically coordinated way. Walking is a high-quality locomotive movement we should engage in each day. It has a harmonizing effect on the entire central nervous system. Walking is stress-reducing and gets us outdoors in fresh air and exposed to seasonal changes. Eye exercises should be done daily to strengthen optic responses. Include a spa retreat, walking expedition, or wilderness adventure in your next holiday plans. You can also massage your scalp or exercise reflexology points on your feet and hands. Exercise your skin by using a natural, dry, soft, bristle brush or washcloth to rub your skin prior to your daily shower or bath.

15. *Expose Yourself to Sunlight and Fresh Air* Expose your skin, without sunglasses, glasses, or contact lenses, to the sun for 10 minutes in the early morning and/or 10 minutes in the late afternoon. Never look at the sun directly. Let the sun's rays enter your eyes indirectly. Sunbathing produces vitamin D in your body, and in wise moderation, builds up your skin's tolerance. Never allow yourself to burn, and avoid the midday sun. Many people actually have a sun-deficient lifestyle. Sunlight should be considered a photonutrient. The skin, as an organ of excretion, removes approximately two pounds of waste daily! Moderate early-morning and/or late-afternoon sun exposure also allows your underexposed skin to be revitalized by natural air currents.

16. *Use Natural Clothing, Cosmetics, and Hygiene Products* Bacteria and viruses grow rapidly on surfaces that continually alternate between being wet then dry. Put hydrogen peroxide on your toothbrush before and after you use it. Rinse it off with hot water. Do not use sponges that breed bacteria; rather, use recycled paper towels. Two or three times a day after washing your hands well and using a scrub brush on your nails, sprinkle some hydrogen peroxide on your hands, especially allowing it to get under your fingernails. Leave on for 30 seconds and rinse off with warm water. This kills parasites and bacteria hitch-hiking under your nails that enter your body when you touch your ears, eyes, nose, or mouth.

One of the worst breeding grounds for bacteria is the kitchen dishcloth. At the end of each day, put the used dishcloth in your laundry basket. Do not dry it out and reuse it the next day. Every day, start with a fresh, clean dishcloth.

The dye on clothes or bedsheets can be absorbed by your skin. Consider using natural, unbleached, cotton pillowcases, bedsheets, and undergarments. Use natural, chemical-reduced cosmetics, and for women, unbleached, pure cotton personal-hygiene products. Check that your shampoos, soaps, toothpaste, mouthwash, and deodorant are not loaded with petroleum by-products and chemicals. Purchase these products in whole-food stores and ask store staff to guide you in your choices.

17. *Save Antibiotics for Serious Health Crises* You do not need to use antibiotics for a regular cold. Always consult a knowledgeable health professional before using an antibiotic. If you do choose to use an antibiotic, use a suitable homeopathic remedy: a "live" culture, organic yogurt; a

green drink with many probiotic cultures to restore your beneficial "good" bacteria population. Do not have mercury amalgams (fillings) put in your teeth. If you do have some, consider having them removed by a nutritionally conscious dentist. Use raw, fresh garlic daily as your natural antibiotic. Daily use of garlic detoxifies the body and protects it against infection by enhancing immune function. To maximize garlic's superlative antibacterial, antiviral, and antiparasitical activity, use it the way I do. Before going to sleep at night, finely chop 1 to 2 cloves of garlic. Put the chopped garlic on a tablespoon and swallow it with water. Do not chew it. There will be absolutely no garlic odor on your breath if you do not chew the garlic. Your first morning bowel movement will have a garlic odor. This is a wonderful sign that this Superfood was active in your GI tract while you were sleeping and regenerating. Garlic tirelessly patrols your intestinal tract all night long, as a "toxic-garbage cop" helping to neutralize, dismantle, and eliminate bacteria, viruses, parasites, and carcinogens.

18. *Get Sufficient Sleep* Determine the number of hours of sleep you require to regenerate yourself. As mentioned above, use natural, unbleached, cotton sheets, pillowcases, and sleepwear. Allow fresh air to enter the room you sleep in. Some people rejuvenate quickly with a 20-minute "power nap" during some portion of the day. Practice your breathing and meditation prior to falling asleep to both relieve and deepen yourself. Honor your sleep debt; keeping a regular bedtime and waking time schedule reduces daytime sleepiness.

19. *Supplement Your Spiritual Fitness Program* Proper meditation calms our anxieties, minds, bodies, and emotions. Prayer, as a natural cycle with meditation, is a selfless process that deepens us into the awareness of the changeless soul.

　　Also remember, it takes more muscles to frown than smile. Be good, do good, be both accountable and responsible. Consider volunteering time to an environmental project, a prison, a school, or a hospital. You may want to include inspirational reading, singing, listening to calming music, writing short stories, poetry, or letters as part of your daily spiritual fitness program.

20. *Superfoods Must Be Part of Your Dietary Strategy* Age-proof your cells with Superfoods! Why fuel yourself with low-octane fuels that are guaranteed to give you fewer miles per gallon and predictable, poorer performance. Incorporate fresh fruits, vegetables, small amounts of whole grains, sea vegetables, sprouts, soy-derived products, legumes,

fat-free cottage cheese, free-range eggs, seeds, nuts, lean meat, wild game, and poultry raised with no antibiotics or growth hormones. Use fresh fish, but avoid most shellfish, which may be contaminated.

Eat some raw food at each meal for their enzyme content. This could include nuts and seeds sprinkled on whole-grain cereals, salads, crunchy veggie sticks or slices, herbal garnishes, or colorful veggie condiments.

Try to include a soy protein source such as miso, tempeh, firm tofu, texturized soy protein, soy beverage, or soy isolate protein powder at least three days a week. Use sea vegetables as seasoning and fresh herbs as garnishes. Use small amounts of salt-free butter and never use margarine. Use one tablespoon of extra-virgin, expeller-pressed "green" olive oil daily on your salad, and 1 to 2 tablespoons, depending on your body size, of organic, expeller-pressed flaxseed or hemp seed oil, sprinkled, unheated, on your vegetables. Purchase opaque containers that have been flushed and sealed with inert gas like nitrogen or argon.

Read labels carefully and avoid foods that contain hydrogenated or partially hydrogenated oils or palm oils, as their long-term use causes cumulative damage. If you can't pronounce a word on a label, don't eat the food. Minimize your intake of any fried foods. Remember, "fat-free" does not mean "problem-free."

Have a green drink like GREENS+ daily. It is a convenient alkalizing food that allows you to incorporate a wide variety of ocean vegetables, organically grown grasses, phytochemical-rich herbs, antioxidant-supportive foods, and a wide spectrum of dairy-free "friendly" bacteria that give your intestines layer upon layer of protection, controlling yeast overpopulation, such as candida albicans.

Your Superfoods dietary strategy is a natural preventive approach to health and healing. Modern medicine is no doubt powerful, but it remains a poor substitute for prevention based on a sound dietary strategy. Eating Superfoods means you are choosing the very best food source. If you don't adopt a Superfoods dietary strategy, you will never reach your optimum health and healing potential, let alone wellness. Remember, your health is won or lost each day at the cellular level.

Eat wisely, live long and healthy, and be happy!

The Power of Eating Superfoods

HEALTH REFLECTION

Let your kitchen be the innovative forefront of your Superfoods dietary strategy, for creative, delicious, and health-giving foods!

Eat as if your life depended on it.
Ronnie Deauville, nutritional researcher

Congratulations! Your choice to eat a more healthful diet is one of the most exciting and personally empowering decisions you can make.
Dr. Neal Barnard, M.D., *Eat Right, Live Longer*

In this chapter, Jeanne Marie Martin has put together recipes, using my suggestions, that take advantage of all the dietary principles covered in this book. Some of the world's most delightful cuisines have been skillfully using Superfoods for centuries.

Superfoods are delicious, satisfying, and very simple to prepare. You can get all the ingredients you'll need at health food stores, supermarkets, and produce stands. You will spend less money on food, since Superfood menu planning makes it possible to use less processed, less expensive ingredients, which don't require costly packaging.

7 Superfood Recommendations for the Kitchen

- Purchase a variety of fresh, seasonal, unprocessed foods.
- Buy organically grown ripe fruits, colorful vegetables, whole grains, and fragrant herbs.
- Do not leave perishable foods out at room temperature for more than two hours.
- Read food labels carefully and eliminate those that contain food dyes and chemical additives such as MSG (monosodium glutamate or sodium benzoate as examples).

- Rinse meat, poultry, and fish before cooking.
- Thoroughly disinfect all utensils and surfaces that come in contact with raw meats and poultry.
- Sprout legumes for 24 hours before cooking and use Nova Scotia dulse, for added iodine, in the cooking.

Dining-Out Tactics

Eating out has become a way of life for North Americans, who eat two out of every five meals away from home. Often we view dining out as a time to splurge, a "time out" when good nutrition doesn't count. Use the suggestions below and you can easily incorporate the Power of Superfoods at any type of eatery.

- Balance your meal with a salad, a vegetable, a small portion of meat, fish, or a vegetarian entrée. Skip the bread and the dessert.
- Look over the entire menu. Restaurants frequently feature healthful dishes low in fat and salt to meet the demands of a growing number of health-conscious consumers.
- Ask your server how a food is prepared, and if it is not to your expectations, request it made-to-order. You can also request changes or substitutions.
- Ask for sauces on the side. Most of an entrée's fat and calories come from the sauce.
- Rather than fat-laden creamy dressings, ask for organic, extra-virgin olive oil and put one tablespoon on your salad.
- Ask for steamed vegetables and add a dash of lemon, mustard, or a herb to liven up the dish.

Make It Work for You—The Recipes

In this chapter you will find menu ideas to get you started. At first you may spend a bit more time preparing food, but as you become familiar with the recipes and preparation techniques of Superfoods, you will be able to create your own recipes or make adjustments to your present favorite recipes to bring them to the healthful criteria of the Power of Superfoods. Your diet will be more interesting and varied as it becomes more healthful. The Power of Superfoods dietary strategies will work for you.

A Note on Salt and Salt Substitutes

In the following recipes we have reduced the salt without compromising the taste. To further reduce salt, substitute the following ingredients in recipes:

- For bouillon cubes, use no-salt or low-salt bouillon cubes.
- For broths and stocks, use no-salt or low-salt broths or stocks.
- For Gomashio, use only a little Celtic sea salt.
- For tamari soy sauce, use no-salt or low-salt tamari and dilute with water.
- For vegetable broth powder, use no-salt or low-salt broth powder.
- Dilute Bragg's Aminos with water.

Also see Salt Substitutes in the glossary for many tasty options.

Easy-to-Use, Energy-Boosting Recipes by Jeanne Marie Martin

❖ APPETIZERS AND SNACKS ❖

Green Magic Dip

(Serves 4 or more)

3 cups firmly packed spinach or 2 cups chopped asparagus or water-packed artichoke hearts

7 to 8 oz. regular/firm tofu, cut in 4 to 6 chunks

2 Tbs. chopped fresh parsley or
3 tsp. dried parsley flakes

2 tsp. tamari soy sauce, Mock Tamari Soy Sauce, or substitute

1/2 to 1 tsp. finely chopped raw onion or prepared horseradish

1 tsp. dill weed

1 tsp. basil

1/2 tsp. paprika

1/4 tsp. oregano

1/4 tsp. marjoram

1/4 tsp. thyme

Several dashes sea kelp and cayenne red pepper

1 to 2 tsp. green drink powder (optional)

1/2 cup water chestnuts or mung bean sprouts, chopped

1 small red bell pepper, chopped

1/4 to 1/2 cup sliced black olives (optional)

Steam the green vegetable for 4 minutes. Add the tofu and steam for another 6 to 8 minutes. Place the vegetables and tofu and all but the last 3 ingredients in a food processor or food mill and process until smooth. (If a blender is used, add a few drops of water and stop the blender several times and stir.) Steam the water chestnuts or mung beans for 4 to 5 minutes. Mix them along with the red pepper and olives into the vegetable/tofu mixture. Serve the dip with raw or steamed vegetable dippers. Keeps 1 to 2 days refrigerated. Do not freeze.

Cauliflower Curry Dip

(Serves 4 or more)

1 cup chopped cauliflower

1/4 cup milk substitute (soy, nut, oat, or rice milk)

1 small clove garlic, minced

1 tsp. curry powder

1/4 tsp. finely chopped onion

1/4 tsp. Celtic sea salt or substitute

1/4 tsp. cumin powder (cominos)

Few dashes ginger

Couple dashes cayenne red pepper

1/4 tsp. turmeric for more yellow color (optional)

Steam the cauliflower for 12 minutes or until tender. Combine all the ingredients in a food processor or blender and process until smooth. Serve warm or chilled with raw or steamed vegetable dippers. Keeps 2 to 3 days refrigerated. Do not freeze.

Orange Sweet Potato Dip

(Serves 4 or more)

2 cups chopped orange sweet potatoes (yams), rinsed 2 or 3 times

Flavorings #1

1/2 to 3/4 tsp. cinnamon

1 to 3 tsp. unsalted butter or organic extra-virgin olive oil

Couple dashes nutmeg

Couple dashes allspice or cloves

Celtic sea salt or substitute to taste

2 to 4 Tbs. ground or chopped raw nuts or seeds (optional)

Flavorings #2

1/2 cup finely chopped onion, sautéed in 1 to 2 tsp. unsalted butter or organic extra-virgin olive oil

1 Tbs. tamari soy sauce, Mock Tamari Soy Sauce, or substitute

Cayenne red pepper and Celtic sea salt or substitute to taste

2 to 4 Tbs. ground or chopped raw nuts or seeds (optional)

Steam the orange sweet potato for about 20 minutes or until tender, almost mushy. Use a food processor or small-holed hand masher to mix all the ingredients in Flavorings #1 or #2 with the steamed potato. Serve hot with raw or steamed vegetable dippers. Keeps 3 to 5 days refrigerated. Do not freeze.

Artichoke Nut Dip

(Serves 3 to 4)

7 to 8 oz. regular/firm tofu, cut in 4 to 6 chunks

1/2 cup chopped water-packed artichoke hearts

1/3 cup raw cashews, almonds, filberts, or pecans

3 to 4 Tbs. fresh lemon or lime juice

2 Tbs. chopped chives or green onion tops (green part only)

2 to 3 tsp. organic extra-virgin olive oil

Celtic sea salt or substitute to taste

1/2 to 1 tsp. green drink powder (optional)

Steam the tofu and artichoke hearts for 5 minutes. Leave raw or bake whole nuts on a dry flat pan in a single layer in a preheated 325°F oven for 4 to 7 minutes. Combine everything in a food processor and process until smooth. Chill and serve with raw or steamed vegetable dippers. Keeps 3 to 6 days refrigerated. Do not freeze.

Nutty Veggie Dip

(Serves 4 to 6)

2 1/2 cups chopped asparagus, broccoli, or carrots, or 3 to 4 cups packed spinach

1/2 cup sesame tahini, sunflower butter, almond butter, filbert butter, or cashew butter

3 to 4 tsp. finely chopped fresh parsley or 2 tsp. dried parsley flakes

1/2 tsp. basil

1/2 tsp. dill weed

1/2 tsp. tarragon (if carrots are used)

Celtic sea salt or substitute to taste

Several dashes ground seaweed or Nova Scotia dulse

Several dashes cayenne red pepper

1 small clove garlic, minced, or 1/4 to 1/2 tsp. prepared horseradish (optional)

Steam the vegetable until tender. Combine everything in a food processor and process until smooth. Serve with raw or steamed vegetable dippers as a snack or pour warmed over whole grains as a main dish. Keeps 1 to 3 days refrigerated. Do not freeze.

Yogurt Carrot Juice Delight

(Serves 1)

3 to 4 oz. freshly made organic carrot juice (or homemade refrigerated juice made within 12 hours)

6 to 8 oz. plain, low-fat, live-culture yogurt

Pour the juice over the yogurt and serve immediately.

Tangy Marinated Vegetables

(Serves 4 or more)

1/3 cup organic extra-virgin olive oil

2 to 3 Tbs. raw flax or pumpkin seed oil

2 Tbs. apple cider vinegar or 1 Tbs. fresh lemon
juice

1/4 tsp. Celtic sea salt or 1 to 2 tsp. tamari soy
sauce or substitute

1/2 tsp. dried parsley flakes, crushed

1/4 tsp. oregano

1/4 tsp. basil

Few dashes cayenne red pepper

Few dashes ground seaweed, or Nova Scotia
dulse

2 cups raw vegetables, chopped or sliced (bell
peppers, cucumbers, green beans, broccoli,
cauliflower, zucchini, mushrooms, tomatoes)

1 green onion or 1/4 cup chives, finely chopped
(optional)

Combine all the ingredients except the vegetables and beat well. Add the vegetables and onions and toss gently. Let soak 1 to 2 hours or more in the refrigerator, tossing 2 to 4 times. Drain the vegetables and let sit at room temperature for 5 to 8 minutes before serving.

Yogurt Nut Butter Dip

(Serves 2 to 4)

1/2 cup plain, low-fat, live-culture yogurt

1/3 cup sesame tahini, sunflower butter, pumpkin
seed butter, almond butter, or filbert butter

2 to 3 Tbs. fresh lemon juice

1 1/2 Tbs. chopped fresh parsley or 2 tsp. dried
parsley flakes

1 small clove garlic, minced

1/2 tsp. dill weed

1/4 tsp. ground cumin (cominos)

Several dashes cayenne red pepper

Mix all ingredients together well with a fork or wire whisk. Serve with steamed or raw vegetable dippers. Keeps refrigerated 1 to 3 days. Do not freeze.

Festive Black Bean Dip

(Serves 4 to 6)

1 cup dry black beans,* soaked 8 hours and sprouted for 12 hours

1 cup chopped onion

2 to 4 garlic cloves, minced

3 Tbs. finely chopped fresh parsley or 1 Tbs. dried parsley flakes

1/2 to 3/4 tsp. Celtic sea salt or substitute

Several dashes ground seaweed, or Nova Scotia dulse

1/2 tsp. ground cumin (cominos)

Cayenne red pepper to taste

Optional Toppings:

1 cup chopped tomatoes, salsa and/or guacamole

1 to 2 green onions, chopped very fine

Red bell pepper, diced

2 to 3 tsp. finely chopped jalapeño peppers or other hot peppers

Cook the beans in water for 1 to 1 1/2 hours or until very tender. Add the onion and garlic and cook another 20 minutes. Drain, saving 1/2 cup bean juice. Place bean mixture and remaining main ingredients in a food processor and process until smooth. Thin with reserved bean juice for thinner dip if you choose. Serve with one or more of the optional toppings. Eat with raw or steamed vegetable dippers, whole-grain pita, chipatis, or rye crackers. Keeps 6 to 7 days refrigerated and freezes well (without toppings).

*Pinto, kidney, adzuki, and red beans can also be substituted for black beans.

Tofu Mock Egg Salad

(Serves 3 to 4)

12 to 14 oz. regular/firm tofu, finely crumbled

2 stalks celery or 1/2 green pepper, very finely chopped

1 medium tomato, seeded, very finely chopped and towel-dried

5 to 7 green onion tops (green part only), finely chopped

1/4 to 1/2 tsp. garlic powder

1/4 tsp. paprika

Vegetable sea salt to taste or mix Celtic sea salt and green drink powder about half and half

Several dashes cayenne red pepper

Few dashes ground seaweed, or Nova Scotia dulse

Several dashes turmeric for yellow color (optional)

1/4 tsp. celery seed (optional)

1 to 2 tsp. parsley (optional)

Combine all ingredients in a bowl and stir well, but gently. Serve with rye crackers or whole-grain pita or chipatis. It can also be stuffed into tomatoes, bell peppers, or celery sticks. Keeps 2 to 4 days refrigerated. Do not freeze.

❖ DRESSINGS ❖

Zesty Herbs and Oil Dressing

(Makes 1 1/2 cups)

1 cup organic extra-virgin olive oil

1/2 cup raw flax or pumpkin seed oil

2 to 4 Tbs. apple cider vinegar or 2 Tbs. fresh lemon juice

2 Tbs. finely chopped fresh parsley or 1 Tbs. dried parsley flakes

3 to 4 tsp. finely chopped fresh basil or mint leaves or 1/2 tsp. dried leaves

2 tsp. finely chopped fresh dill weed or other green herb or 1/4 tsp. dried dill weed or other herb

2 tsp. tamari soy sauce or Mock Tamari Soy Sauce or 1 tsp. paprika

1 tsp. finely chopped fresh thyme or 1/4 tsp. dried thyme

1 tsp. green drink powder (optional)

1/2 to 3/4 tsp. Celtic sea salt or substitute

1/4 tsp. ground seaweed, or Nova Scotia dulse

Several dashes cayenne red pepper

1 clove garlic, minced, or 1 Tbs. finely chopped green onion (optional)

Mix all ingredients well using a fork or wire whisk and refrigerate for several hours or overnight. This dressing tastes naturally sweet and keeps about one week in a metal-lidded, bacteria-free glass jar. Refrigerate immediately after each use.

Yogurt and Herb Dressing

(Makes 1 cup)

1 cup plain, low-fat, live-culture yogurt

1 to 2 cloves garlic, minced, or 1 to 2 finely chopped green onions

1 Tbs. finely chopped fresh parsley or 1 tsp. dried parsley flakes

1 to 2 tsp. dried dill weed

1 to 3 tsp. fresh lemon or lime juice (optional)

1/4 to 1/2 tsp. paprika (optional)

Several dashes cayenne red pepper

Mix all ingredients with a fork. Chill and serve. Keeps refrigerated for 2 to 5 days (less if lemon or lime juice used).

Dill Cucumber Dressing (Oil-Free)

(Makes 1 1/2 cups)

1 medium organic cucumber, seeded (peeling optional, if organic)

1/2 cup pure water or plain, low-fat, live-culture yogurt

1 1/2 Tbs. finely chopped fresh dill weed or 2 tsp. dried dill weed

1 Tbs. finely chopped fresh parsley or 1 tsp. dried parsley flakes

1 to 2 cloves garlic, minced, or 2 to 3 green onions, chopped

Several dashes cayenne red pepper

Several dashes ground seaweed, or Nova Scotia dulse

Celtic sea salt or substitute to taste

Process all ingredients well in a blender. Chill and serve within 2 to 4 days for freshness and best flavor. Keep refrigerated.

Avocado Green Dressing

(Makes 1 1/2 cups)

2 ripe medium avocados

4 to 5 tsp. finely chopped fresh parsley or 2 tsp. dried parsley flakes

1/4 cup organic extra-virgin olive oil

2 to 3 Tbs. fresh lemon or lime juice

1 to 2 Tbs. raw flax, pumpkin seed or hemp seed oil

1/4 tsp. prepared horseradish or onion powder, or to taste

1/8 to 1/4 tsp. Celtic sea salt or substitute

Cayenne red pepper to taste

Few dashes ground seaweed, or Nova Scotia dulse

Process all ingredients in a blender or food processor and correct seasonings to taste. Chill. Serve on salads, vegetable dishes, or whole-grain recipes. Keeps 1 to 3 days refrigerated.

Easy Yogurt Dressing

(Makes 1 cup)

1 cup plain, low-fat, live-culture yogurt

2 tsp. dried dill weed

Cayenne red pepper to taste

Mix all ingredients well. Chill and serve. Keeps 4 to 6 days refrigerated.

Quick and Easy Salad Dressings

- Squeeze fresh lemon or lime juice over any green salad.
- Squeeze fresh grapefruit juice over any green salad.
- Top a salad with fresh, low-fat, live-culture yogurt and fresh chopped green herbs or fresh citrus juice.
- Mix organic extra-virgin olive, flax, pumpkin, or hemp oil(s) with a squeeze of fresh citrus juice or apple cider vinegar.

Sam Graci's Favorite Garnishes For Salads, Soups, and Entrées:

- Sprouts: alfalfa, clover, mung, red pea, hot radish, lentil, or sunflower
- Chopped parsley, Italian parsley, or cilantro
- Chopped or minced green onions, red onions, garlic, or chives
- Chopped exotic greens: arugula, endive, escarole, red oak, sorrel, dandelion leaves, mizuna, mesclun, radicchio
- Grated carrot, beet, white radish, zucchini, turnips, or peeled and grated kohlrabi
- Diced red, orange, yellow, green, or purple bell peppers
- Finely grated ginger root or horseradish
- Chopped fresh green herbs: basil, oregano, dill weed, thyme, sage, rosemary, marjoram, tarragon, mint, chevil
- Finely grated orange yam (sweet potato) or yellow sweet potato
- Sprinkle of soy lecithin granules or green drink powder

❖ SALADS ❖

Great Green Salad

(Serves 2)

8 to 12 large lettuce leaves (leaf, red, bibb, or Boston), torn in bite-sized pieces

1 small handful exotic greens (see Sam's Garnishes, above), torn

1 small or medium tomato, cut in thin wedges, or 6 to 8 radishes, sliced in thin rounds

1/4 organic cucumber or English cucumber or 1/4 small zucchini, sliced in 1/4-inch-thick rounds

1/2 bell pepper (red, yellow, purple, orange, or green), cut in thin strips (optional)

2 to 3 tsp. loosely chopped fresh parsley, chives, or green onions (optional)

Toss everything together and mix with your favorite dressing. Prepare as close to mealtime as possible for optimum freshness and flavor.

Spinach Sunshine Salad

(Serves 2)

1 small bunch spinach, leaves only, torn

1 cup quartered and chopped zucchini chunks

2 small carrots, finely grated

1/2 small or medium avocado, chopped, or 2 stalks celery, sliced, or 1/2 cup steamed asparagus, chopped and chilled

Toss the spinach and green vegetables together. Garnish each serving with half the grated carrot for a "sunny" topping and serve with any dressing soon after preparing. Does not store well.

Sweet Beet Salad

(Serves 2)

8 to 12 large lettuce leaves (leaf, red, bibb, or Boston), torn

1 handful of sprouts (see Sam's Garnishes, above)

1 fresh lemon (or lime), juiced

1 bell pepper (red, yellow, purple, orange or green), cut in thin strips

1/2 avocado, chopped, or 1/2 cup chopped water-packed artichoke hearts

2 small or 1 medium fresh red beet, finely grated

Toss together lettuce, sprouts, pepper, and avocado. Divide into servings and spread the beets over the top. (Adding beet to the mixture will dye the whole salad red.) Squeeze 1 to 2 tsp. of lemon or lime juice over the beets and serve with an oil-based or creamy dressing. Eat fresh. Does not store well.

Zesty Zucchini Salad

(Serves 2)

1 small zucchini, grated

1 medium tomato or 1 red or orange bell pepper, cut in chunks, or 6 to 8 radishes, sliced thin

2 stalks celery, sliced

8 to 12 spinach leaves, torn small

1 handful sprouts (see Sam's Garnishes, above) (optional)

Toss all ingredients gently together and serve with any dressing. Eat fresh. Do not store.

Rainbow Grated Salad

(Serves 2)

8 large leaves leaf or romaine lettuce (stalks/spines removed), thinly chopped or shredded

1/2 small zucchini or 1/2 peeled kohlrabi, grated

1 to 2 carrots, finely grated

4 to 6 red radishes, finely grated (optional)

1/2 yellow summer squash or yellow bell pepper, grated (optional)

1 small fresh beet, finely grated

Toss all the ingredients except the beet. Sprinkle it on top or around the edge of the salad bowl. Serve immediately with a creamy dressing like avocado or yogurt. Do not store.

Kohlrabi Coleslaw

(Serves 2)

1 1/2 to 2 cups peeled and grated kohlrabi

1/2 cup finely grated carrot

1/2 cup grated red bell pepper or 1/2 cup finely grated fresh beet

2 to 3 tsp. finely chopped chives or green onion tops (optional)

1/2 cup grated zucchini, organic cucumber or English cucumber (optional)

Tofu mayonnaise (available at health food stores) (optional)

Mix all ingredients except the beet, if used. Arrange on two plates. Top with grated beet, if used. (Adding beet to the mixture will dye the whole salad red.) Choose a creamy yogurt or avocado dressing or mix with tofu mayonnaise if desired. Eat fresh.

Exotic Greens Salad

(Serves 2)

3 to 4 cups exotic greens (See Sam's Garnishes, p.228), torn slightly or left whole

1 medium tomato, cut in thin wedges, or 1 medium red bell pepper, cut in thin strips

2 to 3 tsp. loosely chopped fresh parsley optional)

1 small handful edible flowers (optional)

4 water-packed artichoke hearts, drained, quartered, and steamed 4 to 5 minutes, or 8 to 12 black olives, halved lengthwise and left raw or steamed 3 to 4 minutes, or 1/2 avocado, cut in thin slices

Arrange the greens artistically on a plate and place other ingredients on top. Toss with an oil-based dressing or dribble a creamy dressing on top. Eat fresh. Do not store.

Layered Vegetable Salad

(Serves 4)

Layer 1
10 to 12 large lettuce leaves (leaf, red, bibb, or
    Boston), chopped

Layer 2
2 large tomatoes or 2 medium red bell peppers,
    cut in small chunks

Layer 3
2 cups quartered and chopped zucchini, organic
    cucumber, or English cucumber

Layer 4
2 to 3 medium carrots, finely grated

Layer 5
I large bunch spinach, chopped

Layer 6
1 to 2 beets, finely grated
1 Tbs. fresh lemon or lime juice (optional)

In a glass bowl (preferably one with straight sides) place layers 1 through 5. Toss the beet in the citrus juice, and sprinkle on top of the salad. Serve with any suitable dressing. Eat fresh. Do not store. (Grated vegetables do not store well.)

❖ SOUPS ❖

Great Greens Soup

(Serves 2 to 3)

4 to 6 bunches mixed greens: spinach, beet
    greens, chard, kale, and/or mustard greens
2 to 3 green onions, finely chopped
1 small clove garlic, minced
1 cup vegetable stock, cooking liquid from
    beans, or milk substitute
1 tsp. basil
1 tsp. dill weed
1/2 to 3/4 tsp. Celtic sea salt or substitute

1/2 tsp. marjoram
1/2 tsp. thyme
2 tsp. vegetable broth powder or 1 unsalted
    vegetable bouillon cube
2 to 4 dashes powdered ginger or 1/4 tsp. fresh-
    squeezed ginger juice
Several dashes of Nova Scotia dulse or ground
    seaweed and cayenne red pepper

Choose firm, bright, or dark green leaves. Remove any blemishes. Wash the greens and chop lightly. Steam until tender. Place the cooked greens with remaining ingredients in a blender and process until smooth. Transfer to a soup pot and simmer 15 to 20 minutes. Serve hot with garnishes. This wholesome soup is rich in iron and minerals. Keeps 1 to 2 days refrigerated. Do not freeze.

Savory Seaweed Soup

(Serves 6)

6 cups water, stock, broth, or vegetable bouillon (unsalted)

2 to 3 carrots, sliced thin

3 to 4 stalks celery, chopped

1 large onion, chopped

1/3 to 2/3 oz. dried seaweed (wakami or kombu are best) or 4 to 6 oz. fresh, edible seaweed, rinsed and chopped

1 to 2 unsalted vegetable bouillon cubes

4 tsp. finely chopped fresh parsley or 2 tsp. dried parsley flakes

Several dashes ground Nova Scotia dulse or seaweed

Few dashes cayenne red pepper

1/2 tsp. Celtic sea salt or substitute (optional)

1 cup mushrooms, sliced or chopped (shiitake, oyster, portobello, chanterelle, Chinese enoki, morel, cepe, or the traditional white-button or brown cremini) (optional)

1/3 cup dark miso

1 to 2 Tbs. organic extra-virgin olive oil (optional)

Heat 2 to 3 tablespoons of the liquid in a medium soup pot and sauté the carrots, celery, onions, and seaweed until crunchy tender. Add all the remaining ingredients except the miso and oil. Stir well. Bring the soup to just under a boil, then simmer for 25 to 35 minutes. Turn off the heat. Remove one cup of broth and blend or mash with the miso until smooth. (Do not cook the miso as it destroys valuable minerals and enzymes.) Return it to the soup. Add organic olive oil. Let the soup sit, covered, for 5 to 10 minutes. Stir and serve immediately. Keeps 5 to 7 days refrigerated. Do not freeze. Leftover soup can be reheated on low heat but do not boil.

Perfect Parsley Soup

(Serves 4 to 6)

4 cups chopped cauliflower or small white and purple turnips

1 cup water, stock, broth, or vegetable bouillon (unsalted)

1 large bunch spinach leaves

1 1/2 cups milk substitute (soy, nut, oat, or rice milk)

1 packed cup coarsely chopped fresh parsley

2 unsalted vegetable bouillon cubes or 3 tsp. vegetable broth powder

2 to 3 Tbs. tamari soy sauce or substitute

3 tsp. finely chopped onion

1 small clove garlic, minced

1 tsp. paprika

1 tsp. basil

Celtic sea salt (or substitute) and cayenne red pepper to taste

1 cup very finely chopped parsley

1 to 2 Tbs. unsalted organic butter or organic extra-virgin olive oil

Steam the cauliflower or turnip for 4 minutes. Add the washed spinach leaves and continue steaming for another 4 to 6 minutes or until both are very tender. Place in a blender with all other ingredients except finely chopped parsley and the oil or organic butter. Process until smooth. Transfer to a medium soup pot and stir in the finely chopped parsley. Simmer on low heat for 14 to 18 minutes. Remove from heat, correct the seasonings, and add oil or butter. Serve garnished with extra sprigs of parsley and Sam's Garnishes (p.228). Serve with legumes or whole grains and optional salad. Keeps fresh for 3 to 6 days refrigerated. Do not freeze.

Rainbow Soup

(Serves 6 to 8)

2 cups water, vegetable stock, or broth (unsalted)

2 cups cooking liquid from beans or vegetable bouillon (unsalted)

1/2 to 3/4 cup dry brown pot barley, buckwheat, kasha, or quinoa

5 to 6 large tomatoes, chopped, or 28-oz. can tomatoes, cored and chopped with the juice

1 medium onion, finely chopped (about 1 cup)

2 to 3 medium carrots, sliced 1/4-inch thick (about 1 cup)

1 cup celery, sliced 1/4-inch thick

1 cup finely chopped broccoli

1 cup chopped zucchini or yellow summer squash

1 cup fresh or frozen green peas (optional)

2 unsalted vegetable bouillon cubes or 2 to 3 Tbs. tamari soy sauce, Mock Tamari Soy Sauce, or substitute

2 tsp. vegetable broth powder

1/4 cup chopped fresh parsley or 2 Tbs. dried parsley flakes

1 tsp. each: basil and dill weed

3/4 tsp. Celtic sea salt or substitute

1/4 tsp. ground seaweed, or Nova Scotia dulse

Several dashes cayenne red pepper

Few drops stevia up to 1/4 tsp. or 1 to 2 tsp. honey or other sweetener (optional)

Place liquids, barley, and vegetables (except the peas, if used) in a medium soup pot. Bring to a boil on high heat, then simmer for 40 minutes. Add the remaining ingredients and simmer another 20 to 30 minutes. Serve hot. Keeps 5 to 7 days refrigerated. Best if not frozen.

Broccoli Bean Soup

(Serves 10 to 12)

2 cups dry pinto or adzuki beans, soaked 6 to 8
hours and sprouted for 12 hours

12 cups pure water, vegetable stock, or broth
(unsalted)

4 cups chopped broccoli

1 large onion, finely chopped (about 2 cups)

3 to 4 Tbs. tamari soy sauce, Mock Tamari Soy
Sauce, or substitute

1/3 cup finely chopped fresh parsley or 3 Tbs.
dried parsley flakes

4 tsp. vegetable broth powder

2 unsalted vegetable bouillon cubes

1 tsp. basil

1/2 to 1 tsp. Celtic sea salt or substitute

1/2 tsp. cumin powder (cominos) or paprika

1/4 to 1/2 tsp. dill weed

1/4 tsp. ground seaweed, or Nova Scotia dulse

Cayenne red pepper to taste

Few drops to 1/4 tsp. stevia or 1 to 2 tsp. honey
or other sweetening (optional)

2 Tbs. miso

2 Tbs. organic extra-virgin olive oil or unsalted
buttter

Garnish: 1 to 2 cups sprouts (see Sam's
Garnishes, p.228)

Cook the beans in liquid until very tender. Add enough water or stock to make a total of 12 cups. Add broccoli and onion and simmer for 20 minutes. Add the remaining ingredients, except the miso, oil, or unsalted butter, and garnishes. Cook another 20 minutes on medium heat. Place 4 cups of the soup, with the miso, oil, or butter in a blender or food processor. Process until smooth, then return to the soup. Serve hot. An easy-to-digest and nutritious soup, high in calcium and protein. Keeps 5 to 7 days refrigerated and may be frozen.

Lentil Vegetable Pottage

(Serves 5 to 6)

1 cup dry brown/green lentils

5 cups pure water, vegetable stock, broth or
bouillon (unsalted)

6 stalks celery, chopped

3 to 4 medium carrots, chopped small

1 large onion, finely chopped

2 cloves garlic, minced

2 unsalted vegetable bouillon cubes or 2 Tbs.
tamari soy sauce or substitute

1/4 cup finely chopped fresh parsley or 3 tsp.
dried parsley flakes

1 tsp. Celtic sea salt or substitute

1 tsp. basil

1 tsp. vegetable broth powder

1/2 tsp. dill weed

1/2 tsp. oregano

1/2 tsp. thyme

1/8 tsp. cayenne red pepper or to taste

Several dashes ground seaweed, or Nova Scotia
dulse

1 medium or large red bell pepper, finely
chopped (optional)

1 Tbs. organic extra-virgin olive oil (optional)

Place the dry lentils, water, celery, carrots, onion, and garlic in a medium soup pot and bring to a boil on high heat. Simmer for 1 hour until the lentils are very tender. Add remaining ingredients except organic oil and simmer another 15 to 25 minutes, stirring occasionally. If desired, blend 1 to 2 cups of the soup and return it to the rest for richer, fuller flavor and added body. Correct spices. Add oil just before serving. Serve hot. Keeps 5 to 7 days refrigerated or may be frozen.

Vegetable Red Lentil Soup

(Serves 8 to 12)

10 cups pure water, stock, broth, or vegetable bouillon (unsalted)

1 1/2 cups dry red lentils

4 stalks celery, chopped

1 medium to large stalk broccoli, finely chopped

1 small zucchini, sliced in half moons

2 1/2 to 3 cups chopped yam/orange sweet potato (1 large or 2 small), rinsed 2 to 3 times

3 large carrots, chopped (about 1 1/2 cups or bit more)

1 large onion, chopped (about 1 1/2 to 2 cups)*

3 cloves garlic, minced*

3 Tbs. tamari soy sauce or substitute

1/2 cup finely chopped fresh parsley or 3 Tbs. dried parsley flakes

3 unsalted vegetable bouillon cubes or 4 tsp. vegetable broth powder

1 to 1 1/2 tsp. Celtic sea salt or substitute

1 tsp. basil

1 tsp. paprika

1 tsp. oregano

1/4 tsp. ground seaweed, or Nova Scotia dulse

8 to 10 dashes cayenne pepper or to taste

Few drops up to 1/4 tsp. stevia sweetener or 1 to 2 tsp. honey or other sweetening (optional)

1 to 2 Tbs. organic extra-virgin olive oil (optional)

Steam the yams and carrots for 10 minutes then place them with the water, lentils, celery, broccoli, and zucchini in a large soup pot. Bring to a boil, then simmer 30 to 45 minutes. Sauté the onion and garlic* in water. Add onion and garlic (or horseradish) and remaining ingredients except oil to the soup pot. Simmer for another 20 to 25 minutes. Add oil if desired. Serve hot. This soup is a meal in itself but may be served with other accompaniments. Keeps 5 to 7 days refrigerated. May be frozen, but is best served fresh.

*Instead of onions and garlic, add 4 to 5 tsp. prepared horseradish to the soup with last ingredients, if desired.

Creamy Carrot or Orange Sweet Potato Soup

(Serves 4)

4 cups chopped and rinsed orange sweet potatoes (yams) or 4 cups chopped carrots

1 3/4 to 2 cups milk substitute, vegetable stock, or
broth (unsalted)

2 unsalted vegetable bouillon cubes or 1 1/2 Tbs.
tamari soy sauce or substitute

2 tsp. finely chopped onion

4 tsp. finely chopped fresh parsley or 2 tsp. dried
parsley flakes

2 tsp. dill weed or tarragon, crushed

1/2 tsp. Celtic sea salt or substitute

Several dashes ground seaweed, or Nova Scotia
dulse

Cayenne red pepper to taste

1/4 to 1/2 tsp. crushed, dried mint leaves (optional)

2 to 3 Tbs. unsalted butter or 1 to 2 Tbs. organic
extra-virgin olive oil

Garnishes: chopped chives or green onion tops or
chopped, fresh parsley or see Sam's Garnishes,
p.228.

Steam the orange vegetable until tender. Place all ingredients except organic oil in a blender or food processor and process until smooth. Transfer to a small soup pot and simmer for 10 minutes. Do not boil. Serve hot with unsalted butter or organic olive oil added after cooking, and garnish(s). Keeps refrigerated for 2 to 5 days. Do not freeze.

Wild Rice Celery Soup

(Serves 4 to 6)

2 cups chopped celery

2 oz. (4 Tbs.) regular/firm tofu

3 1/4 cups milk substitute (soy, nut, oat, or rice
milk)

2 cups cooked wild rice (about 1/2 to 2/3 cup dry)

2 to 3 Tbs. tamari soy sauce, Mock Tamari Soy
Sauce, or substitute

2 Tbs. finely chopped onion

1 small or medium clove garlic, minced

3 Tbs. chopped fresh parsley or 4 to 5 tsp. dried
parsley flakes

1 tsp. vegetable broth powder or 1/2 unsalted
vegetable bouillon cube

1/2 tsp. Celtic sea salt or substitute

1/2 tsp. paprika or 2 pinches saffron

Few dashes ground seaweed or Nova Scotia dulse

Few dashes cayenne red pepper

1 to 2 Tbs. unsalted butter or 1 Tbs. organic extra-
virgin olive oil (optional)

Garnish: 1/4 cup chopped chives or green onion
tops or sprouts

Steam the celery and tofu for 7 to 9 minutes or until tender. Place all ingredients, except the organic oil or unsalted butter and garnishes and 1/4 to 1/3 cup of the wild rice in a blender. Process until smooth. Transfer the blended mixture to a medium soup pot. Add the remaining whole rice. Cover and bring to a low boil over medium heat. Simmer 20 to 30 minutes, stirring occasionally. Remove from heat and add oil or butter and garnishes. Serve hot. Keeps 3 to 5 days refrigerated. Best if not frozen.

❖ SAUCES ❖

Tasty Nut or Seed Sauce

(Makes about 3 1/2 cups)

1 cup nut or seed butter (almond, cashew, or filbert butter, or sesame tahini or sunflower butter)

1 cup oven-toasted nuts or seeds, ground (use same nut or seed as used for butter)

1 3/4 cups milk substitute (soy, nut, oat, or rice milk)*

2 oz. (4 Tbs.) regular/firm tofu*

2 Tbs. arrowroot powder

2 to 3 Tbs. finely chopped onion

1 Tbs. tamari soy sauce or substitute or 2 tsp. vegetable broth powder

2 cloves garlic, crushed

1 unsalted vegetable bouillon cube

1/2 tsp. paprika

1/2 tsp. powdered saffron or 1 g saffron strands (optional)

Celtic sea salt or substitute to taste

Several dashes cayenne red pepper or to taste

Squeeze of ginger-root juice or lemon or lime juice (optional)

Few drops to 1/4 tsp. stevia or 1 tsp. honey or maple syrup or 1 Tbs. apple, peach or pear juice (optional)

Place all the ingredients in the blender and liquefy. Transfer to a saucepan. Cook on medium-low heat, stirring regularly, until thickened, about 20 minutes. Serve on vegetables, whole grains, or casseroles. Keeps 4 to 6 days refrigerated or may be frozen.

* Instead of the milk substitute and tofu, use 2 cups liquid from cooking beans (optional).

Naturally Sweet Onion Sauce

(Makes 2 to 3 cups)

1/2 cup cooking liquid from brown beans like pinto, kidney, or adzuki beans, broth, or vegetable bouillon (unsalted)

4 cups finely chopped or sliced onions

2 to 4 Tbs. tamari soy sauce or Mock Tamari Soy Sauce, or 1 unsalted vegetable bouillon cube

1 Tbs. organic extra-virgin olive oil or unsalted butter

In a skillet (preferably cast-iron), heat 2 to 3 tablespoons of the bean cooking liquid on high, and sauté the onion for 2 to 3 minutes or until tender. Add the remaining liquid and tamari and simmer, covered, for 1 hour. Remove from heat and stir in the organic oil. Serve hot over whole grains and/or vegetables or as a gravy or topping for casseroles. The onions turn deliciously sweet during the long simmering process. Keeps 7 to 10 days refrigerated. May be frozen but is best fresh. This recipe can be used as a mushroom substitute in some recipes.

Orange Yam Sauce

(Makes about 3 cups)

4 cups peeled and chopped orange yams (orange sweet potatoes)

1/3 to 1/2 cup milk substitute (soy, nut, oat, or rice milk)

2 to 3 Tbs. finely chopped fresh parsley (optional)

1 Tbs. tamari soy sauce or substitute or 1 unsalted vegetable bouillon cube

2 tsp. finely chopped onion

1 tsp. basil (optional)

3/4 to 1 tsp. curry powder

1/4 tsp. each oregano and thyme (optional)

1/4 to 1/2 tsp. Celtic sea salt or substitute

Several dashes cayenne red pepper or to taste

Several dashes ground seaweed or Nova Scotia dulse (optional)

1/2 tsp. prepared horseradish or 1 small clove garlic, minced, or 1/4 cup finely chopped chives or green onions (optional)

Rinse the yam several times and steam until tender. Use a food processor or masher to mix all the ingredients. Transfer to a saucepan or double boiler and cook, covered, on low heat until hot throughout, about 15 minutes. Stir regularly. Serve hot on vegetables or whole grains. Keeps 3 to 5 days refrigerated. Best fresh but may be frozen.

Mock Cheese Sauce

(Makes 1 1/2 cups)

1/2 cup engivita yeast or other good-tasting yellow nutritional yeast (not baking yeast)

3 Tbs. flour (amaranth, teff, kamut, spelt, oat, millet, brown rice, or quinoa)

4 tsp. arrowroot powder

1/2 tsp. Celtic sea salt

1 cup pure water

1 Tbs. organic extra-virgin olive oil

1 to 2 tsp. prepared Dijon or yellow mustard, or 1/2 to 1 tsp. dry mustard (optional)

In a saucepan, mix the yeast, flour, arrowroot powder, and sea salt. Add the water and mix thoroughly with a wire whisk. Cook over medium heat, stirring or whisking constantly, until the mixture thickens and begins to bubble slightly. Add oil and mustard, heat another 30 seconds, and serve over vegetables and/or whole grains instead of regular cheese sauce. Keeps 2 to 4 days refrigerated. Do not freeze.

❖ MAIN DISHES ❖

Vital Vegetable Bean Stew

(Serves 6 to 8)

1 1/2 cups dry pinto, romano, kidney, or black beans, soaked 6 to 8 hours and sprouted for 12 hours

4 medium carrots, chopped small

1/2 cauliflower or 3 to 4 small white and purple turnips, chopped in 1-inch chunks

1 stalk broccoli, chopped (about 1 1/2 to 2 cups)

1 extra-large or 2 medium onions, chopped

4 to 6 Jerusalem artichokes, finely chopped (optional)

3 to 4 small red-skinned potatoes, cut in 1-inch chunks (optional)

5 to 6 stalks celery, in 1-inch chunks

1 to 2 red bell peppers, cut in 1-inch chunks

1 small zucchini or yellow summer squash, quartered and cut in 1-inch chunks

8 to 12 water chestnuts, chopped or sliced, or 1/2 to 1 cup mung bean sprouts* (optional)

2 Tbs. tamari soy sauce, Mock Tamari Soy Sauce, or substitute

4 tsp. vegetable broth powder or 2 unsalted vegetable bouillon cubes

1/3 cup fresh chopped parsley or 2 Tbs. dried parsley flakes

1 tsp. Celtic sea salt or substitute

1 tsp. basil

1 tsp. dill weed

1/2 tsp. paprika or cumin powder (cominos)

1/4 tsp. ground seaweed, or Nova Scotia dulse

1/4 tsp. thyme

Several dashes cayenne red pepper or to taste

In a large pot cook the beans for 1 to 1 1/2 hours or until very tender. Steam the carrots, cauliflower, turnips, broccoli, Jerusalem artichokes, and potatoes for 6 to 8 minutes, until slightly tender. When the beans are done, drain off all but two cups of the cooking water. Add all other ingredients (except mung bean sprouts, if used) and simmer for 20 to 30 minutes or until all vegetables are tender but not mushy. Serve hot. A complete meal by itself, especially high in protein and calcium. Keeps up to 7 days refrigerated and freezes well.

* If mung bean sprouts are used, do not add until the last 10 minutes of cooking.

Mock Meatballs

(Serves 4)

2 to 3 Tbs. pure water, stock, broth, or vegetable bouillon (unsalted)

1 large onion, finely chopped (about 1 1/2 cups)

1 cup finely chopped broccoli or asparagus

1 cup finely chopped carrots or orange yams (rinse yams, if used)

1 cup finely chopped celery or bell pepper

1/2 cup finely chopped water chestnuts, almonds, or pecans

1/2 cup finely chopped black olives, or water-packed artichoke hearts

2 to 3 cloves garlic, minced or pressed

2 Tbs. vegetable broth powder or 2 unsalted vegetable bouillon cubes

2 to 3 tsp. tamari soy sauce or substitute

3 to 4 Tbs. chopped fresh parsley or 4 tsp. dried parsley flakes

1 tsp. basil

1 tsp. paprika

1 tsp. dill weed

1/2 tsp. marjoram

1/2 tsp. thyme

1/4 tsp. Celtic sea salt or substitute

2 cups crumbled regular/firm tofu or cooked whole grain (brown rice, millet, brown pot barley, kasha, or quinoa)

1/2 cup ground raw almonds, filberts, pecans, or sunflower seeds

2 Tbs. bean flour (soy, chickpea, or brown lentil flour)

In a skillet, heat the water or liquid on high until bubbly and sauté the onions for 1 minute, stirring regularly. Add the broccoli/asparagus and carrots/yams and sauté for another 2 to 3 minutes. Add all the remaining ingredients except the last three, and sauté another 2 minutes. Remove from the heat. In a large bowl mix the remaining three ingredients together and add the vegetable mixture to them, mixing thoroughly. Form the mixture into balls, using 1/8 to 1/4 cup for each ball. Place the balls on an oiled flat pan and bake in a preheated 400°F oven for 18 to 22 minutes until firm, browned, and hot. Serve with a gravy, tomato sauce, Naturally Sweet Onion Sauce, or any special sauce along with other vegetables and whole grains or legumes. The meatballs keep 5 to 7 days refrigerated and may be frozen although they are best fresh.

Mock Meat Loaf

(Serves 4)

Organic extra-virgin olive oil

1 recipe for Mock Meat Balls

Sesame or sunflower seeds, raw, hulled

Paprika (optional)

Oil a large loaf pan or small square casserole dish. Line the bottom of the pan with wax paper and oil it again. Gently press the Mock Meatballs mixture into the pan and shape a smooth, slightly rounded top. Press sesame or sunflower seeds into the top and sprinkle on paprika for added color. Bake uncovered in a preheated 375°F oven for 40 to 50 minutes until browned and firm. Cool 5 to 10 minutes before slicing. Serve with a favorite sauce and vegetable side dishes. Keeps up to 7 days refrigerated or may be frozen.

Planter's Pie (Vegetarian Shepherd's Pie)

(Serves 4)

2 medium heads cauliflower or 1 large butternut
  or buttercup squash or 4 to 6 large orange
  yams or red-skinned potatoes

1 unsalted vegetable bouillon cube

2 to 3 Tbs. pure water, stock, broth, or vegetable
  bouillon (unsalted)

1 to 1 1/4 cups diced onions

1 cup diced carrots

1 cup diced celery or broccoli or asparagus

8 to 10 oz. regular firm tofu, mashed

2 1/2 to 3 cups tomato sauce

1 cup fresh or frozen green peas or 1 cup diced
  zucchini

Several dashes Celtic sea salt

Organic extra-virgin olive oil (optional)

Steam the cauliflower, yams, or potatoes (if squash is substituted, it may be baked) about 12 to 15 minutes or until tender. Mash with the vegetable bouillon cube until smooth and all lumps are gone. Set aside. (The mashed vegetable should equal 3 1/2 to 4 cups.) In a large skillet (preferably cast-iron), heat the water or other liquid and sauté the onion for 1 minute. Add the carrots and celery and sauté for 2 to 3 minutes until somewhat tender. Add the mashed tofu and sauté 1 to 2 minutes more. Heat the tomato sauce and add to the sautéed mixture, along with the peas and sea salt. Spread the sautéed mixture in a 2 1/2-quart baking dish 2 to 3 inches high (a 9" x 13" pan works well). Spread on an even layer of mashed vegetables and smooth. Bake in a preheated 350°F oven for 40 to 45 minutes until hot throughout, very tender, and the mashed vegetables on top have "set" and become a bit firm. Top with organic olive oil before serving if desired. This is a complete meal in itself but may be served with salad. Keeps 4 to 6 days refrigerated and is best if not frozen. Bake to reheat.

Spaghetti Squash

(Serves 2)

1 medium spaghetti squash

3 to 4 cups tomato sauce, Tasty Nut or Seed Sauce, Naturally Sweet Onion Sauce, Mock Cheese Sauce, or other sauce, heated (p.238)

Boil a whole spaghetti squash in a large pot of water for 55 to 75 minutes or until tender enough for a knife to slide in easily. (If preferred, cut the squash in half lengthwise, remove the seeds and pulp, and bake cut side down on a flat baking sheet in a preheated 350°F oven for 35 to 45 minutes or until tender.) While the squash is cooking, prepare or heat the sauce. Cut the squash in half lengthwise and scrape out and discard the seeds and pulp. Use a fork to scrape the edible squash from its skin and place it on a plate. Cover the hot squash with the heated sauce and serve. The squash can be steamed or baked to reheat and keeps 4 to 6 days refrigerated.

Herb Scrambled Tofu with Vegetables

(Serves 2-3)

14-16 oz. regular/firm tofu, cut into 4 to 6 pieces

2-4 Tbs. pure water, stock, broth, or vegetable bouillon (unsalted)

3-4 green onions, diced

1/2 cup finely chopped red bell pepper or finely grated carrot

1/2 cup finely chopped asparagus or broccoli or zucchini

1 Tbs. tamari soy sauce or substitute or 1 unsalted vegetable bouillon cube, broken up

3-4 tsp. finely chopped fresh parsley

1 tsp. finely chopped fresh basil or dill weed or 1/4 tsp. dried basil or dill weed

1/2 tsp. Celtic sea salt or substitute

1/2 tsp. curry powder or 1/4 tsp. cumin powder plus 1/4 tsp. paprika

Several dashes cayenne red pepper to taste

1 Tbs. organic extra-virgin olive oil (optional)

Steam the tofu for 4 to 5 minutes unless very fresh. Mash and set aside. In a cast-iron skillet or metal frying pan, heat the liquid until bubbly and sauté the onions and vegetables for about 2 minutes. Add the tofu and remaining ingredients except the oil or butter, and sauté for 4 to 6 minutes more. Remove from heat and stir in the organic oil. Serve immediately, alone or with other vegetables. Delicious topped with a sauce or salsa. Keeps 2 to 4 days refrigerated. Do not freeze.

Tangy Three Bean Chili

(Serves 6 to 8)

1 cup dry pinto beans, soaked 8 hours and
   sprouted for 12 hours

1 cup kidney beans, soaked 8 hours and sprouted for 12 hours

1/2 cup chickpeas, soaked 10 to 12 hours and
   sprouted for 12 hours

1/4 cup pure water, stock, broth, or vegetable
   bouillon (unsalted)

2 medium onions, chopped (about 2 cups)

4 to 6 cloves garlic, minced

1 to 2 green, yellow, or red bell peppers,
   chopped (optional)

12 to 13 oz. tomato paste

4 to 5 large tomatoes (cored and chopped)
   or 28-oz. can tomatoes,

2 to 3 Tbs. tamari soy sauce or substitute

2 Tbs. chopped fresh parsley or 1 Tbs. dried
   parsley flakes

3 to 4 tsp. chili powder

1 tsp. Celtic sea salt or substitute

1 tsp. oregano

1 tsp. crushed red chili peppers or 1 to 2 fresh
   hot peppers, chopped

1/2 tsp. ground seaweed or Nova Scotia dulse

1/4 tsp. cumin seeds or 1/2 tsp. cumin powder
   (cominos)

1/16 to 1/4 tsp. cayenne red pepper

2 Tbs. organic extra-virgin olive oil (optional)

1 cup cooked millet or white quinoa (optional)

Combine beans and cook in water for about 1 1/2 to 2 hours or until tender. Meanwhile, heat the liquid in a large cast-iron or steel skillet and sauté the onions and garlic for 2 to 3 minutes. Add the bell pepper, and sauté another 2 to 3 minutes. Add the remaining ingredients (except the beans and oil) and simmer for 35 to 50 minutes. When the beans are ready, drain them and save the liquid. Mix the sauce and beans together and add some of the extra bean cooking liquid (about 1/4 to 1/2 cups or so) if needed to bring the chili to a desired consistency. Add millet or quinoa now if desired. Cook the chili for 20 to 25 minutes. Remove from heat, add the oil, and serve with bread or a cooked whole grain and green vegetables and/or a salad. Keeps refrigerated for 6 to 8 days and freezes well.

For Chili Soup, add 2 cups or more of tomato juice during the last 20 minutes of cooking and correct seasonings as desired.

Spinach Tofu Stuffed Zucchini

(Serves 4)

6 small zucchini, cut in half lengthwise, ends removed

3 large bunches (or 4 small) fresh spinach, lightly chopped

2 to 3 Tbs. pure water, stock, broth, or vegetable bouillon (unsalted)

6 to 8 green onions, finely chopped

1 medium red or orange bell pepper, finely chopped

1/4 cup pine nuts, sunflower seeds, chopped raw almonds, or other nuts

8 to 10 oz. regular/firm tofu, crumbled

2 cloves garlic, minced

3 Tbs. chopped fresh parsley or 1 Tbs. dried parsley flakes

1 1/2 Tbs. tamari soy sauce or substitute or 2 unsalted vegetable bouillon cubes mashed into tofu while sautéing

1 tsp. Celtic sea salt or substitute

1 tsp. curry powder

1 tsp. basil

1/4 tsp. marjoram

1/4 tsp. dill weed

1/4 tsp. thyme

Several dashes cayenne red pepper

Steam the zucchini for 5 to 7 minutes until slightly tender. Steam the spinach separately for about 5 minutes or until tender. In a large skillet, heat the liquid on high heat. Sauté the onions, pepper, and nuts for 2 minutes, stirring constantly. Add remaining ingredients and sauté for another 2 to 3 minutes. Remove from heat and mix with the steamed spinach. Place the strips of zucchini, cut side up and touching each other, in a low baking dish, with 1/4 inch or more of water on the bottom. Cover the zucchini with the spinach-tofu mixture. Bake in a preheated 350°F oven for 12 to 16 minutes until everything is hot and tender throughout. Serve immediately by itself or covered in gravy, tomato sauce, or Mock Cheese Sauce. Serve with whole grains and optional salad. Keeps 2 to 4 days refrigerated. Do not freeze.

❖ SIDE DISHES ❖

Turnip Homefries

(Serves 2)

1/2 cup pure water, stock, broth, or vegetable bouillon (unsalted)

1/2 to 1 tsp. fresh hot peppers, chopped (optional for added flavor)

3 to 4 small white and purple turnips, peeled or unpeeled

1 tsp. dried parsley flakes, crushed

1/2 tsp. dried basil, crushed

1/4 tsp. thyme or dill weed

Few dashes ground seaweed or Nova Scotia dulse

Few dashes cayenne red pepper

Celtic sea salt or substitute (optional)

Pour the liquid into a small dish, add the hot pepper, if used, and let sit 5 to 15 minutes. Chop the turnips into french-fry-size strips or 1/4-inch-thick rounds. In another bowl, mix the parsley, basil, thyme, seaweed, and pepper. Dip the fries or rounds into the liquid, then roll or dip them in the herbs. Lightly salt each one if desired. Place the fries on an oiled baking sheet and bake in a preheated 350°F oven for 20 to 25 minutes, or until the fries are browned and tender. Serve hot. Do not store.

Quick and Easy Winter Squash

(Serves 2 to 4)

1 medium or large acorn, turban, spaghetti, butternut, buttercup, or other medium winter squash or 2 large pieces hubbard or other large winter squash

Celtic sea salt or substitute (optional)

Organic extra-virgin olive oil (optional)

Cut the squash in half and scoop out the seeds and pulp. Place the pieces cut side down on a lightly oiled metal sheet and bake in a preheated 400°F oven for 25 to 40 minutes, or until tender and a knife passes through easily. The skin should be only slightly browned or wrinkled. Serve with sea salt and Sam's Garnishes. Refrigerate for up to 4 to 5 days and steam to reheat. Do not freeze.

Cinnamon Baked Squash

(Serves 2 to 4)

1 medium butternut or buttercup squash   Cinnamon
Pure water

Cut the squash in half from top to bottom. Scoop out the seeds and pulp and discard. Fill each half with water and sprinkle the cut section generously with cinnamon. Place the squash halves in a low baking dish surrounded by 3/4 to 1 inch water. Bake in a preheated 400°F oven for 50 to 65 minutes, or until a knife passes through easily. Cut and serve hot. Keeps refrigerated for 3 to 4 days and is best if not frozen.

❖ MEAT DISHES ❖

Baked Salmon Fillets

(Serves 2)

12 to 16 oz. salmon fillet(s)	1/4 tsp. basil, crushed
2 to 3 Tbs. tamari soy sauce or substitute	Several dashes Celtic sea salt or substitute
2 to 3 tsp. fresh lemon or lime juice	Few dashes cayenne red pepper
1 to 2 tsp. dried parsley leaves, crushed	1/8 tsp. tarragon or dill weed (optional)
1/4 to 1/2 tsp. paprika	Topping/Garnish: 1 to 2 tsp. unsalted butter

Wash the fish and place skin side down in a lightly oiled, low glass baking dish. Add about 1/4 to 1/3 inch water. Pour the tamari then the juice over the fillets. Sprinkle the parsley and other herbs evenly on top. Bake in a preheated 375°F oven, basting once or twice, for 9 to 14 minutes or until fish flakes, changes color, and is cooked evenly throughout. Add a bit of extra hot water around the fish if needed during cooking. Serve with lemon or lime wedges, parsley sprigs and/or fresh chopped parsley, chives or green onion tops, and unsalted butter if desired. Serve with whole grains and vegetables. Keeps 1 to 2 days refrigerated and may be frozen, but best if not frozen.

Herb Baked Sole or Cod

(Serves 2)

1 lb. fresh or thawed sole or cod fillets

2 to 3 Tbs. stock, broth, or vegetable bouillon (unsalted)

1 Tbs. amaranth or teff flour or 1 Tbs. ground almonds or filberts

2 green onions, finely chopped, or 3 tbs. finely chopped chives

1 small clove garlic, minced

1 tsp. finely chopped fresh dill weed or 1/2 tsp. dried dill weed

2 Tbs. finely chopped fresh parsley

1/2 tsp. basil and/or chervil

1/4 tsp. thyme

1/4 tsp. marjoram

1/8 tsp. Celtic sea salt or substitute

Couple dashes tarragon

Several dashes cayenne red pepper

Garnishes: lemon or lime wedges and/or parsley sprigs

Wash the fish and place in an oiled, low baking dish with a cover. Heat the remaining ingredients in a small saucepan for 2 minutes, stirring to remove any lumps. Pour the sauce over the fish, cover the dish, and bake for 25 minutes or until the fish flakes easily and has a uniform texture. Garnish and serve with whole grains, green vegetables and/or a salad. Keeps 1 to 2 days refrigerated and may be frozen, but is best if not.

Herb Garlic Chicken

(Serves 2)

4 large pieces skinless chicken (breasts or legs with thighs)

4 Tbs. low-salt tamari soy sauce or substitute

Lots of dried parsley and paprika

1/2 tsp. basil

1/2 tsp. thyme

Few dashes Celtic sea salt or substitute (optional)

6 very large or 10 to 12 small garlic gloves, crushed

Several dashes cayenne red pepper

Wash the chicken and place in a glass baking dish with about 1/3 inch water in the bottom. Pour the tamari on the chicken pieces, then sprinkle generously with parsley, covering the entire surface of each piece of chicken. Sprinkle on just as much paprika. Sprinkle on basil, thyme, and sea salt. Place the garlic in the water surrounding the chicken. Bake in a preheated 350°F oven for 35 to 45 minutes until tender, and cooked throughout. After the first 10 minutes, baste every 10 minutes with the garlic and juices from the bottom of the dish. Serve with green vegetables and/or salad. Keeps 3 to 4 days refrigerated and may be frozen.

Stuffed Trout or Salmon With Sun-Dried Tomatoes

(Serves 4 to 6)

1 large (2 to 3 lb.) whole rainbow trout or salmon, fresh or thawed

2 to 3 Tbs. stock, broth or vegetable bouillon (unsalted)

1 medium onion, chopped (1 to 1 1/4 cups)

2 cloves garlic, minced

3 Tbs. chopped sun-dried tomatoes (dry, not packed in oil)

2 Tbs. lightly chopped fresh parsley

2 to 3 tsp. chopped fresh basil or 1/4 tsp. dried basil

1/4 tsp. oregano

1/4 tsp. dill weed

1/4 tsp. thyme

1/8 tsp. or less Celtic sea salt (or substitute)

Several dashes cayenne red pepper

3 to 4 green onions, chopped

2 to 3 lemons or limes, sliced in 1/4-inch rounds

Wash and clean the fish. Remove the fins but leave the head and tail. Slice along the belly from the head to the tail. Remove large bones if desired. In a large frying pan or skillet, heat the liquid and sauté the onion and garlic for 2 minutes until fairly tender. Add the sun-dried tomatoes, parsley, basil, oregano, dill, thyme, salt, and pepper, and sauté another 1 to 2 minutes. Remove from heat and stir in the raw green onion. Stuff the mixture evenly into the fish. Place the fish in a lightly oiled baking dish and top with a layer or two of citrus slices. Bake in a preheated 450°F oven for 20 to 25 minutes, or until the flesh is opaque and flakes easily. Serve immediately with green vegetables and/or a salad, whole grains or other dishes. Keeps refrigerated 1 to 2 days and may be baked or steamed to reheat. May be frozen, but is best if not.

Yogurt and Spice Chicken

(Serves 4)

4 large, boneless, skinless chicken breasts

1 cup plain, low-fat, live-culture yogurt

1/3 cup fresh lemon juice

3 to 4 cloves garlic, minced

2 tsp. curry powder

1 tsp. cinnamon

1/2 tsp. cumin powder (cominos)

1/4 tsp. Celtic sea salt or substitute

Two dashes allspice or cloves

A dash two of nutmeg

Several dashes cayenne red pepper

Cut the breasts in half, wash the chicken, and pat it dry. Make small cuts in the chicken so it can absorb the marinade. Mix the remaining ingredients in a glass bowl* and add the chicken. Turn the chicken to coat well and let marinate, covered, in the refrigerator for 4 hours, turning the chicken 2 to 3 times. Place marinated chicken on an oiled broiling pan and baste with extra marinade. Broil about 2 inches from the heat for 7 to 9 minutes on each side, basting once or twice for each side. Garnish with lemon wedges and parsley sprigs. Serve immediately with vegetables and/or salad. Keeps 1 to 3 days refrigerated and may be frozen.

* Never marinate in a metal bowl if citrus juice is used.

Mediterranean Chicken or Turkey Stew

(Serves 4)

4 cups tomato sauce

1 medium or large chicken, skinned and cut into pieces, or 2 to 3 large pieces of turkey, cut in smaller pieces

8 to 10 water-packed artichoke hearts, sliced

1 cup black olives, cut in half

1/2 cup or more chopped water chestnuts, pine nuts, or chopped blanched almonds

5 to 6 green onions, chopped

1 to 2 cloves garlic, minced

Broth, stock, or vegetable bouillon (unsalted)

Celtic sea salt or substitute to taste

Cayenne red pepper to taste

4 to 6 cups cooked spaghetti squash or steamed cauliflower (optional)

1/2 cup lightly chopped fresh parsley

Heat the sauce in a large saucepan. Wash the poultry and remove any fatty parts. Add the poultry, artichoke hearts, olives, water chestnuts, green onions, and garlic to the sauce. Cover and simmer for 60 to 75 minutes or until the poultry falls off the bone and is very tender. Add 1/2 cup or more stock or other liquid as needed while cooking, if mixture is too thick. Add sea salt and cayenne. Serve over cooked spaghetti squash or cauliflower. Top each serving with parsley. Serve with green vegetables and/or a salad. Keeps 2 to 4 days refrigerated and may be frozen.

❖ GARNISHES ❖

Tempeh

Blocks of this fermented soybean product can be bought at health stores. Cut it into small cubes or pieces and add it to stir-fries for extra protein and enzymes. It may also be sautéed or broken up into bits and added to soups, sauces, and casseroles.

Toasted Nori Seaweed

Place individual sheets of plain nori (not sushi nori) in a preheated 400°F oven. Turn off the oven as soon as the door is closed. Leave for 1 to 3 minutes, until quick-toasted. Another way to toast nori is to lay one sheet at a time over a toaster that is on. Turn it every few seconds until each side and edge is covered and shrivels up a bit. Eat the crunchy sheets immediately, just as they are, or crumble them into soups or over whole grains or sauces. Toasted nori makes a great garnish, side dish, or snack. It is very nutritious and full of minerals. Store in tins, jars or bags for many months. Purchased toasted, or sushi, nori may be eaten as is; however, home-toasted tastes best.

Gomashio/Sesame Salt (No Oil Added)

(Makes about 3/4 cup)

1 cup hulled, white sesame seeds*	2 to 3 Tbs. Celtic sea salt or substitute

Spread the seeds on a dry baking pan and bake in a preheated 300°F oven for 4 to 5 minutes. Stir well and bake another 2 to 4 minutes. Stir again and bake another 2 to 3 minutes until lightly browned and toasty-smelling. (Sesame seeds can also be heated in a dry cast-iron skillet on medium-high heat, stirring almost constantly until browned.) Cool for 5 minutes or more, grind the seeds, 1/4 cup at a time, in a blender or all at once in a food processor or coffee mill. (Traditional gomashio leaves half the seeds whole and grinds the rest. For easier digestion, grind all the seeds as finely as possible.) Mix in the sea salt and keep the gomashio in a jar, to prevent bacteria growth, for 1 to 2 weeks in the refrigerator or longer in the freezer. Sesame seeds are high in calcium, and gomashio adds flavor and nutrients to simple dishes as well as improving fancy dishes. Gomashio can also be used to reduce the amount of salt in recipes and still provide delicious flavor.

*Sunflower seeds may be substituted if desired.

Mock Tamari Soy Sauce

(Makes about 1 to 1/4 cups)

2 1/4 cups cooking liquid from black beans*

3/4 to 1 tsp. Celtic sea salt or substitute

1/8 to 1/4 tsp. ground seaweed or Nova Scotia dulse

1/8 tsp. vegetable powder (or ground, dried vegetables) or 1/6 unsalted vegetable bouillon cube

In a saucepan mix all ingredients together and bring to a boil. Reduce the heat immediately and simmer for 90 minutes, covered, stirring every 15 minutes or so. Use a knife to scrape any spices off the side of the pan while stirring and mix them back into the liquid. Keeps 5 to 7 days refrigerated. Freeze 2 Tbs. servings of the Mock Tamari in ice-cube-tray sections for later use. Once frozen, place the "tamari cubes" in a plastic bag or freezer jar in the freezer.

*Allow the juice to settle and only use clear, dark juice on top. Do not use the cloudy part.

❖ GRAINS AND CEREALS ❖

Cooking Whole Grains

- Grains are generally cooked in 2 or more cups of pure water per 1 cup of grain. Those with digestive troubles should use even more water, 2 1/2 to 3 cups per cup of whole grain.
- Cook grains until they are no longer crunchy, but not soggy or mushy. Grains should be tender and easy to chew. Improperly cooked grains are extremely hard to digest!
- Only a few grains need to be soaked before cooking. These include whole oats, rye, triticale, whole wheat (wheat kernels or berries), kamut, spelt, and rarely wild rice.
- Before cooking, check grains for dirt balls, gravel, husks, and other foreign particles by spreading them out and fingering through them. Discard discolored, distorted grains along with unwanted particles.
- Brown rice and quinoa are usually the only grains that need washing, but you may wash any grain if you feel it needs it.
- To prevent grains from boiling over and to distribute heat evenly, water and grains together should never fill more than 3/4 of the cooking pot.
- Do not add sea salt or organic oil to whole grains until after cooking to preserve nutrients and to make sure they cook properly and are more digestible.
- To prevent burning, make sure the water does not run out, the heat is low, the grain does not become overcooked to the point that it falls apart (this usually takes more than an hour), the grain is not stirred, and the pot is not uncovered.

- When reheating cooked whole grains, add 1/4 to 1/3 cup extra water per cup of grain. Cook the grain, covered, on very low heat until warmed (about 10 to 15 minutes). Brown rice, whole oats, rye, triticale, whole wheat, kamut, and spelt can be reheated by steaming in a vegetable steamer.
- One cup of dry whole grain or cereal makes about 3 to 4 servings.
- The main dish grains can almost always be substituted one for the other in different recipes, except for wild rice, rye, buckwheat, or kasha. Most grains are similar, but differ slightly in taste.
- Wheat, rye, triticale, barley, oats, kamut, and spelt contain gluten. Other grains contain minute amounts of gluten but are not considered gluten grains and are not usually eliminated from gluten-free diets, only from grain-free or celiac diets.

❖ MAIN GRAIN DISHES ❖

Buckwheat and Brown Pot Barley Use about 2 cups water per 1 cup grain. Bring the grain to a boil, then simmer, covered, 20 to 30 minutes or until tender and no longer crunchy, adding extra water if needed. Onions can be cooked with the grain and herbs added during the last 5 minutes of cooking. (Buckwheat does not contain wheat and is essentially gluten-free.)

Kasha (toasted buckwheat—contains no wheat and essentially no gluten) Cook as buckwheat, but use less water and reduce the cooking time to about 20 minutes.

Whole Oats or Whole Rye These are not usually used for main dishes. See Cooked Breakfast Cereals, below.

Basmati Brown Rice Cook like short- or long-grain brown rice, but for 40 to 50 minutes.

Short- and Long-Grain Brown Rice Put rice in a pot and fill it with water. Rub the rice together with your fingers and swish it around to remove extra starches, dirt, and stray husks. Discard all the water. If the water was very cloudy during the first washing, repeat the process once or twice until the water is relatively clear. Put 2 to 2 1/2 cups water per 1 cup rice in the pot. Bring to a boil, then cover and simmer 55 to 65 minutes. When the rice is no longer crunchy but easy to chew and tender, not soggy, it is done. Onions, herbs, and spices can be added during the last 15 to 20 minutes of cooking time. Keep the pot tightly covered while cooking, but it will not hurt to peek. Add extra water for more tender, digestible rice.

Millet Cook as rice, but use 2 1/2 to 3 cups water per 1 cup dry millet. It does not usually need washing. Simmer 50 to 60 minutes and use as a substitute for rice. One of the best grains, high in nutrients and very alkaline, it is especially good for delicate stomachs.

Quinoa (pronounced keen-wah) Rinse thoroughly before cooking by rubbing the grains together well in a pot of water once for white quinoa and 3 to 5 times for brown quinoa, changing the water each time. Rinsing helps remove the saponin, which may irritate digestion and allergies. Use 2 to 3 cups water to 1 cup quinoa. Bring to a boil, cover, and simmer white quinoa 20 to 25 minutes until tender, 10 to 12 minutes for brown quinoa. Add flavorings. Use cooked quinoa in place of rice or millet in main dishes. It is especially tasty when diced zucchini or broccoli is cooked on top of the grain during the entire cooking time.

Wild Rice This is one of the few main-dish grains that may require soaking before cooking. If a brand of rice cooks easily the first time without soaking, it does not need it. If the rice seems too tough after an hour of cooking, next time soak it for 2 to 4 hours in 2 to 3 times as much water. Cook wild rice as you would brown rice. Since wild rice is rich-tasting and can be expensive, it is often mixed with 2 to 6 parts brown rice. Cook the two rices separately, then mix together.

❖ COOKED BREAKFAST CEREALS ❖

Amaranth Although amaranth seed can be cooked as a breakfast cereal, it is not that tasty. It is better to use the flour in recipes or to cook the amaranth with another grain. If desired, cook it in 2 times as much water for a rice-like texture, and 2 1/2 to 3 times as much water for cereal or to add to breads. Cook until tender, about 15 to 20 minutes.

Quinoa Rinse thoroughly. Bring 2 1/2 to 3 1/2 cups water per 1 cup quinoa to a boil and simmer 20 to 30 minutes, covered, until very tender for a porridge-like consistency. Reheat quinoa like millet.

Millet For a soft, cereal-like texture, use 3 to 4 cups water per 1 cup millet. (Washing the grain is optional.) Bring water and millet to a boil and simmer, covered, for 55 to 70 minutes until the millet breaks down and is very soft and mushy. To reheat, break up gently with a fork, add a bit of extra water, and heat on low for 10 to 15 minutes.

Whole Oats or Whole Rye These must be soaked in 2 1/2 cups water per 1 cup grain for several hours or overnight. Then change the water and combine 1 1/2 cups water to 1 cup grain and cook for 45 to 60 minutes until fairly tender for the best digestion. Cook only one or two different grains together. The grains are usually a little bit chewy. Rye is rather heavy and is best mixed with another grain. These grains reheat easily in a bit of water and do not stick. They can also be steamed.

Scotch Oats Soak the oats in 2 times as much water for 2 to 4 hours. Drain the water and use 1 1/4 cups water per 1 cup Scotch oats. Bring to a boil then simmer for 20 minutes, or until tender and no longer crunchy. Add a bit of extra water as needed. Reheat like millet.

Sweet Brown Rice Cook and serve like brown rice, but use 2 1/2 to 3 1/2 cups water per 1 cup rice. Cook for 55 to 65 minutes until tender. This short-grain rice is naturally a little sweeter than other rices and makes a tasty breakfast grain.

Brown Rice Short-grain is tastier but long-grain may be used. Put the rice in a pot of water and rub together with your fingers and swish around to remove extra starches, dirt, and stray husks. Discard the water. If the water was very cloudy during the first washing, repeat once or twice until water is relatively clear. Combine 2 1/2 to 3 cups water per 1 cup rice and bring to a boil, then simmer 60 to 80 minutes. When the rice is no longer crunchy but easy to chew and tender, not soggy, it is done. Extra water is used for breakfast rice along with extra cooking time.

Teff Bring 1/2 cup teff seed and 2 cups water to a boil, then simmer for 15 to 20 minutes or until all the water is absorbed. Mix with another grain if desired for added flavor and texture, as teff, like amaranth, is not especially tasty alone.

How To Cook Legumes Properly For Good Digestion (No Gas!)

1. Measure the beans and sort through them to remove any damaged beans, gravel, dirt balls, or foreign objects.
2. Soak 1 cup of dry beans in 3 to 4 cups of cool or room-temperature water for 8 or more hours, uncovered. Soak chickpeas for 12 or more hours and soybeans or fava beans for at least 24 hours. IMPORTANT: Throw away the water the beans soaked in! This water contains a gas released by the beans while soaking, which in turn gives you gas.
3. Rinse the beans several times and swish them around in fresh water. Let them sit for 6 to 8 hours to begin sprouting. Rinse them thoroughly again and leave another 4 to 6 hours for a total of 12 hours' sprouting time. This reduces gas even further and makes the beans more digestible. After sprouting, rinse again thoroughly.
4. Put the beans in a large pot and add fresh water until the beans are covered by one inch or so of water.
5. Bring the beans and water, uncovered, to a boil.

6. When the beans are boiling, a white foam or froth will generally form on top. Scoop this off and discard it. It contributes to gas.

7. Add extra water if needed so that at least one inch of water remains above the beans in the pot. Turn down the heat so the beans are barely bubbling. Cover.

8. Optional: Add 1 tsp. ground fennel or savory to the beans during the cooking time to improve the beans' digestibility.

9. Cook for 1 1/4 hours or more until the beans are very tender and a bean can easily be mashed with the tongue on the roof of the mouth. Crunchy beans are indigestible for humans.

10. Make sure not to add any oil, salt, or salty ingredients like seaweed or Nova Scotia dulse to beans while they are cooking. These ingredients can toughen the beans so they stay hard. When they are completely tender in the cooking pot, then add these ingredients. Added after the beans are soft, Celtic sea salt, seaweeds, or Nova Scotia dulse help them to become more digestible. Organic extra-virgin oil can only be added after cooking.

Note: 1 cup dry beans makes about 2 1/2 cups soaked or cooked beans.

Eating Beans

Always chew beans slowly. Never eat them quickly or when you are under excessive stress or are tired. If possible, eat some raw foods before eating the beans to aid digestion.

The easiest-to-digest beans are lentils, adzuki beans, pinto beans, black beans, and chickpeas. Those with sensitive digestion should try these first. Those with digestive problems should avoid all beans that are not blended or mashed into recipes, unless and until they adjust to them.

Most people require a few weeks to adjust to beans if they have not been eating them regularly. Digestive aids such as Beano and plant enzymes can be purchased at health food stores.

Epilogue

I believe that lifestyle significantly influences the risk of contracting common diseases and certainly affects the body's ability to heal. Of all the lifestyle choices we make, those concerning food are particularly important because we have tremendous control over those choices.

Western medicine is most interested in treatments that begin "outside," while Eastern medicine is most interested in healing that originates "within." The Superfoods dietary strategy follows the basic principles of Eastern medicine, without denying the use or place that Western medicine has in supporting overall health.

The body *can* self-diagnose and self-heal. Superfoods will keep your body's intrinsic healing mechanisms functioning at peak performance. You can enhance these systems by eating colorful, fresh, organic foods and lean proteins that taste naturally delicious. Spontaneous healing is an everyday occurrence to a body well fed with a Superfoods dietary strategy. Your Superfood choices, including GREENS+, will enhance your health in every conceivable way and continue to provide you with lifelong health.

You will go through a transition period when you discontinue using commercial table salt, sugars, or artificial sweeteners, chemical food enhancers such as MSG, fried foods, excess saturated fats from red meats, or full-fat dairy and mass-produced bakery items. These may taste good, but the price your body pays for eating these foods is not worth it.

The Superfoods dietary strategy is chockfull of wonderfully tasty foods and exciting natural flavors that will please your palate and support your peak performance and optimum health. It will take three to four weeks for your taste buds to fully adapt to your superior Superfoods choices. During this period, you will notice you have more energy, deeper sleep patterns, smoother skin, healthier hair, better concentration, and sharper mental acuity. Once you experience the delicious foods in the Superfoods category, you will realize you have been denying yourself the remarkable tastes of life-giving food. These new flavors will be so delicious, your natural taste buds will no longer find salty, sugary, greasy, or processed foods appealing.

There is no question that I am proposing a radical rearrangement of your lifestyle. But I am proposing it to your benefit. Following the recommendations contained in this book will prolong your years of optimum mental and physical health and dramatically help your body to diagnose and heal itself. By following the Superfoods dietary guidelines, you will restore your health.

We cannot escape time or change the cards that Nature dealt to us genetically. Regardless of what your age is at the moment, what you *can* do is add health to your years. The older you are, the more crucial it is to approach the ideas contained in this book with an open mind. It is vital to realize that wherever you are on your life's journey, you can make a difference in your quality of life and health right now!

Premature aging, debility, and illness are not inevitable. If you learn to listen to your body, you can significantly, predictably, and measurably invigorate your health and healing with Nature's Superfoods. The Superfoods dietary strategy will give you the "survival advantage."

I encourage you to use the practical tools presented in this book wisely. It is as simple as becoming aware of your very next meal—then doing it one meal at a time. You will never regret it. The time to begin is now!

I wish you Abundant Good Health.

Glossary

acidophilus part of the normal bacterial flora, or "friendly" bacteria, in the intestinal tract that helps to digest food and destroy harmful bacteria, viruses, or parasites.

alfalfa, barley, and wheat grass young, tender grasses that are superior sources of chlorophyll, vitamins, minerals, trace minerals, antioxidants, and powerful cell-protecting phytochemicals.

alpha-carotene a vitally important carotenoid; important in helping to destroy cancer cells; must accompany beta-carotene in any multi-vitamin-mineral capsule. *See also* beta-carotene; gamma-carotene

amaranth a tiny seed, originally Mexican, grown in the United States and Eastern Canada; can be puffed or ground into flour; a high-enzyme, high-protein, high-calcium seed (not a grain) with a robust, pleasant, nutlike flavor.

amino acids any of 22 nitrogen-containing organic acids from which proteins are made.

antioxidant a chemical compound that neutralizes the cell-damaging free radicals that are created when oxygen is used inside the body's cells.

apple pectin fiber a fiber that is plentiful in apples; removes harmful metals in the intestines, lowers and helps excrete cholesterol, absorbs excess estrogen, and slows rate of carbohydrate absorption.

arrowroot a white-powdered thickening agent used instead of cornstarch in equal proportions as it is more digestible and more nutritious.

beta-carotene a pro-vitamin the body uses to make vitamin A. *See also* alpha-carotene; gamma-carotene

bilberry a herb that improves vision, particularly night vision; may help prevent vascular disease; brings back elasticity and flexibility to capillary walls.

bioflavonoids potent antioxidant compounds that have antiviral and anti-inflammatory effects; necessary for the stability and absorption of vitamin C and can help to prevent cancer and heart disease; sometimes referred to as vitamin P.

blue-green algae a single-cell aquatic plant that contains 65 percent complete protein and a large array of nutrients; most nutrient-rich blue-green algae is Hawaiian spirulina.

body mass index (BMI) a standardized measurement of fat-versus-lean body composition.

bovine growth hormone (rBGH) synthetic hormones given to commercial dairy cows to increase their production of milk.

butters. *See* nut and seed butters

cachexia a severe state of malnutrition and wasting, as occurs, for example, in certain advanced cancers.

candida albicans generally referred to as candida or candidiasis; a yeast that is a natural constituent of the intestinal tract; long-term use of antibiotics, stress, improper digestion, illness, birth control pills diminishes the balance of "healthy bacteria" and the candida yeast multiplies rapidly, causing a yeast infection; as many as 90 percent of all North Americans suffer from yeast infections at some time in their lives.

carbohydrate any one of many organic substances, all of them of plant origins, that are composed of carbon, hydrogen, and oxygen, and that serve as a major source of energy in the diet. *See also* complex carbohydrates; simple carbohydrates.

carbo-loading a dietary strategy used by endurance athletes to increase glycogen stores in muscles by 50 to 100 percent, prior to a major competition or athletic event; severely exercised muscles are depleted of glycogen intentionally, activating the glycogen-storage enzyme (glycogen synthas) to store the glucose (sugar) from the carbohydrates eaten as glycogen; carbohydrates should be evenly consumed throughout the day to maintain the body's insulin levels; consume ample pure water, as every gram of glycogen requires almost 2.75 grams of water to store it.

carcinogen a substance or agent capable of inducing cancerous changes in cells or tissues.

carotene an orange to yellow color in produce that is converted into vitamin A in the body. *See also* alpha-carotene; beta-carotene; gamma-carotene

cell a very small, complex organic unit consisting of a nucleus, cytoplasm, and a cell membrane; all living tissues are composed of cells.

Celtic sea salt a vacuum-dried sea salt from the clean ocean waters off the coast of Wales; contains 42 various minerals and trace minerals not found in regular sea salt; as salty as regular sea salt and stronger than table salt which contains corn sugar (dextrose) and demoisturizers; one teaspoon Celtic sea salt (or regular sea salt) equals three-quarters teaspoon table salt; more digestible, better assimilated by the body; more beneficial for overall health than table salt, but use in moderate amounts.

chlorella a freshwater, single-celled, green algae (sea vegetable); made up of 60 percent easily digested protein; supplies the nucleic acids RNA and DNA, necessary for healthy cell metabolism and renewal; helps to detoxify the body of heavy metals and pesticides.

chlorophyll a plant compound (green) that stimulates the production of nucleic acids such as DNA and RNA; potent detoxifier and antibiotic, and may help to produce hemoglobin.

cholesterol a complex fatty substance produced by the liver or supplied by animal foods essential for production of cell membranes, hormones, vitamin D, as well as precursors to steroidal hormones; oxidized cholesterol may be deposited in artery linings, thereby causing damage. *See also* HDL (high-density lipoprotein); LDL (low-density lipoprotein)

colonic irrigation cleansing colon with filtered water to remove compacted debris.

complex carbohydrate sugar molecules linked together to make digestible molecules such as glycogen or indigestible molecules of fiber, such as cellulose, bran, pectin, and mucilages.

cruciferous a group of vegetables that have a "cross-shaped" blossom, such as broccoli, brussels sprouts, cabbage, cauliflower, turnips, rutabagas, and mustard greens; help to prevent colon cancer.

daidzein a powerful isoflavone from soybeans shown to have anticarcinogenic properties; organic soy sprouts are the most potent and only unheated source of daidzein.

dairy-free probiotic cultures the "friendly" bacteria necessary for proper digestion and good intestinal health;

grown on brown rice; have natural antibiotic and antimicrobial activity; not derived from yogurt, milk, or dairy products since many people are intolerant of dairy products.

degenerative disease loss of capacity of cells, tissues, and organs to function normally; causes include imbalances of nutrients, deficiency of essential nutrients, excess of toxins, or presence of an interfering substance.

detoxification cleanse eating a periodic mono-diet or diet of raw juices for several days to allow the body to work less hard at digesting and use some of its energy for healing.

dulse a type of red seaweed that can be ground and added in small amounts to recipes for flavor and nutrients. *See also* Nova Scotia dulse

echinacea a herb that enhances the immune system, has antiviral, antifungal properties, and stimulates the production of white blood cells.

eicosanoids short-lived hormones that are influenced by the foods a person eats; there are both good and bad eicosanoids; optimum health is achieved when a proper balance of eicosanoids is maintained; excessive levels of insulin, caused by eating high-glycemic foods, disrupts this balance and forms too many bad eicosanoids.

eicosapentaenoic acid (EPA) found in large quantities in cold-water fish; the main fat from which the body manufactures series 3 prostaglandins that decrease inflammation, blood pressure, and water retention by inhibiting production of proinflammatory, artery-constricting series 2 prostaglandins.

engivita yeast a tasty variety of yellow, edible yeast that can be used in recipes, sprinkled on popcorn or other foods to add cheeselike flavor and lots of B vitamins, protein, and other nutrients; not a baking yeast; store in a glass jar, in a cool, dry place; does not require refrigeration.

enzyme a protein produced by the body to speed up and catalyze (initiate) all chemical reactions; the enzyme itself is not changed or altered in the reaction.

essential fatty acid (EFA) either of two fatty acids the body cannot make and must get from food; these two EFAs are linoleic acid (omega-6 EFA) and alpha-linolenic acid (omega-3 EFA); called "good" fats; finest sources are cold-water fish, fish oils, organic flaxseed oil, and hemp seed oil. *See also* omega-3; omega-6; omega-6:3 balance

essential nutrient any of the nearly 45 nutrients that are known to be necessary for the body to operate well and self-heal; there are 20 minerals, 13 vitamins, 10 amino acids, and 2 essential fatty acids that must come from foods, as the body cannot manufacture them.

fat a combination of fatty acids and glycerol (the same slippery liquid used to make soaps and skin lotions); greasy to the touch and will not dissolve in water; some fats are solid like butter or the fat on meat; other fats are liquid, such as vegetable oils or the fat in fish; some fats are necessary for superior health, and some fats are destructive to basic health. *See also* saturated fats

fiber any of several indigestible complex carbohydrates that make up the "roughage" of plant material; they soak up excess estrogens, eliminate cholesterol, and promote bowel regularity.

flavonoid any of a large group of crystalline compounds found in foods that assist with vitamin C absorption and are powerful antioxidants as well as phytochemicals.

flax in seed or oil form, highly nutritious and rich in essential fatty acid omega-3; grind raw seeds in coffee grinder and sprinkle on foods or use organic oils on salads or added, unheated, to lightly cooked or raw vegetables.

free radical an atom or group of atoms that is highly chemically reactive because it has a single unpaired electron which, wanting to be paired, steals electrons from other pairs; free radical damage is believed to be partly responsible for a wide range of disorders including cancer and heart disease.

free radical scavenger a substance that removes or destroys free radicals.

gamma-carotene a vitally important carotenoid; important in helping to destroy cancer cells; must accompany beta-carotene in any multi-vitamin-mineral capsule. *See also* alpha-carotene; gamma-carotene

genistein an isoflavone exclusively found in soy that has been shown to inhibit breast and prostate cancer; only unheated source is organic soy sprouts.

ginkgo biloba an antioxidant-rich herb that increases dopamine, which aids in mental alertness, memory retention, and balance; improves circulation by inhibiting plaque deposits in arteries.

ginseng (Siberian) a herb that improves mental performance and enhances energy level; helps body to adapt to or cope with stress by normalizing body functions.

glucose a simple sugar that is the principal source of energy for the body's cells.

glycemic index the rate at which a carbohydrate is converted to glucose and enters the bloodstream; the higher the glycemic index for a food, the faster it will raise blood sugar levels and therefore increase insulin secretion.

glycogen a chain of sugar molecules, linked together, that is the main form in which glucose is stored in the body, primarily in the liver and muscles; it is converted back into glucose, as needed, to supply energy for the brain or muscles.

grape seed extract contains unique bioflavonoids called proanthocyanidins that are potent antioxidants that help prevent brain cells from aging; aids in the maintenance of small blood vessels, inhibits the release of enzymes that promote inflammation, and brings back elasticity and flexibility to connective tissue.

green drink natural food formulas made from organic, nutrient-rich land and sea vegetables that are superior detoxifiers, blood cleansers, and bowel regulators; a superior source of alkalizing foods full of chlorophyll, vitamins, minerals, trace minerals, enzymes, antioxidants, and phytochemicals; available in powdered form or capsules to be mixed with liquid before use; greens+ (GREENS+) is an example.

green tea a source of potent phytochemicals that help to prevent heart disease and cancer, as well as lower cholesterol levels; organic Japanese-grown green teas appear to be preferred sources.

HDL (high-density lipoprotein) called the "good" cholesterol; body's major carrier of cholesterol to the liver for excretion in the bile.

homocysteine made from the amino acid methionine, which comes in protein-rich foods, especially meats; excess levels of homocysteine damage the linings of arteries, allowing cholesterol to build up on rugged edges of scars that can lead to fatal blockages. (See Appendix 2, under Superfood Tips)

human growth hormone made in the pituitary gland; responsible for stimulating growth in child's body, triggers onset of sexual maturity in adolescents, stimulates both bones and muscles to grow in adolescents; peak production occurs during sleep.

hydrogenation a commercial process by which liquid oils are turned into hard fats by saturating their carbon atoms with hydrogen so they will not go bad; hydrogenated foods should be avoided.

hypoglycemia a lower-than-normal level of glucose in the blood, usually resulting from excessive insulin secretion from the pancreas or from eating high-glycemic foods.

intestinal flora the "friendly" bacteria present in the intestines; essential for the absorption of nutrients, production of B vitamins, destruction of bacteria and viruses; necessary to keep yeast (fungus) like candida in check.

intravenous chelation therapy dripping a solution intravenously that chelates (binds to) heavy metals and removes them from the blood.

isoflavone a class of phytochemicals that inactivates excess estrogen and destroys enzymes produced by cancer genes; they are a group of flavonoids found prominently in legumes, especially soybeans.

kamut a Mediterranean variety of wheat more digestible and higher in protein than regular wheat; about 50 percent of people allergic to wheat can tolerate kamut grain and flour.

kelp/sea kelp a type of dark seaweed that can be ground and added in small amounts to recipes for flavor and nutrients. (Use with caution, too iodine-intense.)

LDL (low-density lipoprotein) called the "bad" cholesterol; carries cholesterol through the bloodstream; high levels enhance risk of coronary heart disease.

licorice root a herb used to invigorate the performance of the pancreas, spleen, and heart; contains glycyrrhizic acid that appears to have anti-inflammatory properties necessary for treating arthritis and blocking tumor growth. (Caution: if you have high blood pressure, consult a health professional before using.)

macronutrient a compound such as protein or minerals (e.g. essential amino acids or calcium) needed in large amounts for normal body function. *See also* micronutrient

metabolism all biochemical functions and changes in the body that make physical life possible.

micronutrient a compound such as a trace mineral or certain vitamins (e.g. iodine or riboflavin) needed only in small amounts for normal body function. *See also* macronutrient

milk substitutes plant-based liquids primarily used in place of milk in recipes; beans, nuts, seeds, whole grains, and leafy greens replace the nutrients of milk in a plant-based diet; purchase soy and rice milk substitutes in health food stores or supermarkets; blend two to three tablespoons ground, raw cashews, blanched almonds, or rolled oats with enough pure water to equal one cup until smooth to make your own nut or oat milk; strain if desired.

milk thistle a herb that contains a unique type of flavonoid with potent antioxidant ability called silymarin; stimulates production of new liver cells and detoxifies the liver.

millet highly alkaline grain that is very mild on the stomach, easy to digest, and especially good for babies, the elderly, and for people with ulcers or allergies; higher in vitamins and minerals than most other grains, rice included; has a tasty, nutty flavor; can be used instead of rice or with it in many recipes; golden-brown or yellow millet is the best; whiter millet is lesser-quality.

mono-dieting a dietary strategy of consuming raw fruits and vegetables or their juices and salads for one or more days to cleanse the body, add enzymes, and rejuvenate general health.

Nova Scotia dulse a purple-red algae or sea vegetable rich in rare trace minerals such as ubium, iodine, and boron; an alkalizing food that contains a well-balanced array of sea-source micronutrients.

nut and seed butters ground-up raw nuts or seeds mixed with oil and used in place of peanut butter in recipes for more nutrients, flavor, and digestibility; drain excess oil before using in recipes.

nutrient a substance needed by the body to maintain health; examples are vitamin C, vitamin E, the pro-vitamins such as beta-carotene, trace minerals, such as iodine, and structural minerals, such as calcium.

omega-3 a fatty acid essential to human health but which is lacking in most North American diets; omega-3 fats are essentail fatty acids (omega-3 EFAs) that the body uses to make series 3 prostaglandins, which prevent the negative effects of series 2 prostaglandins, by preventing their production; sources of omega-3 are fish oils, flaxseed oils, and hemp seed oils.

omega-6 a fatty acid essential to human health that is amply supplied by the North American diet; from omega-6 EFAs, the body makes series 1 and 2 prostaglandins; excess of series 2 prostaglandins causes inflammation, increased blood pressure, water retention, sticky blood platelets, and decreased immune response; sources of omega-6 are olive oil, canola oil and sunflower seed oil.

omega6:3 balance it is necessary to have a balance of omega 3 and omega 6 EFAs in the diet for optimum health; the ideal ratio is 6 omega - 6 EFAs to 1 omega - 3 EFAs; the current ratio in most North American diets is a dangerously imbalanced one of about 24 omega - 6 EFAs to 1 omega - 3 EFAs.

optimum nutrition results in supporting the best possible physical health and accelerated healing in the body.

organically grown a term used to describe foods that are grown without the use of synthetic chemicals, such as pesticides, herbicides, fungicides, or anti-ripening chemicals.

oxidation a chemical reaction in which oxygen reacts with another substance, resulting in a chemical change; most oxidation reactions result in some form of spoilage or rapid deterioration.

pH (potential of hydrogen) a scale used to measure the relative acidity or alkalinity of substances; scale runs from 0 to 14, with 7 being neutral; numbers below 7 denote increased acidity and numbers above 7 denote increased alkalinity.

phytochemical powerful, cell-protecting chemicals found in all plants to protect the body from diseases.

phosphatidyl choline (PC) the most active part of soy lecithin and comprises approximately 22 percent of premium-quality lecithin; a dipolar molecule that emulsifies extra cholesterol deposited on artery walls and eliminates it from the body; vital to peak memory, a healthy heart, and proper transmission of signals from one cell to another.

phytoestrogens a compound structurally similar to human estrogen that is found in plants; can bind with estrogen receptors in the body and is believed to protect against breast and prostate cancer, which are both hormone-dependent cancers.

plaque injurious substances such as free calcium or fatty deposits that build up on body tissues, causing health problems (plaque buildup in arteries is the leading cause of cardiovascular disease; on the teeth it can lead to gum disease; in the brain, it can lead to Alzheimer's disease.)

polyphenols a potent phytochemical and antioxidant found in green tea; destroys cancer cells, lowers cholesterol levels, promotes fat burning, and regulates both blood sugar and insulin levels.

prostaglandins any number of hormone-like chemicals that are made in the body from essential fatty acids; directly influence production of many hormones and enzymes and regulate blood pressure, the inflammatory response, and blood-clotting time.

protein any of a great many complex nitrogen-based organic compounds made up of various combinations of amino acids; proteins are basic constituents of all animal and vegetable tissues; the body makes the specific proteins it requires for repair and growth from amino acids in the foods we eat or manufactured from other amino acids already in the body; muscle tissue, hormones, and enzymes are basically made of protein.

protein-carbohydrate-fat-fiber ratio protein, fat, and fiber, eaten with carbohydrates, work together to decrease insulin secretion caused by carbohydrates; protein stimulates glucagon, which reduces insulin secretion, and fat and fiber slow down the rate of entry of any carbohydrate to further insulin secretion.

quinoa (pronounced "keen-wah") a quick-cooking, essentially gluten-free, high-protein, very digestible grain; white and brown small, round varieties are available; good for allergies.

salt substitutes use gomashio (sesame salt) to reduce salt amounts in recipes or buy salt-substitute herb blends in a health food store or supermarket; also try ground seaweeds, especially Nova Scotia dulse in a saltshaker, tasty yellow nutritional yeast like engivita, unsalted vegetable broth powders, extra-ground dried herbs, or chopped fresh herbs to flavor foods and replace salt; low-salt or no-salt tamari soy sauces or Mock Tamari Sauce can also reduce or replace salt.

SAMe (S-adenosyl-methionine) the activated form of the amino acid methionine and is naturally converted to cysteine in the body; a potent antioxidant; stimulates cartilage growth and reverses osteoarthritis; alleviates depression; reduces the pain and fatigue of fibromyalgia; is an effective pain reducer; if taken as a supplement consult with a health professional and use 600 mg daily, always taken with its cofactors B_6, B_{12}, and folic acid. (See Appendix 2, under Superfood Tips.)

saturated fats unhealthy fats associated with increased incidence of the bad fat low-density lipoprotein (LDL).

saw palmetto a herb that helps to prevent testosterone from binding to cells in the prostate gland and to treat benign prostate hypertrophy (BPH).

sea salt derived from vacuum-dried sea salt; contains an array of valuable minerals and trace minerals (e.g. iodine) that are not found in regular table salt. *See also* Celtic sea salt

sesame tahini *See* tahini/sesame tahini

simple carbohydrate a simple sugar, for example, glucose, fructose, lactose, and table sugar (sucrose); absorbed into the bloodstream rapidly and can cause hypoglycemia, diabetes, and cardiovascular problems.

sodium-potassium pump the shifting of sodium and potassium across cell membranes, creating electricity; the force that operates muscles, organs, and many bodily functions.

soy lecithin a nutritional powerhouse food containing fatty acids, glycerol, and phosphatidyl choline (PC); a strong alkalizing food usually extracted from soybeans; a vital part of the structure of the membranes of all cells and organs; the brain is 30 percent lecithin by dry weight; premium-quality soy lecithin contains 22 percent phosphatidyl choline (PC), vital to peak memory, a healthy heart, and proper transmission of signals from one cell to another.

soy sprouts organically and hydroponically grown (i.e., without soil), are the best source for two special phytochemi-cals called genistein and daidzein, which may prevent breast or prostate cancer.

spelt a European grain closely related to wheat; like kamut in nutrients and qualities, sometimes a good substitute for regular wheat grains or flour.

stevia/honeyleaf a potent South American herbal sweetener also grown in the Orient; 1/10 teaspoon of powder or a few drops of liquid are as sweet as a heaping tablespoon of other sweeteners, with virtually no calories; it is a low-glycemic food that does not raise insulin levels; mixes easily in either hot or cold liquids or foods.

stress physical or mental tension related to external, biochemical, or emotional factors.

Superfood the most nutrient-rich and completely absorbable food in any classification of protein, carbohydrates, fat, or fiber; contains powerful antioxidants, disease-preventive phytochemicals, and a wide range of colors; allows the body a supply of balanced energy and supports accelerated healing; examples are Hawaiian spirulina, phosphatidyl choline, alfalfa, barley, and wheat grasses, milk thistle, and Japanese green tea, greens+ (GREENS+) is an example.

tahini/sesame tahini a peanut butter-like spread made with ground, hulled white sesame seeds and oil; excess oil can be drained from tahini before using in recipes; sesame butter is made from unhulled brown sesame seeds.

tamari soy sauce a naturally fermented soybean liquid unlike most soy sauces, with no artificial additives, usually aged in wood six months or more; all tamaris are soy sauces but not all soy sauces are tamaris; wheat-free, low-salt varieties are best; try Mock Tamari Soy Sauce to avoid soy or reduce salt intake.

tapioca flour a white, starchy, slightly sweet, gluten-free, grain-free flour usually derived from cassava root and used instead of milk powder in some recipes or to lighten up heavier flours.

T-cell a cell that is a crucial part of the immune system needed to defend the body from bacteria, viruses, parasites, fungus, and cancer cells.

teff a tiny Ethiopian seed that has five times the iron, calcium, and potassium of any other grain; high in protein and fiber; gluten- and grain-free; use half a cup of seeds as substitute for one cup sesame seeds in recipes, or use the flour with lighter flours or to add nutrients to dishes.

tocopherol (tocopheryl) a potent, fat-soluble antioxidant known as vitamin E; reduces the propensity of low-density lipoproteins (LDL) from oxidizing.

trans-fatty acids acids that are destructive to human health in which the hydrogen atoms or carbon atoms involved in a double bond are situated on opposite sides of the fatty chain; found in margarine and commercial baked goods.

vegan a person who eats no animal products such as meat, fish, poultry, eggs, milk, or dairy products.

xenobiotics chemicals or compounds foreign to the body that causes metabolic stress to the proper functioning of a healthy cell. Examples are pain relievers, pesticides, food preservatives, food colorings, recreational drugs, and prescription drugs.

Appendix 1
Publications and Online Resources

The following newsletters are informative, up-to-date publications, to keep you apprised of current research on nutrition and its practical application to Superfood dietary strategies.

1. *Health and Healing*
   By: Dr. Julian Whitaker, M.D.
   Phone: 800-539-8219
   Monthly issues
   One-year subscription $39.95 U.S.
   Two-year subscription $79.90 U.S.

   A vibrant publication, informative, practical, and encouraging. It is presented in an easy-to-understand format, with reliable scientific information that is always timely. An absolute must-read newsletter for everyone.

2. *The Green Times*
   By: greens+ Canada
   Phone: 877-500-7888
   Quarterly issues, no charge in Canada

   A publication that features progressive ideas on incorporating Superfoods and nutritious "green drinks" into your daily dietary strategy. Articles are informative, reliable, and easy to read. High-quality presentation and format. Full of practical, up-to-date nutritional advice and information.

3. *The Greens Super News*
   By: Orange Peel Ent. Inc.
   Phone: 800-643-1210
   Bimonthly issues, no charge in the United States

   A newsletter featuring progressive ideas on incorporating Superfoods and nutritious "green drinks" into your daily dietary strategy. Articles explain various Superfoods and the health benefits of using them daily. Contains current scientific research and is highly informative, accurate, and practical.

4. *Life Extension Magazine*
   By: The Life Extension Foundation
   Phone: 800-544-4440
   One-year subscription $75.00 U.S.
   Two-year subscription $135.00 U.S.

   The Life Extension Foundation is a not-for-profit organization dedicated to funding research in gerontology. It also provides easy-to-read research reports on living longer and healthier. Contains in-depth articles on life-extension strategies. The subscription price allows you to purchase products at a membership-only reduced price.

5. *Health Realities*
   By: Queen and Co.
   Phone: (719) 598-4968
   Quarterly Issues
   One-year subscription $50.00 U.S.
   Two-year subscription $95.00 U.S.

A must-read newsletter of exceptional quality for health-care professionals and serious students of health and nutrition. Highly recommended.

6. *Clinical Pearls*
   By: ITServices
   Monthly issues
   Phone: (916) 483-1085
   Yearly subscription $109.00 U.S.

   A publication not for the casual reader. Reviews of 50 to 60 worldwide research papers are clearly presented, half containing commentaries by the editor. Highly recommended for those who want up-to-date research and clinical results in nutrition.

7. *Townsend Letter For Doctors And Patients*
   Editors: Jonathan Collin, M.D., and Alan Gaby, M.D.
   Phone: (360) 385-6021
   One-year subscription $49.00 U.S.
   Two-year subscription $88.00 U.S.

   Published ten times a year as a 150-page magazine. Articles written by various authors. Each edition covers a range of important nutritional topics.

8. *Natural Solutions*
   By: Transitions For Health
   Phone: 800-888-6814
   Quarterly issues, one year $15.95 U.S.
   Subscription is free if you order any of their fine products.

   A must-read for women, especially menopausal or perimenopausal women. Pertinent articles on women's health with practical "how-to" solutions. You can receive a complimentary copy just for phoning. Transitions for Health specialize in state-of-the-art women's nutritional products.

9. *Health World*

   Excellent on-line resource for complementary medicine. Provides free access to Medline, a large database of nutritional information. Just click onto http://healthy.net

10. *International Health News*
    By: Hans R. Larsen, M.Sc.
    Access: on the World Wide Web: http://www.com/healthnews/
    Montly issues
    One-year subscription $25.00 Canadian, $20.00 U.S.

    This quality newsletter provides concise, authoritative research on health, nutrition, and medicine.

11. *Colgan Chronicles*
    By: Michael Colgan, Ph.D.
    Phone: 800-668-2775
    Eight issues a year, subscription $64.00 U.S.

    An accurate and reliable publication with a focus on health-and-physical-fitness issues. Contains a splash of good humor, with progressive tips for those serious about achieving and maintaining peak physical performance.

Appendix 2
Sources for Superfood Rejuvenation Products

Green Drinks

The high-quality "green drinks" referred to in this book are available in leading whole food stores across North America. If you need help to locate a store near you or would like further information, contact the following companies:

In Canada
1. greens+Canada
   317 Adelaide Street West, Suite 501
   Toronto, Ontario M5V 1P9
   Phone: 877-500-7888
   Contact for locations in your area or for information on **greens+**.

In the United States
2. Orange Peel Enterprises, Inc.
   2183 Ponce de Leon Circle
   Vero Beach, Florida 32960
   Phone: 800-643-1210
   Contact for locations in your area or for information on **GREENS+**.

3. Healthy Directions, Inc.
   7811 Montrose Road
   Potomac, Maryland 20854-3394
   Phone: 800-722-8008, ext. 2194E
   Contact for information on **FIBER GREENS+** and Dr. Whitaker's **Greens**.

4. Transitions for Health
   621 SW Alder, Suite 900
   Portland, Oregon 97205
   Phone: 800-888-6814
   Contact for information on **Easy Greens**.

5. Life Extension Foundation
   P.O. Box 229120
   Hollywood, Florida 33022-9120
   Phone: 800-544-4440
   Contact for information on **Herbal Mix**.

6. Green Foods Corporation
   318 North Graves Avenue
   Oxnard, California 93030
   Phone: 805-983-7470
   Contact for information on **Green Magma**.

Information on Organic Produce

Mothers & Others for a Liveable Planet
40 West 20th Street
New York, New York 10011
Phone: (212) 242-0010

Special foods are available in most health food stores and in some supermarkets. If you are unable to obtain any item locally, contact the following:

For complete line of natural and health foods and allergy foods:

Allergy Resources Inc.
P.O. Box 444, 6 Main Street
Guffey, Colorado 80820
In U.S. or Canada: 800-873-3529

For some organic foods, especially nuts, seeds, and dried fruits:

Walnut Acres
Penns Creek, Pennsylvania 17862
In U.S. or Canada: 800-433-3998

Multi-Vitamin-Mineral-Antioxidant Supplement

I highly recommend a daily multi-supplement derived from natural sources. Your local whole food store will carry several selections. Make sure that your choice contains the following:

- beta-carotene, derived from a natural source containing the full range of natural carotenoids such as alpha-carotene, luten, zeaxanthin, and cryptoxanthine;
- vitamin E, in a complex of all the naturally occurring tocopheryls such as d-alpha tocopheryl, beta tocopheryl, gamma tocopheryl, etc.; and
- selenium and chromium picolinate, included at doses of 200 mcgs each and the derived source is from Nutrition 21.

If you have difficulty finding such an advanced formula, call the following:

In Canada
Supplements Plus
Phone: 800-387-4761

In the United States
Healthy Directions, Inc.
Phone: 800-722-8008, ext. 2194E

Healthy Directions has two products that were recently awarded the 1997 New Product Award. The first product, MEMORY ESSENTIALS, helps keep your mental acuity sharp and accurate and prevents aging of the brain. The second product, VISION ESSENTIALS, is an advanced vision support system to prevent macular degeneration and to support optimal eye health and good vision.

Women's Resources

For saliva tests and kits for hormone, bone, food allergies, and osteoporosis assays, contact:

Great Smokies Diagnostic Laboratory
In Canada, phone: 800-268-6200
In the United States, phone: 800-522-4762

There are a group of compounding pharmacies that custom-make natural products for women's hormonal health. These pharmacies offer advice and explanations over the phone, and will send you information packets on "natural" hormone alternatives to hormone replacement therapy (HRT). They will also inform you of doctors in your area who prescribe "natural" hormones. Contact the International Academy of Compounding Pharmacists, who will give you the name of a compounding pharmacist near you.
In Canada and the United States, phone: 800-927-4227

For a superior progesterone cream containing more than 400 mg of progesterone per ounce of cream, contact:

Transitions For Health
In Canada and the United States, phone: 800-888-6814

Books

Take Charge Of Your Body (Women's Health Advisor)
by Dr. Carolyn DeMarco, M.D.
Cost: $25.00 (includes all shipping)
In Canada and the United States: 800-387-4761
A powerhouse of health information for women. This book empowers every woman with detailed explanations of women's unique health issues and includes an extensive resource directory. A must-read!

Natural Woman, Natural Menopause
by Marcus Laux, N.D., and Christine Conrad
HarperCollins, New York. 1997.
A wonderful book that encourages women to use menopause as a positive transformation process, to develop all aspects of womanhood.

Superfood Sprouting Know-How

The recognized master in home sprouting is Steve Meyerowitz, affectionately called "the Sproutman." His informative, step-by-step procedure for home sprouting is found in the book *Sprouts, The Miracle Food*. For this book or sprouting kits or organic seeds and grains to sprout, visit your local whole food store. If you are unable to locate this book or sprouting supplies, contact:

In Canada
Alive Books, (604) 435-1919

In the United States
The Sprout House, (413) 528-5200

Biological Terrain Assessment

To have the pH of your venous blood, saliva, and urine monitored, contact:

In Canada
The Holistic Alternative
Caron DeVita, (604) 925-8932

In the United States
Partners in Wellness
Carone Scott, (425) 558-9339

pH Paper Sources

In Canada
greens+ Canada
1-800-258-0444

In the United States
Orange Peel Enterprises, Inc.
1-800-643-1210

Since chemical preservatives, moisturizers, hydrogenated fats, MSG, sweeteners, and so many other industrial by-products of the petroleum industry are finding their way into our daily food supplies, I highly recommend a little paperback that lets you know what flavors, colors, or artificial preservatives really are. Make sense of food labels with *Your Personal Nutritionist: Food Additives* by Ed Blonz (Signet, 1997, $4.00 U.S. or $5.50 Canadian).

Health and Medical Hot Lines

- Alcohol and Drug Helpline: 800-252-6465
- Nutrition and Dietetics: 800-366-1655
- Prostate Information: 800-543-9632
- Pesticides Network: 800-858-7378
- Anorexia nervosa (eating disorders): 503-344-1144
- Herbal Research Foundation: 800-748-2617

The Alternative Hotline

I encourage you to join the Health Action Network Society (HANS), an international clearinghouse of alternative-health information. The annual fee to join is $25.00 U.S. or $35.00 Canadian. For phone numbers, health information alternative therapies, self-help groups, and a lot more, contact The Alternative Hotline at: 1-888-437-4267 toll free, and 604-435-0512; E-mail: hans@.hans.org; Web site: http://www.hans.org

Attention Deficit Disorder and Learning Disabilities

In Canada, contact Children and Adults With Attention Deficit Disorders at (604) 222-4043; and in the United States at (954) 587-3700 or at 800-233-4050.

My favorite support group is the Center for New Discoveries in Learning, in Windsor, California. Call them at (707) 837-8180. Through the center, you can obtain their wonderful book *What's Food Got To Do With It*. Two highly dedicated women, Dr. Sandra Hills, N.D., and Pat Wyman, M.A., are the powerhouses in developing diets, videos, cassettes, and literature designed to help you work with your child naturally, with great success. They apply the Superfood dietary strategy I recommend for all attention deficit disorders or learning disabilities.

Recommended Cookbooks

Jane Fonda, *Cooking For Healthy Living*. Turner Publishing, 1996.

Bessie Jo Tillman, M.D., *The Natural Healing Cookbook*. Rudra Press, 1995.

Natural cookbooks for healthy living by Jeanne Marie Martin are masterpieces of tasty, imaginative recipes and valuable information from a chef extraordinaire. Her cookbooks are:
- *All Natural Allergy Cookbook*
- *Complete Candida Yeast Guidebook*
- *Eating Alive* (with Jonn Matsen, N.D.)
- *For The Love of Food*
- *Hearty Vegetarian Soups & Stews*
- *Light Cuisine*
- *Recipes For Romance*
- *Return To The Joy of Health* (with Zoltan Rona, M.D.)
- *Vegan Delights*

Phone:　*In Canada*: Alive Books, 604-435-1919
　　　　In the United States: Nutri-Books, 303-778-8383

Health Clinics

The following clinics offer residential programs for evaluation, treatment, education, motivation, exercise, and Superfood dietary strategies.

In Canada
Eco-Med Wellness Centre
Parksville, British Columbia
Phone: (250) 468-7133
Staffed by Dr. Stephen Kaprouski, N.D.

Mountain Trek Fitness Retreat & Health Spa
Nelson, British Columbia
Phone: 800-661-5161; or Web site: http://www.hiking.com
Staffed by a resident Naturopathic Doctor (N.D.) and many health-care professionals. Offers a large array of up-to-date health-care alternatives.

In the United States
The Whitaker Wellness Institute
4321 Birch Street, Suite 100
Newport Beach, California 92660
Phone: (714) 851-1550
Staffed by Dr. Julian Whitaker and other physicians.

In Europe
Nowo Balance Klinik Bruneck
Tegernsee, Germany
Phone: 011-49-802-98-765 or 011-49-802-98-235
Staffed by Dr. Christiane May-Ropers, M.D., and Professor Dr. David Schweitzer, Ph.D., M.D.

Superfood Tips

St.-John's-wort

If you feel depressed, try using the herb St.-John's-wort. It is effective only for mild or moderate depression and should not be relied upon for severe depression. Most health professionals recommend taking a 300 mg capsule, 3 times a day. It takes 4 to 6 weeks for St.-John's-wort to begin to work.

SAMe

If you feel depressed, consult your health-care professional and try SAMe (S-adenosyl-methionine), which relieves depression in a week or less. SAMe is the activated form of the amino acid methionine and is naturally converted in the body to the amino acid acysteine.

Use 600 mg daily for 2 weeks and 400 mg daily thereafter.

SAMe is available from The Life Extension Foundation.

In Canada and the United States, phone: 800-544-4440

Homocysteine

Protein-rich foods such as meats contain an amino acid called methionine, which converts to another amino acid called homocysteine. Excess levels of homocysteine damage artery linings in both men and women, which scars the inner lining deeply. Cholesterol builds up inside the scarred arteries; this can lead to fatal blockages. The Superfoods dietary strategy supplies lots of fruits, vegetables, beans, legumes, whole grains, and lean protein, all sources rich in vitamins B12, B6, and folic acid that prevent the buildup of homocysteine. For added protection, check that your daily multi-vitamin-mineral-antioxidant supplement contains at least 50 to 75 mg of vitamin B6, 100 mcg of vitamin B12, and 400 mcg of folic acid, to protect your arteries from homocysteine buildup.

Blood Types

Each person has unique nutritional needs as well as inherent biochemical strengths and weaknesses, because of genetic variations. We are all biochemically different from each other. Professor Roger Williams, of the

University of Texas, coined the phrase "biochemical individuality," as he documented the variation in individuals for various nutrients.

Each person must make adjustments, in their personal Superfood dietary strategy, to properly meet the specific requirements of their own biochemical individuality. One method of fine-tuning your Superfood diet is to work closely with a qualified health professional who can help you determine your blood type. Dr. Peter D'Adamo has written a book specifically on blood types—*Eat Right 4 Your Type* (Putnam, 1997)—in which he describes the four blood types: O, A, B, and AB. Each blood type has specific nutritional requirements, as follows:

Blood type O   individuals require more protein and fewer carbohydrates such as grains.

Blood type A   do well on a vegetarian diet of high carbohydrates and a low fat intake.

Blood type B   should use a wide variety of beans, grains, legumes, vegetables, fruit, and does well with meat in their diet.

Blood type AB   do well with moderate amounts of protein, fat, and carbohyrates.

Knowing your blood type helps you to fine-tune your Superfoods dietary strategy to your daily nutritional needs.

References

Introduction The Power of Change

Krauss, R.M. 1991. The Tangled Web of Coronary Risk Factors. *American Journal of Medicine* 90 (suppl.2A):365–415.

Mertz, W. 1987. *Trace Elements In Human and Animal Nutrition.* 5th ed. New York: Academic Press.

Multiple Risk Factor Trial Research Group. 1982. Multiple Risk Factor Intervention Trial. Risk Factor Changes and Mortality Results. *Journal of the American Medical Association* 248:1465–77.

Nissinen, A., and K. Stanley. 1989. Unbalanced Diets as a Cause of Chronic Disease. *American Journal of Clinical Nutrition* 49:993–98.

Prigogine, I., and L. Stenger. 1984. *Order Out of Chaos: Man's New Dialogue With Nature.* New York: Bantam Books.

Spencer, J.G.C. 1954. The Influence of the Thyroid in Malignant Disease. *British Journal of Cancer* 8, no. 393:214–30.

Vanderpas, J.B. 1990. Iodine and Selenium Deficiency Associated With Cretinism in Northern Zaire. *American Journal of Clinical Nutrition* 52:1087–93.

Walker, M. 1997. Nutritional Enhancement for the Disabled. *Explore More Magazine* 20, 21:35–39.

William, R.J. 1956. *Biochemical Individuality.* New York: Wiley Publications.

Chapter 1 Eating Your Way to Better Health

Conner, M. et al. 1985. Primitive Diets of our Ancestors. *New England Journal of Medicine* (January 31):4–8.

Masoro, E.J. 1990. Assessment of Nutritional Components in Prolongation of Life and Health By Diet. *Proceedings of the Society for Experimental Biology and Medicine* 193:31–34.

Smith, L. 1993. Primitive Diet Health Today. *Health Naturally Magazine* (October/November):22–25.

Subar, A.F. et al. 1995. Fruit and Vegetable Intake in the United States: The Baseline Survey of the Five a Day for Better Health Program. *American Journal of Health Promotion* 9(5):352–60.

Voet, D., and J.G. Voet. 1990. "Enzymes." In *Biochemistry*, 316–28, 355–90. New York: John Wiley and Sons.

Chapter 2 An Introduction to Superfoods

Armstrong, B., and R. Doll. 1975. Environmental Factors and Cancer Incidence and Mortality in Different Countries With Specific Reference To Dietary Practices. *International Journal of Cancer* 15:617–31.

Cancer: What You Eat Can Affect Your Risk. 1995. *Mayo Clinic Health Newsletter* (September).

Canfield, I.M., J.W. Forage, and J.G. Valenzuela. 1992. Carotenoids as Cellular Antioxidants. *Proceedings of the Society for Experimental Biology and Medicine* 200:260–65.

Hayflick, L. 1994. *How And Why We Age*, 222–62. New York: Ballantine Books.

Lewis, M.A. Cancer-Protective Factors in Fruits and Vegetables: Biochemical and Biological Background. 1993. *Pharmacology and Toxicology* 725:116–34.

More Than a Hill of Beans: Soy Research Takes Off. 1995. *American Institute for Cancer Research Newsletter* (Fall).

Neher, T.O., and J.Q. Koeng. 1994. Health Effects of Outdoor Air Pollution. *American Family Physician* 49:1397–404.

Nordmann, R., C. Ribiere, and H. Rouach. 1992. Implication of Free Radical Mechanisms in Ethanol-induced Cellular Injury. *Free Radical Biology and Medicine* 12:219–58.

Those Mighty Phytochemicals. 1995. Beyond The Benefits of Broccoli. *Environmental Nutrition Newsletter*. (Spring).

Zhang, Y., P. Talady, C.G. Cho, and G.H. Posner. 1992. A Major Inducer of Anti-carcinogenic Protective Enzymes From Broccoli. *Proceedings of the National Academy of Sciences* 89:2399–403.

Chapter 3 Use Superfoods Daily

Barnard, N.D. 1990. *The Power On Your Plate*, 50–132. Summerton, Tenn.: Book Publishing Co.

Borek, Carmia. 1995. *Maximize Your Life Span With Antioxidants*, 45–75. New Cannaan, Conn.: Keats Publishing.

Grover, S.A. et al. 1994. *Life Expectancy Following Dietary Modification or Smoking Cessation*. Archives of International Medicine 154:1697–704.

Grower, J.D. 1988. A Role For Dietary Lipids and Antioxidants in the Activation of Carcinogens. *Free Radical Biology and Medicine* 5:95–111.

Masoro, E.J. 1990. Assessment of Nutritional Components in Prolongation of Life and Health By Diet. *Proceedings of the Society for Experimental Biology and Medicine*, 193:31–34.

Murray, M.T. 1995. *The Healing Power of Herbs*. Rocklin, Calif.: Prima Publishing.

Wang, H. et al. 1996. Total Antioxidant Capacity of Fruits. *Journal of Agriculture and Food Chemistry* 44:701–5.

Whitaker, J. 1997. Hypertension Report 1:39–44. Potomac, Maryland: Philips Publishing, Inc.

Chapter 4 Green Drinks: Nutritional Life Insurance

Balch, J.F., and P.A. Balch. 1997. *Prescriptions for Nutritional Healing*. Garden City Park, New York: Avery Publishing Group.

Bewicke, D., and B.A. Potter. 1984. *Chlorella the Emerald Food*. Berkeley: Ronin Publishing.

Donsbach, K.W. 1988. *Alfalfa*. Rosarito Beach, Baja California, Mexico: Wholistic Publications.

Hagiwara, Y. 1986. *Green Barley Essence*. New Canaan, Conn.: Keats Publishing.

Henrikson, R. 1989. *Spirulina*. Laguna Beach, Calif: Ronore Ent., Inc.

Hills, S., and P. Wyman. 1997. *What's Food Got To Do With It?* Windsor, Calif.: The Center for New Discoveries in Learning.

Hobbs, C. 1987. *Milk Thistle*. Capitola, Calif.: Botanica Press.

Phytochemical Properties of Cancer-fighting Foods. 1995. Harvard Health Letter. Green Revolution (Special Supplement) (April 1).

Sehnert, K.W. 1989. The Garden Within. *Health World Magazine* 52 (November):63–67

Weil, A. 1997. Beyond Ritalin. *Self-Healing Newsletter*. (March:) 1–6.

Whitaker, J. This Green Drink Can Help Arthritis. *Health and Healing Newsletter* 5, no. 1 (January 1995).

———. 1997. My Program For People With ADD. *Health and Healing* 7, no. 3 (March): 4–6.

Chapter 5 The Acid-Alkaline Balance
Part 1 Acid Runs Batteries, Not Your Body

Brodan, V. et al. 1974. Effects of Sodium Glutamine Infusion On Ammonia Formation During Intense Exercise In Man. *Nutrition Report International* 9:223–35.

Danforth, W.H. 1965. Activation of Glycolytic Pathways In Muscle. *Circulation*. New York: Academic Press, 285–98.

Guyton, A.C. 1986. *Textbook of Medical Physiology*. 7th ed.,   410–92. Philadelphia: W.B. Saunders Co.

Itodgman, C.D. et al. 1958. *Handbook of Chemistry and Physics*. 40th ed., 1700–749. Cleveland: Chemical Rubber Pub. Co.

Kirkpatrick, C.T., ed. 1992. *Illustrated Handbook of Medical Physiology*, 340–85. New York: John Wiley and Sons.

Porter, R., and J. Whelan, eds. 1981. Human Muscle Fatigue Physiological Mechanism. London, England: Ditmur Medical.

Whitfield, J.F. 1990. *Calcium Cell Cycles and Cancer*. New York: CRC Press, Inc.

Yanick, P. 1995. Functional medicine update. Townsend Letter for Doctors. (May):34–40.

Part 2 How Foods Affect Your Acid-Alkaline Balance

Aihara, H. 1986. *Acid and Alkaline*. Oroville, Calif.: George Ohsawa Macrobiotic Foundation.

Black, R. 1985. "Metabolic Acid-base disturbances." *Intensive-Care Medicine*, edited by Irwin, R. et al., 596–609. Boston: Little, Brown.

Flessner, M., and M. Knepper. 1983. *Renal Acid-base Balance in Disease of the Kidney*. 5th ed., Vol.1:207–32. Boston: Little, Brown.

Fogelman, A.M. From Fatty Streak to Myocardial Infarction: An Inflammatory Response to Oxidized Lipids. *Circulation*, part 2, (October 1994): 1–8.

Manz, F., and H. Schmidt. 1992. Retrospective Approach To Explain Growth Retardation and Urolithiasis in a Child With Long-term Nutritional Acid Loading. *Z-Ernahrungswiss* 31(2), (June):121–29.

Morter, M.T. 1997. *Dynamic Health*, 275–99. Rogers, Arkansas: Morter Health System.

Queen, H.L. 1994. Free Radical Therapy, Part IV, Acidemia and Free Calcium Excess. *Health Realities* 13, no. 4:1–56.

Thode, J. et al. 1982. Evaluation of New Semi-automatic Electrode System for Simultaneous Measurement of Ionized Calcium and pH. *Scandinavian Journal Clinical Laboratory Investigation* (4)(S) (September):407–15.

Chapter 6 The High-Performance Superdrink—Yes, Water!

Batmanghelidj, F. 1995. *Your Body's Many Cries For Water*, 13–75. Falls Church, Virginia: Global Health Solutions.

Dahl, L.K. 1972. Salt and Hypertension. *American Journal of Clinical Nutrition* 25:231–44.

Dyckner, T., and P.O. Wester. 1987. Potassium–Magnesium Depletion in Patients With Cardiovascular Disease. *American Journal of Medicine* 82, (suppl.3A):111–17.

Espiner, E.A. 1987. The Effect of Stress on Salt and Water Balance. *Bailliere's Clinical Endocrinology and Metabolism* 1(2):370–95.

Goldstein, D.J. et al. 1987. Increase In Mast Cell Number and Altered Vascular Permeability in Thirsty Rats. *Life Sciences* 60:1591–602.

Humes, H.D. 1986. Disorders or Water Metabolism, Fluids and Electrolytes. *American Journal of Physiology*, 118–49.

Robertson, R.P., and M. Chin. 1973. A Role For Prostaglandin E in Defective Insulin Secretion and Carbohydrate Intolerance in Diabetes Mellitus. *Journal of Clinical Investigations* 60:747–53.

Chapter 7 Color Your Plate With Superfoods

Colbin, A. 1986. *Food and Healing*, 148–96. New York: Ballantine Books.

Diamond, H. 1995. *You Can Prevent Breast Cancer*, 197–210. San Diego: Pro Motion Publishing.

Weil, A. 1996. *Spontaneous Healing*, 136–53. 1996. New York: Ballantine Books.

Whitaker, J. 1996. *Is Heart Surgery Necessary?*, 144–60. Washington, D.C.: Regnery Publishing.

Chapter 8 The Clean Machine-Periodic Mono-Dieting

Connor, W. 1972. The Key Role of Nutritional Factors in the Prevention of Coronary Heart Disease. *Preventive Medicine* 1:31–37.

Glick, D. 1992. New Age Meets Hippocrates. *Newsweek* (July 13).

Kolonel, L. 1981. Nutrient Intakes In Relation To Cancer Incidence in Hawaii. *British Journal of Cancer* 44:63–69.

Masoro, E.J. 1990. Assessment of Nutritional Components In Prolongation of Life and Health By Diet. *Proceedings of the Society for Experimental Biology and Medicine* 193:31–34.

Chapter 9 Fuel, For Peak Performance

Albrink, M.J. 1978. Dietary Fiber, Plasma Insulin, and Obesity. *American Journal of Clinical Nutrition* 31:S277–79.

Anderson, J.W. 1983. Plant Fiber and Blood Pressure. *Annals of International Medicine* 98(part 2):842.

Aparicio, M. et al. 1989. Effects of a Ketoacid Diet on Glucose Tolerance and Tissue Insulin Sensitivity. *Kidney International Supplement* 27:S231–S235.

Brisson, R.J. et al. 1988. Dietary Fiber in Relation to Prognostic Indicators in Breast Cancer. *Journal of the National Cancer Institute* 8:819–25.

Colgan, M., M.S. Fielder, and L. Colgan. 1991. Micronutrient Status of Endurance Athletes Affects Hematology and Performance. *Journal of Applied Nutrition* 43:17–36.

Foster-Powell, K., and J.B. Miller. 1995. International Tables of Glycemic Index. *American Journal of Clinical Nutrition* 62:871S–893S.

Hawley, H.P., and G.B. Gordon. 1976. The Effect of Long Chain Free Fatty Acids on Human Neutrophil Function and Structure. *Laboratory Investigation* 34:216–22.

Hollenbeck, C., and G.M. Reaven. 1987. Variations in Insulin-Stimulated Glucose Uptake in Healthy Individuals With Normal Glucose Tolerance. *Journal Clinical Endocinol Metabolism* 64:1169–73.

How Much Protein Do Athletes Really Need? 1987. *Tufts University Diet and Nutrition Letter* 5:1.

Jenkins, D.J.A. et al. 1987. Low-glycemic Index Diet In Hyperlipidemia: Use of Fractional Starchy Foods. *American Journal of Clinical Nutrition* 46:66–71.

Mitropoulos, K.A. et al. 1994. Dietary Fat Induces Changes in Factor VII Coagulant Activity Through Effects on Plasma Stearic Acid Concentration. *Arteriosclerosis and Thrombosis Journal* 14:214–22.

Recommended Dietary Allowances. 1989. 10th ed. Westport, Conn: National Academy Press.

Remer, T., and F. Manz. 1994. Estimation of the Renal Net Acid Excretion by Adults Consuming Diets Containing Variable Amounts of Protein. *American Journal of Clinical Nutrition* 59:1356–61.

Sears, B., and B. Lawren. 1995. *Enter The Zone*. New York: Harper Collins.

Vegetarian Diets. 1988. Position Paper of the American Dietetic Association. *Journal of the American Dietetic Association* 88:351–55.

Von Schacky, C., S. Fishcher, and P.C. Weber. 1985. Long Term Effect of Dietary Marine Omega-3 Fatty Acids Upon Plasma and Cellular Lipids, Platelet Function, and Eicosanoid Formation in Humans. *Journal of Clinical Investigation* 76:1626–31.

Wallace, G., and L. Bell, eds. 1983. *Fiber in Human and Animal Nutrition*. The Royal Society of New Zealand.

Ward, G.M. et al. 1982. Insulin Receptor Binding Increased by High-Carbohydrate, Low-fat Diet in Non-Insulin-Dependent Diabetics. *European Journal of Clinical Investigation* 12:93.

Watson, R.R. 1986. Immunological Enhancement by Fat-soluble Vitamins, Minerals and Trace Metals: A Factor in Cancer Prevention. *Cancer Detection and Prevention* 9:67–77.

Chapter 10 Say Goodbye to Dieting

Beunett, W., and J. Gurn. 1982. *The Dieter's Dilemma*. New York: Basic Books.

Carlton, A., and I. Lillios. 1986. The Fattening of America. *Journal American Dietetic Association* 86:367–68.

Does It Matter What You Weigh? 1997. *Newsweek* (April 21).

Fat Times. 1995. *Time* magazine (January 16).

Kern, P.A. et al. 1990. Lipoprotein Lipase as the Mechanism For Collecting Digested Fat. *New England Journal of Medicine* 322:1053.

Pavlou, K.N. 1985. Muscle Burns Fat. *Medical Science Sports and Exercise* 17:466–71.

Schyltz, Y., and J.P. Flatt. 1989. Body Fat Retention and Eating Fat. *American Journal of Clinical Nutrition* 50:307–14.

Simopoulos A., and R.J. Wurtman, eds. 1987. *Human Obesity*. New York: New York Academy of Sciences.

Storlien, L.H. 1987. Flax Oil Helps To Lose Fat. Science 237:885.

Wade, G.N. 1983. Eating and Gaining Weight. *Physiological Behavior* 29:710.

Chapter 11 Exercise Your Way to Optimum Health

Cade, R. et al. 1984. Effect of Aerobic Exercise Training on Patients With Systemic Arterial Hypertension. *American Journal of Medicine* 77:785–90.

Dulbo, A.G., and D.S. Miller. 1989. Ephedrine, Caffeine and Aspirin: Over-the-counter Drugs That Interact To Stimulate Thermogenesis in the Obese. *Nutrition* 5:7.

Lawson, S. et al. 1987. Effect of a 10-week Aerobic Exercise Program on Metabolic Rate, Body Composition, and Fitness In Lean, Sedentary Females. *British Journal of Clinical Practice* 41:684-688.

Lennon, D. et al. 1985. Diet and Exercise Training Effects on Resting Metabolic Rate. *International Journal of Obesity* 9:39–47.

Prigogine, I., and I. Stenger. 1984. *Order Out Of Chaos: Man's New Dialogue With Nature.* New York: Bantam Books.

Scaravelli, V. 1996. *Awakening The Spine.* San Francisco: Harper Collins.

Woolf-May, K. et al. 1997. Effects of an 18-Week Walking Program on Cardiac Function In Previously Sedentary or Relatively Inactive Adults. *British Journal of Sports Medicine* 31:48–53.

Zusman, R.M. 1986. Alternative Antihypertensive Therapy. *Hypertension* 8:837–42.

Chapter 12 Breathing for Relaxation and Stress Management

Benson, H., and W. Proctor. 1984. *Beyond The Relaxation Response.* Berkeley, Calif: Putnam-Berkeley Inc.

Davis, M. et al. 1995. *The Relaxation and Stress Reduction Workbook.* 4th ed. Oakland, Calif.: New Harbinger Publications.

Eliot, R.S. 1994. *From Stress To Strength: How To Lighten Your Load And Save Your Health.* New York: Bantam Books.

Hendricks, G. 1995. *Conscious Breathing.* New York: Bantam Books.

Sovik, R. 1997. Channel Breathing Purification. *Yoga International* (February-March).

Weissler, V. 1996. Transforming Stress Into Stillness. Relaxation cassette tapes available from 800-826-1550.

Chapter 13 Superfoods and Supernutrition for Women

Arnold, S. et al. 1996. Synergistic Activation of Estrogen Receptors with Combinations of Environmental Chemicals. *Science* 272:1489–92.

Benowitz, N.L. 1990. Clinical Pharmacology of Caffeine. *Annual Review of Medicine* 41:277–88.

Brisson, R.J. et al. 1988. Dietary Fat In Relation To Prognostic Indicators In Breast Cancer. *Journal of the National Cancer Institute* 8:819–25.

Chou, T. 1992. Wake Up And Smell The Coffee: Caffeine, Coffee and the Medical Consequences. *Annual Review of Medicine* 157:544–53.

Hankin, J.H. 1993. Role of Nutrition In Women's Health. *Journal of the American Dietetic Association* 93, no. 9:994–99.

Nelson, M.E. et al. 1991. A Walking Program and Increased Dietary

Calcium In Post Menopausal Women: Effect on Bone. *American Journal of Clinical Nutrition* 53:1304–11.

Pesticides In Food. 1987. Hearings of the Subcommittee On Oversight and Investigations of the Committee on Energy and Commerce, 100th Congress, 1st Session (April 30):47.

Some Calories Count More Than Others. 1988. *Tufts University Diet and Nutrition Letter* 6:2.

Tomascz, A. 1994. Multiple-antibiotic Resistant Pathogenic Bacteria: A Report on the Rockefeller University Workshop. *New England Journal of Medicine* 330:1247–51.

Weil, A. 1995. Chapter 11, "How Not To Get Cancer," and Chapter 12, "How To Protect Your Immune System." In *Natural Health, Natural Medicine*. Boston: Houghton Mifflin.

Chapter 14 Superfoods and Supernutrition Mostly For Men

Does stress kill? 1995. Consumers report on health. *Consumer Magazine* (July).

Dodging Cancer With Diet. 1995. *Nutrition Action Health Letter* (January-February):4–6.

Gallagher, M. 1996. Ageless Muscle. *Muscle and Fitness Magazine* (January):162–65.

Kesaniemi, Y.A., S. Tarpila, and T. Miettinen. 1990. Low vs. High Dietary Fiber And Serum, Biliary and Fecal Lipids in Middle-aged Men. *American Journal of Clinical Nutrition* 51:1007–12.

Lichtenstein, A.H. et al. 1994. Hypercholesterolemic Effect of Dietary Cholesterol in Diets Enriched in Polyunsaturated and Saturated Fat. *Arteriosclerosis and Thrombosis Journal* 14:168–75.

Thiebolt, L., S. Berthelay, S., and J. Berthelay. 1971. Preventive and Curative Action of Bark Extract of Pygeum Africanum, On Prostatic Adenoma. *Therapie* 26, no. 3:575–80.

Walker, M. 1991. Saw Palmetto Extract Relief For Benign Prostatic Hypertrophy (BPH). *Townsend Letter For Doctors* (February-March):107–10.

Chapter 15 Spiritual Fitness

Dossey, L. 1993. *Healing Words*. San Francisco: HarperCollins.

———. 1996. *Prayer Is Good Medicine*. San Francisco: HarperCollins.

Pert, C.B. et al. 1985. Neuropeptides And Their Receptors: A Psychosomatic Network. *Journal of Immunology* 135:820S–826S.

Sarno, J. 1991. *Healing Back Pain: The Mind-body Connection*. New York: Warner Books.

Thich Nhat Hanh. 1976. *The Miracle of Mindfulness*. Boston: Beacon Press.

Index

About the Author

Sam Graci

Sam Graci is an internationally renowned lecturer, consultant, and researcher in the field of optimum human health and nutrition for maintenance of proper health and accelerated healing. He is the formulator and developer of the world-renowned and multi-award-winning greens drink GREENS+.

Sam is a graduate of the University of Western Ontario, in London, Ontario, in adolescent psychology and chemistry, and has further degrees in education, special education, and counseling. He taught postgraduate courses at Brock University, in St. Catharines, Ontario.

He has traveled extensively throughout the world interviewing researchers, reviewing research, and collecting information about medicinal plants, vegetables, fruits, grains, legumes, sea vegetables and their organic-growing techniques.

On the cutting edge of nutritional research and study, Sam is the author of many relevant, progressive articles on nutrition and health for magazines and newspapers. His thinking is revolutionary, yet his explanations are simple and logical. Sam Graci successfully integrates and unifies a variety of scientific research, presenting it in practical applications.

A thought-provoking and enthusiastic speaker, Sam is a popular and frequent guest speaker on television and radio talk shows.

Sam and his wife, Elvira, enjoy a regime of hiking in nature, kayaking, bicycling, and running, balanced with stretching and breathing relaxation. At the core of his life, meditation and quiet reflection give his life's work sustenance and substance. He enjoys following a precise Superfoods dietary strategy.

About the Contributors

Harvey Diamond

Harvey Diamond has dedicated more than 28 years to the development of a true wellness lifestyle. An internationally known author, lecturer, and health consultant, he is one of the modern pioneers of the natural-foods and health movement. His groundbreaking book, *Fit for Life* has sold nearly 12 million copies worldwide. *Fit for Life* has been translated into 29 languages and is one of the most popular books on health and nutrition ever written. His knowledgeable, compassionate, and witty style gives millions of people information they can use immediately to acquire and maintain optimal health.

For additional information, call Fit for Life at 800-889-9989.

Jeanne Marie Martin

Jeanne Marie Martin lectures internationally on topics concerning natural foods and holistic lifestyles. Her 25 years of experience have led her to write ten health cookbooks and more than 250 magazine articles.

As a nutrition consultant, Jeanne Marie has worked with more than 30 holistic-medical doctors, naturopaths, and chiropractors whose clients have special health problems. She specializes in creating customized diets for people with candida albicans, chronic fatigue syndrome, high or low blood sugar, heart problems, cancer, as well as devising nutritional programs for athletes, pregnant women, and people with weight-control concerns.

Jeanne Marie also frequently teaches cooking classes in the Seattle and Vancouver areas. She lectures on nutrition at universities, schools, hospitals, clinics, and on television and radio talk shows. For further information, phone (604) 878-8787, P.O. Box 4391, Vancouver, B.C., V6B 3Z8.

David Schweitzer, Ph.D., M.D.

Dr. David Schweitzer has medical degrees in both Eastern and Western medicine. He is an international authority in natural and Oriental medicine, and has many awards for his humanitarian work. He has successfully combined Western science and Eastern philosophy into one holistic medicine. As president of the International Albert Schweitzer Society, he believes that each of us is called to create our own "Lambarene," the hospital in Africa founded by Albert Schweitzer, a genuine community based on unconditional love and mutual support.

Originally from Austria, David Schweitzer is now practicing in London, England, at The Essential Health Clinic.

Julian Whitaker, M.D.

Dr. Julian Whitaker is the editor of North America's leading monthly health newsletter *Health & Healing*, which specializes in practical approaches to optimal health and longevity. He has practiced medicine for more than 20 years, after receiving degrees from Dartmouth College, in Hanover, New Hampshire, and Emory University, in Atlanta, Georgia.

Dr. Whitaker has long been an advocate of living a healthy life. To this end, he lectures in North America on using his exclusive "Whitaker Program" and natural therapies to maximize physical, mental, and emotional wellness. He is one of the world's foremost authorities on both preventive and longevity medicine.

Over the past two decades, thousands of patients worldwide have come to the Whitaker Wellness Institute in Newport Beach, California, for a one-week program of medical testing, treatment, and education designed for their individual health problems.

Dr. Whitaker is the author of six major books: *Reversing Heart Disease*; *Reversing Diabetes*; *Reversing Health Risks*; *A Guide To Natural Healing*; *Is Heart Surgery Necessary?*; and *Shed 10 Years in 10 Weeks*. These books and information about the Whitaker wellness programs are available from the Whitaker Wellness Institute at (714) 851-1550.